WITH WOLFE IN CANADA THE WINNING OF A CONTINENT

WITH WOLFE IN CANADA THE WINNING OF A CONTINENT

G. A. (George Alfred) Henty

www.General-Books.net

Publication Data:

Title: With Wolfe in Canada the Winning of a Continent
Author: Henty, G. A. (George Alfred), 1832-1902
Reprinted: 2010, General Books, Memphis, Tennessee, USA
Bisac subject codes: FIC014000, FIC032000, HIS006000, HIS036020, JUV016000, JUV030030,

How We Made This Book for You
We made this book exclusively for you using patented Print on Demand technology.
First we scanned the original rare book using a robot which automatically flipped and photographed each page.
We automated the typing, proof reading and design of this book using Optical Character Recognition (OCR) software on the scanned copy. That let us keep your cost as low as possible.
If a book is very old, worn and the type is faded, this can result in numerous typos or missing text. This is also why our books don't have illustrations; the OCR software can't distinguish between an illustration and a smudge.
We understand how annoying typos, missing text or illustrations, foot notes in the text or an index that doesn't work, can be. That's why we provide a free digital copy of most books exactly as they were originally published. You can also use this PDF edition to read the book on the go. Simply go to our website (www.general-books.net) to check availability. And we provide a free trial membership in our book club so you can get free copies of other editions or related books.
OCR is not a perfect solution but we feel it's more important to make books available for a low price than not at all. So we warn readers on our website and in the descriptions we provide to book sellers that our books don't have illustrations and may have numerous typos or missing text. We also provide excerpts from books to book sellers and on our website so you can preview the quality of the book before buying it.
If you would prefer that we manually type, proof read and design your book so that it's perfect, simply contact us for the cost. Since many of our books only sell one or two copies a year, unlike mass market books we have to split the production costs between those one or two buyers.

Limit of Liability/Disclaimer of Warranty:
The publisher and author make no representations or warranties with respect to the accuracy or completeness of the book. The advice and strategies in the book may not be suitable for your situation. You should consult with a professional where appropriate. The publisher is not liable for any damages resulting from the book.
Please keep in mind that the book was written long ago; the information is not current. Furthermore, there may be typos, missing text or illustration and explained above.

WITH WOLFE IN CANADA THE WINNING OF A CONTINENT

book prepared by Martin Robb

**With Wolfe in Canada
Or The Winning of a Continent
by G. A. Henty**

1894

Contents
Preface.
Chapter 1: A Rescue.
Chapter 2: The Showman's Grandchild.
Chapter 3: The Justice Room.

Chapter 4: The Squire's Granddaughter.
Chapter 5: A Quiet Time.
Chapter 6: A Storm.
Chapter 7: Pressed.
Chapter 8: Discharged.
Chapter 9: The Defeat Of Braddock.
Chapter 10: The Fight At Lake George.
Chapter 11: Scouting.
Chapter 12: A Commission.
Chapter 13: An Abortive Attack.
Chapter 14: Scouting On Lake Champlain.
Chapter 15: Through Many Perils.
Chapter 16: The Massacre At Fort William Henry.
Chapter 17: Louisbourg And Ticonderoga.
Chapter 18: Quebec.
Chapter 19: A Dangerous Expedition.
Chapter 20: The Path Down The Heights.
Chapter 21: The Capture Of Quebec.

Preface.
My Dear Lads,

In the present volume I have endeavoured to give the details of the principal events in a struggle whose importance can hardly be overrated. At its commencement the English occupied a mere patch of land on the eastern seaboard of America, hemmed in on all sides by the French, who occupied not only Canada in the north and Louisiana in the south, but possessed a chain of posts connecting them, so cutting off the English from all access to the vast countries of the west.

On the issues of that struggle depended not only the destiny of Canada, but of the whole of North America and, to a large extent, that of the two mother countries. When the contest began, the chances of France becoming the great colonizing empire of the world were as good as those of England. Not only did she hold far larger territories in America than did England, but she had rich colonies in the West Indies, where the flag of England was at that time hardly represented, and her prospects in India were better than our own. At that time, too, she disputed with us on equal terms the empire of the sea.

The loss of her North American provinces turned the scale. With the monopoly of such a market, the commerce of England increased enormously, and with her commerce her wealth and power of extension, while the power of France was proportionately crippled. It is true that, in time, the North American colonies, with the exception of Canada, broke away from their connection with the old country; but they still remained English, still continued to be the best market for our goods and manufactures.

Never was the short-sightedness of human beings shown more distinctly, than when France wasted her strength and treasure in a sterile contest on the continent of Europe, and permitted, with scarce an effort, her North American colonies to be torn from her.

All the historical details of the war have been drawn from the excellent work entitled Montcalm and Wolfe, by Mr. Francis Parkman, and from the detailed history of the Louisbourg and Quebec expeditions, by Major Knox, who served under Generals Amherst and Wolfe.

Yours very sincerely,

G. A. Henty.

Chapter 1: A Rescue.

Most of the towns standing on our seacoast have suffered a radical change in the course of the last century. Railways, and the fashion of summer holiday making, have transformed them altogether, and great towns have sprung up where fishing villages once stood. There are a few places, however, which seem to have been passed by, by the crowd. The number yearly becomes smaller, as the iron roads throw out fresh branches. With the advent of these comes the speculative builder. Rows of terraces and shops are run up, promenades are made, bathing machines and brass bands become familiar objects, and in a few years the original character of the place altogether disappears.

Sidmouth, for a long time, was passed by, by the world of holiday makers. East and west of her, great changes took place, and many far smaller villages became fashionable seaside watering places. The railway, which passed by some twelve miles away, carried its tens of thousands westward, but left few of them for Sidmouth, and anyone who visited the pretty little place, fifteen years back, would have seen it almost as it stood when our story opens a century ago.

There are few places in England with a fairer site. It lies embosomed in the hills, which rise sharply on either side of it, while behind stretches a rich, undulating country, thickly dotted with orchards and snug homesteads, with lanes bright with wildflowers and ferns, with high hedges and trees meeting overhead. The cold breezes, which render so bare of interest the walks round the great majority of our seaside towns, pass harmlessly over the valley of the Sid, where the vegetation is as bright and luxuriant as if the ocean lay leagues away, instead of breaking on the shore within a few feet of the front line of houses.

The cliffs which, on either side, rise from the water's edge, are neither white like those to the east, nor grey as are the rugged bulwarks to the west. They are of a deep red, warm and pleasant to the eye, with clumps of green showing brightly up against them on every little ledge where vegetation can get a footing; while the beach is neither pebble, nor rock, nor sand, but a smooth, level surface sloping evenly down; hard and pleasant to walk on when the sea has gone down, and the sun has dried and baked it for an hour or two; but slippery and treacherous when freshly wetted, for the red cliffs are of clay. Those who sail past in a boat would hardly believe that this is so, for the sun has baked its face, and the wind dried it, till it is cracked and seamed, and makes a brave imitation of red granite; but the clammy ooze, when the sea goes down, tells its nature only too plainly, and Sidmouth will never be a popular watering place for children, for there is no digging sand castles here, and a fall will stain light dresses and pinafores a ruddy hue, and the young labourers will look as if they had been at work in a brick field.

But a century since, the march of improvement had nowhere begun; and there were few larger, and no prettier, seaside villages on the coast than Sidmouth.

It was an afternoon in August. The sun was blazing down hotly, scarce a breath of wind was stirring, and the tiny waves broke along the shore with a low rustle like that of falling leaves. Some fishermen were at work, recaulking a boat hauled up on the shore. Others were laying out some nets to dry in the sun. Some fisher boys were lying asleep, like dogs basking in the heat; and a knot of lads, sitting under the shade of a boat, were discussing with some warmth the question of smuggling.

"What do you say to it, Jim Walsham?" one of the party said, looking up at a boy some twelve years old, who was leaning against a boat, but who had hitherto taken no part in the discussion.

"There is no doubt that it's wrong," the boy said. "Not wrong like stealing, and lying, and that sort of thing; still it's wrong, because it's against the law; and the revenue men, if they come upon a gang landing the tubs, fight with them, and if any are killed they are not blamed for it, so there is no doubt about its being wrong. Then, on the other hand, no one thinks any the worse of the men that do it, and there is scarce a one, gentle or simple, as won't buy some of the stuff if he gets a chance, so it can't be so very wrong. It must be great fun to be a smuggler, to be always dodging the king's cutters, and running cargoes under the nose of the officers ashore. There is some excitement in a life like that."

"There is plenty of excitement in fishing," one of the boys said sturdily. "If you had been out in that storm last March, you would have had as much excitement as you liked. For twelve hours we expected to go down every minute, and we were half our time bailing for our lives."

An approving murmur broke from the others, who were all, with the exception of the one addressed as Jim Walsham, of the fisher class. His clothing differed but little from that of the rest. His dark blue pilot trousers were old and sea stained, his hands and face were dyed brown with exposure to the sun and the salt water; but there was something, in his manner and tone of voice, which showed that a distinction existed.

James Walsham was, indeed, the son of the late doctor of the village, who had died two years previously. Dr. Walsham had been clever in his profession, but circumstances were against him. Sidmouth and its neighbourhood were so healthy, that his patients were few and far between; and when he died, of injuries received from being thrown over his horse's head, when the animal one night trod on a stone coming down the hill into Sidmouth, his widow and son were left almost penniless.

Mrs. Walsham was, fortunately, an energetic woman, and a fortnight after her husband's death, she went round among the tradesmen of the place and the farmers of the neighbourhood, and announced her intention of opening a school for girls. She had received a good education, being the daughter of a clergyman, and she soon obtained enough pupils to enable her to pay her way, and to keep up the pretty home in which her husband lived in the outskirts of Sidmouth.

If she would have taken boarders, she could have obtained far higher terms, for good schools were scarce; but this she would not do, and her pupils all lived within distances where they could walk backwards and forwards to their homes. Her evenings she devoted to her son, and, though the education which she was enabled to give him would be considered meagre, indeed, in these days of universal cramming, he learned as much as the average boy of the period.

He would have learned more had he followed her desires, and devoted the time when she was engaged in teaching to his books; but this he did not do. For a few hours in the day he would work vigorously at his lessons. The rest of his time he spent either on the seashore, or in the boats of the fishermen; and he could swim, row, or handle a boat under sail in all weather, as well or better than any lad in the village of his own age.

His disposition was a happy one, and he was a general favourite among the boatmen. He had not, as yet, made up his mind as to his future. His mother wanted him to follow his father's profession. He himself longed to go to sea, but he had promised his mother that he would never do so without her consent, and that consent he had no hope of obtaining.

The better-class people in the village shook their heads gravely over James Walsham, and prophesied no good things of him. They considered that he demeaned himself greatly by association with the fisher boys, and more than once he had fallen into disgrace, with the more quiet minded of the inhabitants, by mischievous pranks. His reputation that way once established, every bit of mischief in the place, which could not be clearly traced to someone else, was put down to him; and as he was not one who would peach upon others to save himself, he was seldom in a position to prove his innocence.

The parson had once called upon Mrs. Walsham, and had talked to her gravely over her son's delinquencies, but his success had not been equal to his anticipations. Mrs. Walsham had stood up warmly for her son.

"The boy may get into mischief sometimes, Mr. Allanby, but it is the nature of boys to do so. James is a good boy, upright and honourable, and would not tell a lie under any consideration. What is he to do? If I could afford to send him to a good school it would be a different thing, but that you know I cannot do. From nine in the morning, until five in the afternoon, my time is occupied by teaching, and I cannot expect, nor do I wish, that he should sit moping indoors all day. He had far better be out in the boats with the fishermen, than be hanging about the place doing nothing. If anything happened to me, before he is started in life, there would be nothing for him but to take to the sea. I am laying by a little money every month, and if I live for another year there will be enough to buy him a fishing boat and nets. I trust that it may not come to that, but I see nothing derogatory in his earning an honest living with his own hands. He will always be something better than a common fisherman. The education I have striven to give him, and his knowledge that he was born a gentleman, will nerve him to try and rise.

"As to what you say about mischief, so far as I know all boys are mischievous. I know that my own brothers were always getting into scrapes, and I have no doubt, Mr. Allanby, that when you look back upon your own boyhood, you will see that you were not an exception to the general rule."

Mr. Allanby smiled. He had come rather against his own inclinations; but his wife had urged him to speak to Mrs. Walsham, her temper being ruffled by the disappearance of two favourite pigeons, whose loss she, without a shadow of evidence, most unjustly put down to James Walsham.

The parson was by no means strict with his flock. He was a tall man, inclined to be portly, a good shot and an ardent fisherman; and although he did not hunt, he was frequently seen on his brown cob at the meet, whenever it took place within a reasonable distance of Sidmouth; and without exactly following the hounds, his knowledge of the country often enabled him to see more of the hunt than those who did.

As Mrs. Walsham spoke, the memory of his old school and college days came across him.

"That is the argumentum ad hominem, Mrs. Walsham, and when a lady takes to that we can say no more. You know I like your boy. There is much that is good in him; but it struck me that you were letting him run a little too wild. However, there is much in what you say, and I don't believe that he is concerned in half the mischief that he gets credit for. Still, you must remember that a little of the curb, just a little, is good for us all. It spoils a horse to be always tugging at his mouth, but he will go very badly if he does not feel that there is a hand on the reins.

"I have said the same thing to the squire. He spoils that boy of his, for whom, between ourselves, I have no great liking. The old man will have trouble with him before he is done, or I am greatly mistaken."

Nothing came of Mr. Allanby's visit. Mrs. Walsham told James that he had been there to remonstrate with her.

"I do not want to stop you from going out sailing, Jim; but I wish you would give up your mischievous pranks, they only get you bad will and a bad name in the place. Many people here think that I am wrong in allowing you to associate so much with the fisher boys, and when you get into scrapes, it enables them to impress upon me how right they were in their forecasts. I do not want my boy to be named in the same breath with those boys of Robson's, or young Peterson, or Blame."

"But you know I have nothing to do with them, mother," James said indignantly. "They spend half their time about the public house, and they do say that when Peterson has been out with that lurcher of his, he has been seen coming back with his coat bulged out, and there is often a smell of hare round his father's cottage at supper time. You know I wouldn't have anything to do with them."

"No, Jim, I am sure you would not; but if people mix up your name with theirs it is almost as bad for you as if you had. Unfortunately, people are too apt not to distinguish between tricks which are really only the outcome of high spirit, and a lack of something better to do, and real vice. Therefore, Jim, I say, keep yourself from mischief. I know that, though you are out of doors so many hours of the day, you really do get through a good deal of work; but other people do not give you credit for this. Remember how your father was respected here. Try to act always as you would have done had he been alive, and you cannot go far wrong."

James had done his best, but he found it hard to get rid of his reputation for getting into mischief, and more than once, when falsely suspected, he grumbled that he might just as well have the fun of the thing, for he was sure to have the blame.

As Jim Walsham and his companions were chatting in the shade of a boat, their conversation was abruptly broken off by the sight of a figure coming along the road. It was a tall figure, with a stiff military bearing. He was pushing before him a large box, mounted on a framework supported by four wheels. Low down, close to the ground, swung a large flat basket. In this, on a shawl spread over a thick bed of hay, sat a little girl some five years old.

"It is the sergeant," one of the boys exclaimed. "I wonder whether he has got a fresh set of views? The last were first-rate ones."

The sergeant gave a friendly nod to the boys as he passed, and then, turning up the main street from the beach, went along until he came to a shaded corner, and there stopped. The boys had all got up and followed him, and now stood looking on with interest at his proceedings. The little girl had climbed out of her basket as soon as he stopped, and after asking leave, trotted back along the street to the beach, and was soon at play among the seaweed and stones.

She was a singularly pretty child, with dark blue eyes, and brown hair with a touch of gold. Her print dress was spotlessly clean and neat; a huge flapping sunbonnet shaded her face, whose expression was bright and winning.

"Well, boys," the sergeant said cheerfully, "how have you been getting on since I was here last? Nobody drowned, I hope, or come to any ill. Not that we must grumble, whatever comes. We have all got to do our duty, whether it be to march up a hill with shot and shell screaming and whistling round, as I have had to do; or to be far out at sea with the wind blowing fit to take the hair off your head, as comes to your lot sometimes; or following the plough from year's end to year's end, as happens to some. We have got to make the best of it, whatever it is.

"I have got a grand new set of pictures from Exeter. They came all the way down from London town for me by waggon. London Bridge, and Windsor Castle, with the flag flying over it, telling that the king–God bless his gracious majesty–is at home.

"Then, I have got some pictures of foreign parts that will make you open your eyes. There's Niagara. I don't know whether you've heard of it, but it's a place where a great river jumps down over a wall of rock, as high as that steeple there, with a roar like thunder that can be heard, they say, on a still night, for twenty miles round.

"I have got some that will interest you more still, because you are sailors, or are going to be sailors. I have got one of the killing of a whale. He has just thrown a boat, with five sailors, into the air, with a lash of his tail; but it's of no use, for there are other boats round, and the harpoons are striking deep in his flesh. He is a big fish, and a strong one; but he will be beaten, for he does not know how to use his strength. That's the case with many men. They throw away their life and their talents, just because they don't know what's in them, and what they might do if they tried.

"And I have got a picture of the fight with the Spanish Armada. You have heard about that, boys, surely; for it began out there, over the water, almost in sight of Sidmouth, and went on all the way up the Channel; our little ships hanging on to the great Spaniards and giving them no rest, but worrying them, and battering them, till they were glad to sail away to the Dutch coast. But they were not safe there, for we sent fire ships at them, and they had to cut and run; and then a storm came on, and sunk many, and drove others ashore all around our coasts, even round the north of Scotland and Ireland.

"You will see it all here, boys, and as you know, the price is only one penny."

By this time, the sergeant had let down one side of the box and discovered four round holes, and had arranged a low stool in front, for any of those, who were not tall enough to look through the glasses, to stand upon. A considerable number of girls and boys had now gathered round, for Sergeant Wilks and his show were old, established favourites at Sidmouth, and the news of his arrival had travelled quickly round the place.

Four years before, he had appeared there for the first time, and since then had come every few months. He travelled round the southwestern counties, Dorset and Wilts, Somerset, Devon, and Cornwall, and his cheery good temper made him a general favourite wherever he went.

He was somewhat of a martinet, and would have no crowding and pushing, and always made the boys stand aside till the girls had a good look; but he never hurried them, and allowed each an ample time to see the pictures, which were of a better class than those in most travelling peep shows. There was some murmuring, at first, because the show contained none of the popular murders and blood-curdling scenes to which the people were accustomed.

"No," the sergeant had said firmly, when the omission was suggested to him; "the young ones see quite enough scenes of drunkenness and fighting. When I was a child, I remember seeing in a peep show the picture of a woman lying with her head nearly cut off, and her husband with a bloody chopper standing beside her; and it spoiled my sleep for weeks. No, none of that sort of thing for Sergeant Wilks. He has fought for his country, and has seen bloodshed enough in his time, and the ground half covered with dead and dying men; but that was duty–this is pleasure. Sergeant Wilks will show the boys and girls, who pay him their pennies, views in all parts of the world, such as would cost them thousands of pounds if they travelled to see them, and all as natural as life. He will show them great battles by land and sea, where the soldiers and sailors shed their blood like water in the service of their country. But cruel murders and notorious crimes he will not show them."

It was not the boys and girls, only, who were the sergeant's patrons. Picture books were scarce in those days, and grown-up girls and young men were not ashamed to pay their pennies to peep into the sergeant's box.

There was scarcely a farm house throughout his beat where he was not known and welcomed. His care of the child, who, when he first came round, was but a year old, won the heart of the women; and a bowl of bread and milk for the little one, and a mug of beer and a hunch of bread and bacon for himself, were always at his service, before he opened his box and showed its wonders to the maids and children of the house.

Sidmouth was one of his regular halting places, and, indeed, he visited it more often than any other town on his beat. There was always a room ready for him there, in the house of a fisherman's widow, when he arrived on the Saturday, and he generally stopped till the Monday. Thus he had come to know the names of most of the boys of the place, as well as of many of the elders; for it was his custom, of a Saturday evening, after the little one was in bed, to go and smoke his pipe in the taproom of the "Anchor," where he would sometimes relate tales of his adventures to the assembled fishermen. But, although chatty and cheery with his patrons, Sergeant Wilks was a reticent, rather than a talkative, man. At the "Anchor" he was, except when called upon for a story, a listener rather than a talker.

As to his history, or the county to which he belonged, he never alluded to it, although communicative enough as to his military adventures; and any questions which were asked him, he quietly put on one side. He had intimated, indeed, that the father and mother of his grandchild were both dead; but it was not known whether she was the child of his son or daughter; for under his cheerful talk there was something of military strictness and sternness, and he was not a man of whom idle questions would be asked.

"Now, boys and girls," he said, "step up; the show is ready. Those who have got a penny cannot spend it better. Those who haven't must try and get their father or mother to give them one, and see the show later on. Girls first. Boys should always give way to their sisters. The bravest men are always the most courteous and gentle with women."

Four girls, of various ages, paid their pennies and took their places at the glasses, and the sergeant then began to describe the pictures, his descriptions of the wonders within being so exciting, that several boys and girls stole off from the little crowd, and made their way to their homes to coax their parents out of the necessary coin.

James Walsham listened a while, and then walked away to the sea, for there would be several sets of girls before it came to the turn of the boys. He strolled along, and as he came within sight of the beach stopped for a moment suddenly, and then, with a shout, ran forward at the top of his speed.

The little girl, after playing some time with the seaweed, had climbed into a small boat which lay at the edge of the advancing tide, and, leaning over the stern, watched the little waves as they ran up one after another. A few minutes after she had got into it, the rising tide floated the boat, and it drifted out a few yards, as far as its headrope allowed it. Ignorant of what had happened, the child was kneeling up at the stern, leaning over, and dabbling her hands in the water.

No one had noticed her. The boys had all deserted the beach. None of the fishermen were near the spot.

Just before James Walsham came within sight of the sea, the child had overbalanced itself. His eye fell on the water just as two arms and a frightened little face appeared above it. There was a little splash, and a struggle, and the sea was bare again.

At the top of his speed James dashed across the road, sprang down the beach, and, rushing a few yards into the water, dived down. He knew which way the tide was making, and allowed for the set. A few vigorous strokes, and he reached something white on the surface. It was the sunbonnet which had, in the child's struggles, become unfastened. He dived at once, and almost immediately saw a confused mass before him. Another stroke, and he seized the child's clothes, and, grasping her firmly, rose to the surface and swam towards shore.

Although the accident had not been perceived, his shout and sudden rush into the water had called the attention of some of the men, and two or three of them ran into the water, waist deep, to help him out with his little burden.

"Well done, Master Walsham! The child would have been drowned if you had not seed it. None of us noticed her fall over. She was playing on the beach last time I seed her."

"Is she dead?" James asked, breathless from his exertions.

"Not she," the fisherman said. "She could not have been under water a minute. Take her into my cottage, it's one of the nighest. My wife will put her between the blankets, and will soon bring her round."

The fisherman's wife met them at the door, and, taking the child from the lad, carried it in, and soon had her wrapped up in blankets. But before this was done she had opened her eyes, for she had scarcely lost consciousness when James had seized her.

The lad stood outside the door, waiting for the news, when the sergeant hurried up, one of the fishermen having gone to tell him what had happened, as soon as the child had been carried into the cottage–assuring him, as he did so, that the little one would speedily come round.

Just as he came up the door of the cottage opened, and one of the women, who had run in to assist the fisherman's wife, put her head out.

"She has opened her eyes," she said. "The little dear will soon be all right."

"Thank God for His mercies!" the sergeant said, taking off his hat. "What should I have done if I had lost her?

"And I have to thank you, next to God," he said, seizing the boy's hand. "May God bless you, young gentleman! and reward you for having saved my darling. They tell me she must have been drowned, but for you, for no one knew she had fallen in. Had it not been for you, I should come round to look for her, and she would have been gone–gone forever!" and the showman dashed the tears from his eyes with the back of his hand.

"I was only just in time," the lad said. "I did not see her fall out of the boat. She was only a few yards away from it when she came up–just as my eyes fell on the spot. I am very glad to have saved her for you; but, of course, it was nothing of a swim. She could not have been many yards out of my depth. Now I will run home and change my things."

James Walsham was too much accustomed to be wet through, to care anything about his dripping clothes, but they served him as an excuse to get away, for he felt awkward and embarrassed at the gratitude of the old soldier. He pushed his way through the little crowd, which had now gathered round, and started at a run; for the news had brought almost all those gathered round the peep show to the shore, the excitement of somebody being drowned being superior even to that of the peep show, to the great majority; though a few, who had no hope of obtaining the necessary pennies, had lingered behind, and seized the opportunity for a gratuitous look through the glasses.

James ran upstairs and changed his clothes without seeing his mother, and then, taking down one of his lesson books, set to work, shrinking from the idea of going out again, and being made a hero of.

Half an hour later there was a knock at the front door, and a few minutes after his mother called him down. He ran down to the parlour, and there found the showman.

"Oh, I say," the boy broke out, "don't say anything more about it! I do hate being thanked, and there was nothing in swimming ten yards in a calm sea. Please don't say anything more about it. I would rather you hit me, ever so much."

The sergeant smiled gravely, and Mrs. Walsham exclaimed:

"Why didn't you come in and tell me about it, Jim? I could not make out at first what Mr.–Mr.–"

"Sergeant Wilks, madam."

"What Sergeant Wilks meant, when he said that he had called to tell me how grateful he felt to you for saving his little grandchild's life. I am proud of you, Jim."

"Oh, mother, don't!" the boy exclaimed. "It is horrid going on so. If I had swum out with a rope through the surf, there might be something in it; but just to jump in at the edge of the water is not worth making a fuss about, one way or the other."

"Not to you, perhaps, young gentleman, but it is to me," the showman said. "The child is the light of my life, the only thing I have to care for in the world, and you have saved her. If it had only been by stretching out your hand, I should have been equally grateful. However, I will say no more about it, but I shall not think the less.

"But don't you believe, madam, that there was no credit in it. It was just the quickness and the promptness which saved her life. Had your son hesitated a moment it would have been too late, for he would never have found her. It is not likely that your son will ever have any occasion for help of mine, but should there be an opportunity, he may rely upon it that any service I can render him shall be his to the death; and, unlikely as it may seem, it may yet turn out that this brave act of his, in saving the life of the granddaughter of a travelling showman, will not be without its reward."

"Is she all right now?" James asked abruptly, anxious to change the conversation.

"Yes. She soon came to herself, and wanted to tell me all about it; but I would not let her talk, and in a few minutes she dropped off to sleep, and there I left her. The women tell me she will probably sleep till morning, and will then be as well as ever. And now I must go and look after my box, or the boys will be pulling it to pieces."

It was, however, untouched, for in passing the sergeant had told the little crowd that, if they left it alone, he would, on his return, let all see without payment; and during the rest of the afternoon he was fully occupied with successive audiences, being obliged to make his lectures brief, in order that all might have their turn.

After the sergeant had left, James took his hat and went for a long walk in the country, in order to escape the congratulations of the other boys. The next day little Agnes was perfectly well, and appeared with her grandfather in the seat, far back in the church, which he always occupied on the Sundays he spent at Sidmouth. On these occasions she was always neatly and prettily dressed, and, indeed, some of the good women of the place, comparing the graceful little thing with their own children, had not been backward in their criticisms on the folly of the old showman, in dressing his child out in clothes fit for a lady.

Chapter 2: The Showman's Grandchild.

Three months later the showman again appeared at Sidmouth, but did not set up his box as usual. Leaving it at his lodging, he went at once with his grandchild to Mrs. Walsham's.

"I have come, madam," he said after the first inquiries about the child had been answered, "on a particular business. It will seem a strange thing to you for a man like me to ask, but things are not quite as they seem, though I can't explain it now. But I am beating about the bush, and not getting any nearer. I have come to ask, madam, whether you would take charge of the child for two years. Of course I am ready to pay anything that you may think proper."

"But I don't take boarders," Mrs. Walsham said, much surprised at the proposition. "I only take girls who come in the morning and go away in the afternoon. Besides, they are all a good many years older than your grandchild. None of the girls who come to me are under twelve."

"I know, ma'm, I know; and I am sure you must think it a great liberty on my part to ask such a thing," the sergeant said apologetically. "It is not the teaching I want, but just a home for her."

Mrs. Walsham felt puzzled. She did, in her heart, feel it to be a liberty. Surely this wandering showman would find no difficulty in getting his grandchild taken care of among people of his own rank in life. It did seem most singular that he should seek to place the child with her. Mrs. Walsham was not given to thinking what her neighbours would say, but she thought of the buzz of comment and astonishment which her taking the charge of this child would excite. She had been particular in keeping her little school to some extent select, and as it was now as large as she could manage unaided, she was able to make it almost a favour to the farmers' wives to take their girls.

But to do Mrs. Walsham justice, this thought had less influence with her than that of the time and care which would be required by a child of that age in the house. Certainly, she thought, as she looked at her, sitting with her eyes wide open and an expression of grave wonder in her face, "she is a little darling, and as Jim saved her life I have a special interest in her; but this is out of the question."

It was two or three minutes before she answered the showman's last words.

"No, it cannot be done, Sergeant Wilks. No money that could be paid me would make up to me for the charge of a child of her age. I am all day in school, and what could a child, especially one accustomed to be out all day, do with herself? The worry and anxiety would be immense. Were it not for my school, it would be different altogether. A child of that age, especially such a sweet little thing as your granddaughter seems to be, would be a pet and amusement; but as it is, I am sorry to say that it is out of the question. But surely you will have no difficulty in finding plenty of good women who would be glad to take her, and to whom, having children of the same age, she would be no trouble whatever."

"Yes," the sergeant said slowly, "I was afraid you would say that, ma'm. Besides, though you are good enough not to say it, I know that there must be other objections. I know you must be surprised at my wanting her to be with a lady like yourself. So far as money goes, I could afford to pay fifty pounds a year, and perhaps you might get a girl who could look after Aggie while you are busy."

"Fifty pounds a year!" Mrs. Walsham said, greatly surprised. "That is a large sum, a great deal too large a sum for you to pay for the care of such a little child. For half that, there are scores of farmers' wives who would be happy to take her, and where she would be far more happy and comfortable than she would be with me."

"I know I could get plenty to take her," the soldier said, "but I have reasons, very particular reasons, why I wish to place her with a lady for two years. I cannot explain those reasons to you, but you may imagine they must be strong ones, for me to be willing to pay fifty pounds a year for her. That money has been laid by from the day she was born, for that purpose. I have other reasons, of my own, for wishing that she should be at Sidmouth rather than at any other place; and I have another reason," and a slight smile stole across his face, "for preferring that she should be with you rather than anyone else. All this must seem very strange to you, madam; but at the end of the two years, when you know what my reasons were, you will acknowledge that they were good ones.

"God knows," he went on, looking very grave, "what a wrench it will be for me to part with her. How lonely I shall be, as I tramp the country without her pretty prattle to listen to; but I have got to do it sooner or later, and these two years, when I can see her sometimes, will be a break, and accustom me to do without her sweet face.

"Please, madam," he urged, "do not give me a final answer today. I shall not go till Monday, and will call again, if you will let me, that morning; and believe me, if I could tell you all, I could give you reasons which would, I think, induce you to change your mind."

So saying, he made a military salute, took the child's hand in his, and was soon striding along towards the sea.

Mrs. Walsham was some time before she recovered from her surprise. This was, indeed, a mysterious affair. The earnestness with which the old soldier pleaded his cause had moved her strongly, and had almost persuaded her to accept the proposal, which had at first seemed preposterous. Fifty pounds a year, too, was certainly a handsome sum. She could get a girl from the village for two or three shillings a week to look after the child, and go out with her during school hours, and a hundred pounds would be a very handsome addition to the sum which she had begun, little by little, to lay by for Jim's preparation for the medical profession.

In the five years which would elapse, before it would be time for him to enter upon his studies for it, she could hardly hope to lay by more than that sum, and this would at a stroke double it. Certainly it was a tempting offer. She could not do justice to the child, could not give her the care and attention which she ought to have, and which she could have for such a sum elsewhere; but the sergeant knew exactly how she was placed, and if he was willing and anxious for her to assume the charge of the child, why should she refuse this good offer?

However, her pupils were waiting for her in the next room, and with an effort Mrs. Walsham put the matter aside, and went in to them.

When James returned home to dinner, his mother related to him the whole conversation. James was more amused than puzzled.

"It seems a rum idea, mother; but I don't see why you shouldn't take her. She is a sweet little thing, and will be a great amusement. Fifty pounds a year seems a tremendous sum for a man like that to pay; but I suppose he knows his own business, and it will be a great pull for you. You will be able to have all sorts of comforts. I should like it very much. I have often wished I had had a little sister, and she can go out walks with me, you know. It would be like having a big dog with one, only much jollier."

"Yes," his mother said smiling; "and I shouldn't be surprised if you wanted to throw sticks into the water for her to fetch them out, and to be taking her out for a night's fishing, and be constantly bringing her home splashed with that nasty red mud from head to foot. You would be a nice playmate for a little girl, Jim. Perhaps it is that special advantage that the sergeant had in his mind's eye, when he was so anxious to put her with me."

James laughed.

"I would see that she didn't come to any harm, anyhow, you know; and, after all, I suppose it was my picking her out of the sea that had something to do with his first thinking of putting her with you."

"I suppose it had, Jim," she said more seriously. "But what do you think, my boy? You know there are disadvantages in it. There will be a good deal of talk about my taking this showman's grandchild, and some of the farmers' wives won't like it."

"Then let them dislike it," James said indignantly. "The child is as good as their daughters, any day. Why, I noticed her in church looking like a little lady. There was not a child there to compare to her."

"Yes, I have noticed her myself," Mrs. Walsham said. "She is a singularly pretty and graceful child; but it will certainly cause remark."

"Well, mother, you can easily say, what is really the fact, that you naturally felt an interest in her because I picked her out of the water. Besides, if people make remarks they will soon be tired of that; and if not, I can get into some scrape or other and give them something else to talk about."

Accordingly, when Sergeant Wilks called on Monday morning for his answer, Mrs. Walsham told him that she had decided to accept his offer.

"You are aware how I am placed," she said, "and that I cannot give her the care and time which I could wish, and which she ought to have for such a liberal payment as you propose; but you know that beforehand, and you see that for two years' payments I could not sacrifice my school connection, which I should have to do if I gave her the time I should wish."

"I understand, madam," he said, "and I am grateful to you for consenting to take her. She is getting too old now to wander about with me, and since the narrow escape she had, last time I was here, I have felt anxious whenever she was out of my sight. It would not suit me to put her in a farm house. I want her to learn to speak nicely, and I have done my best to teach her; but if she went to a farm house she would be picking up all sorts of country words, and I want her to talk like a little lady.

"So that is settled, ma'm. I am going on to Exeter from here, and shall get her a stock of clothes there, and will bring her back next Saturday. Will it suit you to take her then?"

Mrs. Walsham said that would suit very well; and an hour later the sergeant set out from Sidmouth with his box, Aggie trotting alongside, talking continuously.

"But why am I to stop with that lady, grampa, and not to go about with you any more? I sha'n't like it. I like going about, though I get so tired sometimes when you are showing the pictures; and I like being with you. It isn't 'cause I have been naughty, is it? 'Cause I fell out of the boat into the water? I won't never get into a boat again, and I didn't mean to fall out, you know."

"No, Aggie, it's not that," the sergeant said. "You are always a good girl–at least, not always, because sometimes you get into passions, you know. Still, altogether you are a good little girl. Still, you see, you can't always be going about the country with me."

"But why not, grampa?"

"Well, my dear, because great girls can't go about the country like men. It wouldn't be right and proper they should."

"Why shouldn't it be, grampa?" the child persisted.

"Well, Aggie, I can't exactly explain to you why, but so it is. Men and boys have to work. They go about in ships, or as soldiers to fight for their country, just as I did. Girls and women have to stop at home, and keep house, and nurse babies, and that sort of thing. God made man to be hard and rough, and to work and go about. He made woman gentle and soft, to stop at home and make things comfortable."

Aggie meditated for some distance, in silence, upon this view of the case.

"But I have seen women working in the fields, grampa, and some of them didn't seem very soft and gentle."

"No, Aggie, things don't always go just as they ought to do; and you see, when people are poor, and men can't earn enough wages, then their wives and daughters have to help; and then, you see, they get rough, more like men, because they are not doing their proper work. But I want you to grow up soft and gentle, and so, for a time, I want you to live with that lady with the nice boy who pulled you out of the water, and they will make you very happy, and I shall come and see you sometime."

"I like him," the child said with a nod; "but I would rather be with you, you know."

"And the lady will teach you to read, Aggie. You have learned your letters, you know."

Aggie shook her head, to show that this part of the programme was not particularly to her liking.

"Do you think the boy will play with me, grampa?"

"I daresay he will, Aggie, when you are very good; and you must never forget, you know, that he saved your life. Just think how unhappy I should be, if he had not got you out of the water."

"The water was cold and nasty," Aggie said, "and it seemed so warm and nice to my hands. Aggie won't go near the water any more. Of course, if the boy is with me I can go, because he won't let me tumble in.

"Shall I get into the basket now, grampa? I is tired."

"Oh, nonsense, little woman! you have not walked half a mile yet. Anyhow, you must trot along until you get to the top of this hill, then you shall have a lift for a bit."

And so, with the child sometimes walking and sometimes riding, sometimes asleep in her basket and sometimes chatting merrily to her grandfather, the pair made their way across the country towards Exeter.

There was no little talk in Sidmouth when, on the following Sunday, the showman's grandchild appeared in Mrs. Walsham's pew in church, and it became known that she had become an inmate of her house. It was generally considered that Mrs. Walsham had let herself down greatly by taking the showman's grandchild, and one or two of the mothers of her pupils talked about taking them away. One or two, indeed, called upon her to remonstrate personally, but they gained nothing by the step.

"I do not understand what you mean," she said quietly, "by saying that the child is not fit to associate with my other pupils. She is singularly gentle and taking in her manner. She expresses herself better than any child of her own age in Sidmouth, so far as I know. There are few so neatly and prettily dressed. What is there to object to? Her grandfather has been a sergeant in the army. He bears a good character, and is liked wherever he goes. I do not consider that James or myself are, in any way, demeaned by sitting down to meals with the child, who, indeed, behaves as prettily and nicely as one could wish; and I certainly do not see that any of my pupils can be injuriously affected by the fact that, for an hour or two in the day, she learns her lessons in the same room with them. Had I thought that they would be, I should not have received her. I shall, of course, be sorry if any of my pupils are taken away, but as I have several girls only waiting for vacancies, it would make no difference to me pecuniarily."

And so it happened that Mrs. Walsham lost none of her pupils, and in a short time the wonder died out. Indeed, the child herself was so pretty, and taking in her ways, that it was impossible to make any objection to her personally.

Mrs. Walsham had been struck by the self command which she showed at parting with her grandfather. Her eyes were full of tears, her lip quivered, and she could scarcely speak; but there was no loud wailing, no passionate outburst. Her grandfather had impressed upon her that the parting was for her own good, and child though she was, she felt how great a sacrifice he was making in parting with her, and although she could not keep the tears from streaming down her cheeks, or silence her sobs as she bade him goodbye, she tried hard to suppress her grief.

The pain of parting was, indeed, fully as great to Sergeant Wilks as to his granddaughter; and it was with a very husky voice that he bade her goodbye, and then, putting her into Mrs. Walsham's arms, walked hastily away.

Aggie was soon at home. She and James very quickly became allies, and the boy was ever ready to amuse her, often giving up his own plans to take her for a walk to pick flowers in the hedgerow, or to sail a tiny boat for her in the pools left as the sea retired. Mrs. Walsham found, to her surprise, that the child gave little trouble. She was quiet and painstaking during the half hours in the morning and afternoon when she was in the school room, while at mealtimes her prattle and talk amused both mother and son, and altogether she made the house brighter and happier than it was before.

In two months the sergeant came round again. He did not bring his box with him, having left it at his last halting place; telling James, who happened to meet him as he came into Sidmouth, that he did not mean to bring his show there again.

"It will be better for the child," he explained. "She has done with the peep show now, and I do not want her to be any longer associated with it."

Aggie was delighted to see him, and sprang into his arms, with a scream of joy, as he entered. After a few minutes' talk, Mrs. Walsham suggested that she should put on her hat and go for a walk with him, and, in high contentment, the child trotted off, holding her grandfather's hand. Turning to the left, the sergeant took the path up the hill, and when he reached the top, sat down on the short turf, with Aggie nestling up against him.

"So you are quite well and happy, Aggie?" he asked.

"Quite well, grampa, and very happy; but I do wish so much that you were here. Oh. it would be so nice to have you to go out with every day!"

"I am afraid that cannot be managed, Aggie. I have been busy so long that I could not settle down quietly here. Besides, I must live, you know."

"But wouldn't people give you money for the show if you lived here, grampa? You always got money here the same as other places."

"Yes, my dear, but I could not get fresh pictures every day, and should soon tire them by showing the old house."

"But you are sorry sometimes, grampa, not to have me with you?"

"Yes, Aggie, very sorry. I miss you terribly sometimes, and I am always thinking about you."

"Then why don't you take me away again, grampa?"

"Because, as I told you, Aggie, I want you to learn to read, and to grow up quite a little lady."

"Does reading make one a lady, grampa?"

"No, Aggie, not by itself, but with other things."

"And when I am quite grown up and big, and know how to read nicely, shall I be able to go with you again?"

"We will see about that, Aggie, when the time comes. There is plenty of time yet to think about that."

"But I am getting on very fast, grampa, and the lady says I am a good girl. So it won't be such a very long time before I can leave."

"It will be some time, yet. You have only got to read little words yet, but there are lots of long words which you will come to presently. But Mrs. Walsham tells me that you are getting on nicely, and that you are a very good girl, which pleases me very much; and when I am walking along with my box, I shall like to be able to think of you as being quite comfortable and happy."

"And I go walks with Jim, grampa, and Jim has made me a boat, and he says someday, when it is very fine and quiet, he will take me out in a big boat, like that boat, you know; and he is going to ask you if he may, for the lady said I must not go out with him till he has asked you. And he said he won't let me tumble over, and I am going to sit quite, quite still."

"Yes, Aggie, I don't see any harm in your going out with him. I am sure he will only take you when it is fine, and he will look after you well. You like him, don't you?"

"Oh! I do, grampa; and you know, it was him who got me out of the water, else I should never have come out, and never have seen grampa again; and he has made me a boat. Oh! yes, I do like him!"

"That's right, my dear; always stick to those who are good to you."

A few days after this, as James was sailing the toy boat, for Aggie's amusement, in a pool, a boy sauntered up. He was somewhat taller than James Walsham, and at least two years older. He was well dressed, and James knew him as the nephew and heir of the squire.

It was not often that Richard Horton came down into the village. He was accustomed to be treated with a good deal of deference at the Hall, and to order servants and grooms about pretty much as he chose, and the indifference with which the fisher boys regarded him offended him greatly. He was a spoilt boy. His uncle had a resident tutor for him, but the selection had been a bad one. The library was large and good, the tutor fond of reading, and he was content to let the boy learn as little as he chose, providing that he did not trouble him. As to any instruction beyond books, he never thought of giving it.

The squire never interfered. He was a silent and disappointed man. He attended to his duties as a magistrate, and to the management of his estate, but seldom went beyond the lodge gates. He took his meals by himself, and often did not see his nephew for a week together, and had no idea but that he was pursuing his studies regularly with his tutor. Thus, the character of Richard Horton formed itself unchecked. At the best it was a bad one, but under other circumstances it might have been improved.

Up to the age of ten, he had lived in London with his father and mother, the latter a sister of the squire, who, having married beneath her, to the indignation of Mr. Linthorne, he had never seen her afterwards.

Four years before the story begins, she had received a letter from him, saying that, as her eldest son was now his heir, he wished him to come and live with him, and be prepared to take his place. The Hortons, who had a numerous family, at once accepted the offer, and Richard, hearing that he was going to a grand house, and would no doubt have a pony and all sorts of nice things, left his father and mother without a tear.

He was essentially selfish. He was vain of his good looks, which were certainly striking; and with his changed fortunes he became arrogant, and, as the squire's servants said, hateful; and yet the change had brought him less pleasure than he expected. It was true that he had the pony, that he was not obliged to trouble himself with lessons, that he was an important person at the "Hall;" but he had no playfellows, no one to admire his grandeur, and the days often passed heavily, and there was a look of discontent and peevishness upon his handsome face.

Perhaps the reason why he so seldom came down into Sidmouth, was not only because the fisher boys were not sufficiently impressed with his importance, but because they looked so much happier and more contented than he felt, in spite of his numerous advantages. On this day he was in a particularly bad temper. He had lamed his pony the day before, by riding it furiously over a bad road after it had cast a shoe. The gardener had objected to his picking more than half a dozen peaches which had just come into perfection, and had threatened to appeal to the squire.

Altogether, he was out of sorts, and had walked down to the sea with a vague hope that something might turn up to amuse him. He stood for some little time watching James sail the boat, and then strode down to the edge of the pool. The boat was a model of a smack, with brown sails. James had taken a good deal of pains with it, and it was an excellent model.

Presently, in crossing, she stuck in a shallow some twelve feet from the edge. The intervening stretch of water was a foot deep.

James picked up some small stones and threw them close to her, that the tiny wave they made might float her off. He tried several times without success.

"What's the use of such little stones as that?" Richard said roughly. "You will never get her off like that;" and picking up one as large as his fist, he threw it with some force.

It struck the mast, and broke it asunder, and knocked the boat on to her side. James Walsham uttered an angry exclamation.

"You are a bad boy," Aggie said passionately. "You are a bad boy to break my boat;" and she burst into tears.

"I didn't mean to do it, you little fool!" Richard said angrily, vexed more at his own clumsiness than at the damage it had caused. "What are you making such a beastly noise about?" and he gave her a push.

It was not a hard one, but the ground was slippery, and the child's foot slipped, and she fell at the edge of the pool, her dress going partly into the water. At the same instant, Richard reeled, and almost fell beside her, from a heavy blow between the eyes from James's fist.

"You insolent blackguard!" he exclaimed furiously, "I will pay you for this;" and he rushed at James.

The combat was not a long one. Hard work at rowing and sailing had strengthened Jim Walsham's muscles, and more than balanced the advantage in height and age of his adversary. He had had, too, more than one fight in his time, and after the first sudden burst of passion, caused by the overthrow of Aggie, he fought coolly and steadily, while Richard rained his blows wildly, without attempting to guard his face.

The child, on regaining her feet, ran crying loudly towards the beach, making for two fishermen who were engaged in mending a net some distance away; but before she could reach them to beg for aid for her champion, the fight was over, terminating by a heavy right-handed hit from James, which landed Richard Horton on his back in the pool.

James stood quietly awaiting a renewal of the conflict when he arose, but Richard had had enough of it. One of his eyes was already puffed and red, his nose bleeding, and his lip cut. His clothes were soaked from head to foot, and smeared with the red mud.

"I will pay you out for this, you see if I don't," Richard gasped hoarsely.

"What! have you had enough of it?" James said scornfully. "I thought you weren't any good. A fellow who would bully a little girl is sure to be a coward."

Richard moved as if he would renew the fight, but he thought better of it, and with a furious exclamation hurried away towards the Hall.

James, without paying any further heed to him, waded after the boat, and having recovered it, walked off towards the child, who, on seeing his opponent had moved off, was running down to meet him.

"Here is the boat, Aggie," he said. "There is no great harm done, only the mast and yard broken. I can easily put you in fresh ones;" but the child paid no attention to the boat.

"He is a wicked bad boy, Jim; and did he hurt you?"

"Oh, no, he didn't hurt me, Aggie, at least nothing to speak of. I hurt him a good deal more. I paid him out well for breaking your boat, and pushing you down, the cowardly brute!"

"Only look, Jim," she said, holding out her frock. "What will she say?"

James laughed.

"Mother won't say anything," he said. "She is accustomed to my coming in all muddy."

"But she said 'Keep your frock clean,' and it's not clean," Aggie said in dismay.

"Yes, but that is not your fault, little one. I will make it all right with her, don't you fret. Come on, we had better go home and change it as soon as possible."

They passed close by the two fishermen on their way.

"You gave it to the young squire finely, Master Walsham," one of them said, "and served him right, too. We chanced to be looking at the moment, and saw it all. He is a bad un, he is, by what they say up at the Hall. I heard one of the grooms talking last night down at the 'Ship,' and a nice character he gave him. This thrashing may do him some good; and look you, Master Walsham, if he makes a complaint to the squire, and it's likely enough he will get up a fine story of how it came about–the groom said he could lie like King Pharaoh–you just send word to me, and me and Bill will go up to the squire, and tell him the truth of the matter."

Mrs. Walsham felt somewhat alarmed when her son told her what had happened, for the squire was a great man at Sidmouth, a magistrate, and the owner of the greater part of the place as well as of the land around it; and although Mrs. Walsham did not hold the same exaggerated opinion of his powers as did the majority of his neighbours, who would scarcely have dreamt of opposing it, had the squire ordered anyone to be hung and quartered, still she felt that it was a somewhat terrible thing that her son should have thrashed the nephew and heir of the great man.

In the evening there was a knock at the door, and the little maid came in with eyes wide open with alarm, for she had heard of the afternoon's battle, to say that the constable wished to speak to Mrs. Walsham.

"Servant, ma'am," he said as he entered. "I am sorry to be here on an unpleasant business; but I have got to say as the squire wishes to see Master Walsham in the justice room at ten o'clock, on a charge of 'salt and battery.

"Don't you be afeard ma'am," he went on confidentially. "I don't think as anything is going to be done to him. I ain't got no warrant, and so I don't look upon it as regular business. I expects it will be just a blowing up. It will be just the squire, and not the magistrate, I takes it. He told me to have him up there at ten, but as he said nothing about custody, I thought I would do it my own way and come to you quiet like; so if you say as Master Walsham shall be up there at ten o'clock, I'll just take your word for it and won't come to fetch him. The doctor was allus very good to me and my missus, and I shouldn't like to be walking through Sidmouth with my hand on his son's collar."

"Thank you, Hobson," Mrs. Walsham said quietly. "You can rely upon it my son shall be there punctually. He has nothing to be afraid or ashamed of."

Full of rage as Richard Horton had been, as he started for home, he would never have brought the matter before the squire on his own account. His case was too weak, and he had been thrashed by a boy younger than himself. Thus, he would have probably chosen some other way of taking his vengeance; but it happened that, just as he arrived home, he met his tutor coming out. The latter was astounded at Richard's appearance. His eyes were already puffed so much that he could scarcely see out of them, his lips were cut and swollen, his shirt stained with blood, his clothes drenched and plastered with red mud.

"Why, what on earth has happened, Richard?"

Richard had already determined upon his version of the story.

"A brute of a boy knocked me down into the water," he said, "and then knocked me about till he almost killed me."

"But what made him assault you in this outrageous manner?" his tutor asked. "Surely all the boys about here must know you by sight; and how one of them would dare to strike you I cannot conceive."

"I know the fellow," Richard said angrily. "He is the son of that doctor fellow who died two years ago."

"But what made him do it?" the tutor repeated.

"He was sailing his boat, and it got stuck, and he threw in some stones to get it off; and I helped him, and I happened to hit the mast of his beastly boat, and then he flew at me like a tiger, and that's all."

"Well, it seems to be a monstrous assault, Richard, and you must speak to the squire about it."

"Oh, no, I sha'n't," Richard said hastily. "I don't want any row about it, and I will pay him off some other way. I could lick him easy enough if it had been a fair fight, only he knocked me down before I was on my guard. No, I sha'n't say anything about it."

But Richard's tutor, on thinking the matter over, determined to speak to the squire. Only the evening before, Mr. Linthorne had surprised him by asking him several questions as to Richard's progress and conduct, and had said something about examining him himself, to see how he was getting on. This had caused Mr. Robertson no little alarm, for he knew that even the most superficial questioning would betray the extent of Richard's ignorance, and he had resolved that, henceforth, he would endeavour to assert his authority, and to insist upon Richard's devoting a certain portion of each day, regularly, to study. Should the squire meet the boy anywhere about the house, he must at once notice the condition of his face; and even if he did not meet him, he could not fail to notice it on Sunday, when he sat beside him in the pew. It would be better, therefore, that he should at once report the matter to him.

Without saying a word to Richard of his intentions, he therefore went to the squire's study, and told him what had taken place, as he had learned it from Richard. The squire listened silently.

"Very well, Mr. Robertson. You were quite right to tell me about it. Of course, I cannot suffer my nephew to be treated in this manner. At the same time, I am sorry that it was Walsham's son. I don't know anything about the boy, and should not know him even by sight, but I had an esteem for his father, who was a hard-working man, and, I believe, clever. He used to attend here whenever any of the servants were ill, and I had intended to do something for the boy. I am sorry he has turned out so badly. However, I will have him up here and speak to him. This sort of thing cannot be permitted."

And accordingly, orders were given to the constable. When, in the evening, Mr. Robertson informed Richard what he had done, the boy flew into a terrible passion, and abused his tutor with a violence of language which shocked and astonished him, and opened his eyes to his own culpability, in allowing him to go on his way unchecked. He in vain endeavoured to silence the furious lad. He had been so long without exercising any authority, that he had now no authority to exercise, and, after an angry scene, Richard flung himself out of the room, and left his tutor in a state bordering on consternation.

Chapter 3: The Justice Room.

Richard's feelings were not to be envied, as he lay awake that night, thinking over what had taken place in the morning. It had never, for a moment, entered his mind that his tutor would repeat his statement to the squire, and he would have given a good deal if he had not made it. However, there was nothing for him now but to stick to the story, and he felt but little doubt of the result. He had no idea that any, but the actors in it, had witnessed the scene by the pool, and he felt confident that his uncle would, as a matter of course, take his word in preference to that of this boy, who would naturally tell lies to screen himself. Of course, the child was there, but no one would mind what a baby like that said. Still, it was a nuisance, and he gnashed his teeth with rage at the interference of his tutor in the matter.

"I will get rid of him, somehow, before long," he said. "I will pay him out for his meddling, as sure as my name's Richard Horton. I will get him out of this before three months are gone."

The next morning at breakfast, Richard received a message from the squire that he was to be present at ten o'clock in the justice room, and accordingly, at that hour he presented himself there with a confident air, but with an inward feeling of misgiving.

The squire was sitting at his table, with his clerk beside him. Mr. Robertson was in a chair a short distance off. The constable was standing by the side of James Walsham, at the other end of the room. Mr. Linthorne nodded to his nephew.

"I wish you to repeat the story which you told Mr. Robertson yesterday."

Richard had thought over whether it would be better to soften his story, but as it had already been told to the squire, he had concluded that there would be more danger in contradicting his first version than in sticking to it. Accordingly, he repeated his story almost word for word as he had told it to Mr. Robertson.

"What have you to say to this, James Walsham?" the squire asked. "This is a serious charge, that you without any provocation assaulted and maltreated my nephew."

"I say it is all a lie, sir," James said fearlessly.

The squire uttered a short exclamation of surprise and anger. He had been, at first, favourably impressed with the appearance of the young prisoner, though he had been surprised at seeing that he was younger than his nephew, for he had expected to see a much older boy.

"That is not the way to speak, sir," he said sternly, while the constable pressed a warning hand on James's shoulder.

"Well, sir, it's not true then," the boy said. "It's all false from beginning to end, except that I did strike him first; but I struck him, not because he had thrown a great stone and broken my boat, but because he pushed a little girl who was with me down into the water."

"She slipped down. I never pushed her," Richard broke in.

"Hold your tongue, sir," the squire said sternly. "You have given your evidence. I have now to hear what the accused has to say.

"Now, tell your story."

James now gave his version of the affair.

When he had ended, Mr. Linthorne said gravely, "Have you any witnesses to call?"

"Yes, sir, there are two fishermen outside who saw it."

"Bring them in," the magistrate said to the constable.

Not a word was spoken in the justice room until the constable returned. As James had told his story, the magistrate had listened with disbelief. It had not occurred to him that his nephew could have told a lie, and he wondered at the calmness with which this boy told his story. Why, were it true, Richard was a coward as well as a liar, for with his superior age and height, he should have been able to thrash this boy in a fair fight; yet James's face had not a mark, while his nephew's showed how severely he had been punished.

But his eye fell upon Richard when James said that he had witnesses. He saw an unmistakable look of terror come over his face, and the bitter conviction flashed across him that James's story was the true one.

"There is no occasion to give him the book, Hobson," he said, as the constable was about to hand the Testament to one of the fishermen. "This is a private investigation, not a formal magisterial sitting, and there is no occasion, at this stage, to take any evidence on oath."

"What is your name, my man?"

"John Mullens, your honour."

"Well, just tell me, Mullens, what you know about this business."

"I was a-mending my nets, yer honour, along with Simon Harte, and young Master Walsham was a-sailing his boat in a pool, along with the little gal as lives at his mother's."

"How far were you from the spot where he was?" the squire asked.

"Two hundred yards or so, I should say," the fisherman replied. "We was working behind a boat, but we could see over it well enough. Presently we saw Master Horton come down, and stand alongside the others.

"I said to Simon, 'He is a good-looking young fellow, is the squire's nephew,'" and the fisherman's eye twinkled with a grim humour, as he glanced at Richard's swollen face.

"The boat got stuck, and Master Walsham threw something in close to it to get it off. Then I see Master Horton stoop, and pick up a chunk of stone, and chuck it hard;

and it hit the boat and knocked it over. I see the little girl turn round and say something to Master Horton, and then she put her apron up to her face and began to cry. He gave her a sort of shove, and she tumbled down into the edge of the pool.

"I says to Simon, 'What a shame!' but afore the words was out of my mouth, Master Walsham he hits him, and hits him hard, too. Then there was a fight, but Master Horton, he hadn't a chance with James, who gave him as sound a licking as ever you see'd, and ending with knocking him backwards into the pool. Then he gets up and shakes his fist at James, and then goes off as hard as he could. That's all I know about it."

"It's a wicked lie," Richard burst out. "They have made it up between them. There was nobody there."

"Hold your tongue, sir, I tell you," the squire said, so sternly that Richard, who had risen from his seat, shrank back again and remained silent; while Simon Harte gave his evidence, which was almost identical with that of the other fisherman.

"Have you any other witnesses?" the magistrate asked James.

"Only the little girl, sir, but I did not bring her up. She is so little, I thought it was better she should not come, but I can send for her if you wish it."

"It is not necessary," Mr. Linthorne said. "I have heard quite sufficient. The manner in which you and these fishermen have given your evidence convinces me that you are speaking the truth, and I am sorry that you should have been placed in this position. You will understand that this is not a formal court, and therefore that there is no question of discharging you. I can only say that, having heard the story of what took place at this fight between you and my nephew, I am convinced that you did what any other boy of spirit would have done, under the same circumstances, and that the punishment which you administered to him was thoroughly deserved.

"Good morning!"

James Walsham and his witnesses left the room. Mr. Linthorne rose, and saying to his nephew, "Follow me, sir," went to his study.

Without saying a word as to what had passed, he took down some books from the shelves, and proceeded to examine Richard in them. A few minutes sufficed to show that the boy was almost absolutely ignorant of Latin, while a few questions in geography and history showed that he was equally deficient in these also.

"That will do," the squire said. "Go up to your room, and remain there until I send for you."

An hour after this a dog cart came round to the door. Mr. Robertson took his place in it with his trunk, and was driven away to Exeter, never to return.

For two days Richard remained a prisoner in his room. His meals were brought up to him, but the servant who came with them answered no questions, telling him that the squire's orders were that he was not to hold any conversation with him. There was, indeed, a deep pleasure among the servants at the Hall, at the knowledge that Richard Horton was in disgrace. The exact circumstances of the affair were unknown, for the fishermen had not been present when Richard had told his story, and Mrs. Walsham, who was much shocked when James told her the circumstances, had impressed upon him that it was better to say nothing more about it.

"You are clear in the matter, Jim, and that is enough for you. The squire will, no doubt, punish his nephew for the wicked lies he has told. Some day, you know, the boy will be master here. Don't let us set everyone against him by telling this disgraceful story."

So, beyond the fact that there had been a fight between James Walsham and the squire's nephew, and that Richard Horton had been thrashed, and that the squire himself had said that it served him right, Sidmouth knew nothing of what had taken place in the justice room.

Mr. Linthorne's first impulse had been to send his nephew at once back to his parents, with the message that he would have nothing more to do with him; but, though he had the reputation of being a stern man, the squire was a very kind-hearted one. He was shocked to find that the boy was a liar, and that, to shield himself, he had invented this falsehood against his opponent; but upon reflection, he acknowledged that he himself had been to blame in the matter. He had taken the boy into his house, had assigned to him the position of his heir, and had paid no further attention to him.

Unfortunately, the man he had selected as his tutor had proved false to the trust. The boy had been permitted to run wild, his head was turned with the change in his prospects, his faults had grown unchecked. It was to be said for him that he had not intended, in the first place, to bring his opponent into disgrace by making this false accusation against him, for his tutor had acknowledged that he had said he did not intend to tell him, or to take any step in the matter, and his position of accuser had been, to some extent, forced upon him by the necessity of his confirming the tale, which he had told to account for his being thrashed by a boy smaller than himself.

Yes, it would be unfair upon the boy utterly to cast him off for this first offence. He would give him one more trial.

The result of the squire's reflection was that, on the third day of his imprisonment, Richard was sent for to the study. The squire did not motion to him to sit down, and he remained standing with, as the squire said to himself, a hang-dog look upon his face.

"I have been thinking over this matter quietly, Richard, for I did not wish to come to any hasty conclusion. My first impulse was to pack you off home, and have no more to do with you, but I have thought better of it. Mean and despicable as your conduct has been, I take some blame to myself, for not having seen that your tutor did his duty by you. Therefore, I have resolved to give you another chance, but not here. I could not bear to have a boy, who has proved himself a despicable liar, about me; but I will try and think that this was a first offence, and that the lesson which it has taught you may influence all your future life, and that you may yet grow up an honourable man.

"But you will remember that, henceforth, you are on trial, and that the position in which you will stand by my will, will depend solely and entirely on your own conduct. If you prove, by that, that this lesson has had its effect, that you deeply repent of your conduct, and are resolved to do your best to be henceforth straight, honourable, and true, you will, at my death, occupy the position I have intended for you. If not, not one single penny of my money will you get. I am going to put you in a school where you will be looked strictly after, and where you will have every chance of retrieving yourself. I have just written to a friend of mine, a post captain in his majesty's service, asking him to receive you as a midshipman. I have told him frankly that you have been somewhat over indulged, and that the discipline of the sea life will be of great benefit to you, and have requested him to keep a tight hand over you, and let me know occasionally how you are going on. I have told him that your position as my heir will, to a very large extent, depend upon his reports, and have asked him, in the name of our old friendship, to be perfectly frank and open in them with me. I have said 'he is my eldest nephew, but I have others who will take his place, if he is unworthy of the position, and although I should be sorry if he should be found wanting, I will commit the interests of all the tenants and people on my estate to no one who is not, in every respect, an honourable gentleman.'

"That will do, sir. You need not remain longer in your room, but you will not leave the grounds. My friend's ship is at Portsmouth at present, and doubtless I shall receive an answer in the course of a few days. Until then, the less we see each other, the more pleasant for us both."

There were few more miserable boys in England than Richard Horton, during the week which elapsed before the answer to the squire's letter was received. It cannot be said that, in the true sense of the word, he was sorry for his fault. He was furious with himself, not because he had lied, but because of the consequences of the lie. A thousand times he called himself a fool for having imperilled his position, and risked being sent back again to the dingy house in London, merely to excuse himself for being thrashed by a boy smaller than himself. Mad with his folly, not in having invented the story, but in having neglected to look round, to assure himself that there were no witnesses who would contradict it, he wandered disconsolate about the gardens and park, cursing what he called his fortune.

It was an additional sting to his humiliation, that he knew every servant in and about the house rejoiced at his discomfiture, and he imagined that there was a veiled smile of satisfaction, at his bruised visage and his notorious disgrace with the squire, on the face of every man he met outside, and of every woman who passed him in the house.

During the whole week he did not venture near the stables, for there he knew that he had rendered himself specially obnoxious, and there was nothing for him to do but to saunter listlessly about the garden, until the day arrived that the letter came granting the squire's request, and begging that he might be sent off at once, as the vessel would probably put to sea in a few days.

"Now, Richard," the squire said that evening to him, in a kinder voice than he had used on the last occasion, "you understand exactly how we stand towards each other. That being so, I do not wish to maintain our present uncomfortable relations. You have had your punishment, and, unless I hear to the contrary, I shall assume that the punishment has had its effect. When you return from sea, after your first voyage, you will come home here as if nothing had happened, and this business need never be alluded to between us. If you turn out as I have hitherto believed you to be, I shall receive you as warmly as if my opinion of you had never been shaken.

"I have requested Captain Sinclair to let me know what is the average allowance that the midshipmen receive from their parents, and shall see that you have as much as your messmates. I have also asked him to kindly allow one of his officers to order you a proper outfit in all respects, and to have the bill sent in to me. So now, my boy, you will have a fresh and a fair start, and I trust that you will turn out everything that I can wish."

"I will try, sir. I will indeed," Richard said earnestly; and he spoke from his heart, for the inheritance was very dear to him, and it would be a terrible thing indeed to forfeit it.

For two years after Richard Horton's departure, things went on quietly at Sidmouth. James Walsham continued to make a pet and a playmate of little Aggie. Her out-of-door life had made her strong and sturdy, and she was able to accompany him in all his rambles, while, when he was at work at home preparing fishing lines, making boats, or otherwise amusing himself, she was content to sit hours quietly beside him, chattering incessantly, and quite content with an occasional brief answer to the questions. When he was studying, she too would work at her lessons; and however much she might be puzzled over these, she would never disturb him by asking him questions when so engaged.

She was an intelligent child, and the hour's lesson, morning and afternoon, soon grew into two. She was eager to learn, and rapidly gained ground on Mrs. Walsham's older pupils. During the two years, that lady never had cause to regret that she had yielded to the sergeant's entreaties. Aggie was no trouble in the house, which she brightened with her childish laughter and merry talk; and her companionship, James's mother could not but think, did the boy much good. It softened his manner, and, although he still often went out with the fishermen, he was no longer thrown entirely for companionship upon the boys on the beach.

The sergeant came and went, seldom being more than two months without paying a visit to Sidmouth. The child was always delighted to see her grandfather, and James took to him greatly, and liked nothing better than to stroll up with him to a sheltered spot on the hillside, where he would throw himself down on the grass, while the sergeant smoked his pipe and told him stories of his travels and adventures, and Aggie ran about looking for wildflowers, or occasionally sat down, for a while, to listen also.

The squire lived his usual lonely life up at the Hall. The absence of his nephew, whose ship had sailed for a foreign station, was a relief rather than otherwise to him. It had, from the first, been a painful effort to him to regard this boy as his heir, and he had only done it when heartsick from a long and fruitless search for one who would have been nearer and dearer to him. Nor had he ever taken to the lad personally. The squire felt that there was not the ring of true metal in him. The careless way in which he spoke of his parents showed a want of heart; and although his uncle was ignorant how much the boy made himself disliked in the household, he was conscious, himself, of a certain antipathy for him, which led him to see as little of him as possible.

The two years, for which the sergeant had placed his grandchild with Mrs. Walsham, came to an end. That he did not intend to continue the arrangement, she judged from something he said on the occasion of his last visit, two months before the time was up, but he gave no hint as to what he intended to do with her.

In those weeks Mrs. Walsham frequently thought the matter over. That the sergeant had plans for the child she could hardly doubt. The child herself had told her that she knew of no other relations than her grandfather, and yet he could hardly intend to take her about with him, after placing her for two years in a comfortable home. She was but seven years old now—far too young to go out into a place as servant girl in a farm house. She doubted not that the sergeant had expended the whole of his savings, and she thought him foolish in not having kept her with him for some little time longer, or, if he could not do that, he might have placed her with some honest people, who would have kept her for the sum he had paid until she was old enough to take a place as a nurse girl.

And yet, while she argued thus, Mrs. Walsham felt that the old showman had not acted without weighing the whole matter. There must be something in it which she did not understand. In fact, he had said so when he placed the child with her.

As the time approached, she became more worried at the thought of Aggie leaving her. The little one had wound herself very closely round her heart. The expense of keeping her was small indeed, the cost of her food next to nothing; while the extra girl, whom Mrs. Walsham had taken on when she first came, had been retained but a very short time, James's constant companionship with her rendering the keeping of a nurse altogether unnecessary.

At last she made up her mind that she would offer to keep her on without pay. She and James would miss her companionship sorely, and it could not be considered an extravagance, since the money she had received for her would pay for the cost of her keep for years to come. When Mrs. Walsham's mind was once made up, her only fear was that these mysterious plans of the sergeant would not allow him to leave Aggie with her.

Punctual to the day, Sergeant Wilks arrived, and after a little talk in the parlour, as usual, with James and Aggie present, he formally requested the favour of a conversation with Mrs. Walsham alone.

"Take Aggie for a walk, James. Do not stay out above three quarters of an hour, as your tea will be ready for you then."

"You must have wondered, ma'am, a good deal," the sergeant began when they were alone, "why I, who get my living by travelling the country with a peep show, wished to place my grandchild in a position above her, and to have her taught to be a little lady. It is time now that I should tell you. Aggie is my granddaughter, but she is the granddaughter, too, of Squire Linthorne up at the Hall."

"Bless me!" Mrs. Walsham ejaculated, too astonished for any further expression of her feelings.

"Yes, ma'am, she is the daughter of the squire's son Herbert, who married my daughter Cissie."

"Dear me, dear me," Mrs. Walsham said, "what an extraordinary thing! Of course I remember Herbert Linthorne, a handsome, pleasant young fellow. He was on bad terms, as everyone heard, eight years ago, with his father, because he married somebody beneath—I mean somebody of whom the squire did not approve. A year afterwards, we heard that he was dead, and there was a report that his wife was dead, too, but that was only a rumour. The squire went away just at the time, and did not come back for months afterwards, and after that he was altogether changed. Before, he had been one of the most popular men in this part of the country, but now he shut himself up, gave up all his acquaintances, and never went outside the park gates except to come down to church. I remember it gave us quite a shock when we saw him for the first time–he seemed to have grown an old man all at once. Everyone said that the death of his son had broken his heart.

"And Aggie is his granddaughter! Well, well, you have astonished me. But why did you not tell me before?"

"There were a good many reasons, ma'am. I thought, in the first place, you might refuse me, if you knew, for it might do you harm. The squire is a vindictive man, and he is landlord of your house; and if he came to know that you had knowingly taken in his granddaughter, there was no saying how he might have viewed it. Then, if you had known it, you might have thought you ought to keep her in, and not let her run about the country with your son; and altogether, it would not have been so comfortable for you or her. I chose to put her at Sidmouth because I wanted to come here often, to hear how the squire was going on; for if he had been taken ill I should have told him sooner than I intended."

"But why did you not tell him before?" Mrs. Walsham asked.

"Just selfishness, ma'am. I could not bring myself to run the risk of having to give her up. She was mine as much as his, and was a hundred times more to me than she could be to him. I took her a baby from her dead mother's arms. I fed her and nursed her, taught her her first words and her first prayer. Why should I offer to give her up to him who, likely enough, would not accept the offer when it was made to him? But I always intended to make it some day. It was my duty to give her the chance at least; but I kept on putting off the day, till that Saturday when she was so nearly drowned; then I saw my duty before me."

"I had, from the first, put aside a hundred pounds, to give her more of an education than I could do; but if it hadn't been for that fall into the sea, it might have been years before I carried out my plan. Then I saw it could not go on any longer. She was getting too old and too bold to sit quiet while I was showing my box. She had had a narrow escape, and who could say what might happen the next time she got into mischief? Then I bethought me that the squire was growing old, and that it was better not to put it off too long. So, ma'am, I came to you and made up my mind to put her with you."

"And you had your way," Mrs. Walsham said, smiling, "though it was with some difficulty."

"I expected it would be difficult, ma'am; but I made up my mind to that, and had you kept on refusing I should, as a last chance, have told you whose child she was."

"But why me?" Mrs. Walsham asked. "Why were you so particularly anxious that she should come to me, of all people?"

The sergeant smiled.

"It's difficult to tell you, ma'am, but I had a reason."

"But what was it?" Mrs. Walsham persisted.

The sergeant hesitated.

"You may think me an old fool, ma'am, but I will tell you what fancy came into my mind. Your son saved Aggie's life. He was twelve years old, she was five, seven years' difference."

"Why, what nonsense, sergeant!" Mrs. Walsham broke in with a laugh. "You don't mean to say that fancy entered your head!"

"It did, ma'am," Sergeant Wilks said gravely. "I liked the look of the boy much. He was brave and modest, and a gentleman. I spoke about him to the fishermen that night, and everyone had a good word for him; so I said to myself, 'I can't reward him for what he has done directly, but it may be that I can indirectly.'

"Aggie is only a child, but she has a loving, faithful little heart, and I said to myself, 'If I throw her with this boy, who, she knows, has saved her life, for two years, she is sure to have a strong affection for him.'

"Many things may happen afterwards. If the squire takes her they will be separated. He may get to care for someone, and so may she, but it's just giving him a chance.

"Then, too, I thought a little about myself. I liked to fancy that, even though she would have to go from me to the squire, my little plan may yet turn out, and it would be I, not he, who had arranged for the future happiness of my little darling. I shouldn't have told you all this, ma'am; but you would have it."

"I am glad you brought her to me, Sergeant Wilks, anyhow," Mrs. Walsham said, "for I love her dearly, and she has been a great pleasure to me; but what you are talking about is simply nonsense. My son is a good boy, and will, I hope, grow up an honourable gentleman like his father; but he cannot look so high as the granddaughter of Squire Linthorne."

"More unequal marriages have been made than that, ma'am," the sergeant said sturdily; "but we won't say more about it. I have thought it over and over, many a hundred times, as I wheeled my box across the hills, and it don't seem to me impossible. I will agree that the squire would never say yes; but the squire may be in his grave years before Aggie comes to think about marriage. Besides, it is more than likely that he will have nothing to say to my pet. If his pride made him cast his son off, rather than acknowledge my daughter as his, it will keep him from acknowledging her daughter as his grandchild. I hope it will, with all my heart; I hope so."

"In that case, Sergeant Wilks," Mrs. Walsham said, "let this be her home for the time. Before you told me your story, I had made up my mind to ask you to let her remain with me. You need feel under no obligation, for the money you have paid me is amply sufficient to pay for the expenses of what she eats for years. It will be a real pleasure for me to keep her, for she has become a part of the house, and we should miss her sorely, indeed. She is quick and intelligent, and I will teach her all I know, and can train her up to take a situation as a governess in a gentleman's family, or perhaps–" and she laughed, "your little romance might come true some day, and she can in that case stop in this home until James makes her another."

"You are very kind, ma'am," the sergeant said. "Truly kind indeed; and I humbly accept your offer, except that so long as I live she shall be no expense to you. I earn more than enough for my wants, and can, at any rate, do something towards preventing her from being altogether a burden on your hands. And now, ma'am, how would you recommend me to go to work with the vindictive old man up at the Hall?"

"I shouldn't have thought he was vindictive. That is not at all the character he bears."

"No," the sergeant said, "I hear him spoken well of; but I have seen, in other cases, men, who have had the name of being pleasant and generous, were yet tyrants and brutes in their own family. I judge him as I found him--a hard hearted, tyrannical, vindictive father. I think I had better not see him myself. We have never met. I have never set eyes on him save here in church; but he regarded me as responsible for the folly of his son. He wrote me a violent letter, and said I had inveigled the lad into the marriage; and although I might have told him it was false, I did not answer his letter, for the mischief was done then, and I hoped he would cool down in time.

"However, that is all past now; but I don't wish to see him. I was thinking of letting the child go to the Hall by herself, and drop in suddenly upon him. She is very like her father, and may possibly take his heart by storm."

"Yes," Mrs. Walsham assented. "Now I know who she is, I can see the likeness strongly. Yes; I should think that that would be the best way. People often yield to a sudden impulse, who will resist if approached formally or from a distance. But have you any reason to suppose that he will not receive her? Did he refuse at first to undertake the charge of the child? Does he even know that she is alive? It may be that, all these years, he has been anxious to have her with him, and that you have been doing him injustice altogether."

"I never thought of it in that light," the sergeant said, after a pause. "He never came near his son when he lay dying, never wrote a line in answer to his letters. If a man could not forgive his son when he lay dying, how could he care for a grandchild he had never seen?"

"That may be so, Sergeant Wilks; but his son's death certainly broke him down terribly, and it may be that he will gladly receive his granddaughter.

"But there are the young ones back again. I will think over what you have been telling me, and we can discuss it again tomorrow."

Chapter 4: The Squire's Granddaughter.

The following day another council was held, and Mrs. Walsham told the sergeant that, on thinking it over, she had concluded that the best way would be to take the old butler at the Hall, who had served the family for forty-five years, into their confidence, and to ask him to arrange how best Aggie might be introduced to the squire.

"I have been thinking over what you said, ma'am, and it may be that you are right, and that I have partly misjudged the squire. I hope so, for Aggie's sake, and yet I cannot help feeling sorry. I have always felt almost sure he would have nothing to say to her, and I have clung to the hope that I should not lose my little girl. I know, of course, how much better it will be for her, and have done all I could to make her so that she should be fit for it, if he took her. But it will be a wrench, ma'am. I can't help feeling it will be a wrench;" and the old soldier's voice quivered as he spoke.

"It cannot be otherwise, sergeant," Mrs. Walsham said kindly. "You have been everything to each other, and though, for her good and happiness, you are ready to give her up, it is a heavy sacrifice for you to make."

That afternoon, the sergeant went for a long walk alone with Aggie, and when they returned Mrs. Walsham saw, by the flushed cheeks and the swollen eyes of the child, that she had been crying. James noticed it also, and saw that she seemed depressed and quiet. He supposed that her grandfather had been telling her that he was going to take her away, for hitherto nothing had been said, in her hearing, as to the approaching termination of the stay with his mother.

As they came out of church, Mrs. Walsham had waited for a moment at the door, and had told the butler at the Hall that she wished particularly to speak to him, that afternoon, if he could manage to come down. They were not strangers, for the doctor had attended John's wife in her last illness, and he had sometimes called with messages from the Hall, when the doctor was wanted there.

John Petersham was astonished, indeed, when Mrs. Walsham informed him that the little girl he had seen in her pew, in church, was his master's granddaughter.

"You don't say so, ma'am. You don't say as that pretty little thing is Master Herbert's child! But why didn't you say so afore? Why, I have caught myself looking at her, and wondering how it was that I seemed to know her face so well; and now, of course, I sees it. She is the picture of Master Herbert when he was little."

"I couldn't say so before, John, because I only knew it myself last night. Her grandfather–that is, her other grandfather, you know–placed her with me to educate, and, as he said, to make a little lady of, two years ago; but it was only last night he told me."

"Only to think of it!" the butler ejaculated. "What will the squire say?"

"Yes, that is the point, John. What will the squire say? Her grandfather thinks he will have nothing to say to her."

"Nothing to say to her, ma'am! Why, he will be off his head with joy. Didn't he search for her, and advertise for her, and do all he could to find her for months? It wasn't till he tried for over a year that he gave it up, and sent for Richard Horton to come to him."

"Her grandfather can only judge by what he knows, John. He tells me that the son wrote to his father, over and over again, on his deathbed, and that he never came near him, or took any notice of the letters."

"That's true enough, ma'am," the butler said sadly; "and it is what has pretty nigh broken the squire's heart. He was obstinate like at first, and he took me with him when he travelled about across the sea among the foreigners, and when he was at a place they called Athens, he got a fever and he was down for weeks. We came home by sea, and the winds was foul, and we made a long voyage of it, and when we got home there was letters that had been lying months and months for us, and among them was those letters of Master Herbert's.

"The squire wasn't an hour in the house afore the carriage was round to the door, and we posted as hard as horses could take us right across England to Broadstairs, never stopping a minute except to change horses; and when we got there it was a month too late, and there was nothing to do but to go to the churchyard, and to see the stone under which Master Herbert and his young wife was laid.

"The house where they had died was shut up. There had been a sale, and the man who was the father of Master Herbert's wife was gone, and we learned there had been a baby born, and that had gone too. The squire was like a madman, blaming himself for his son's death, and a-raving to think what must Master Herbert have thought of him, when he never answered his letters. I had a terrible time with him, and then he set to work to find the child; but, as I told you, we never did find it, or hear a word of it from that time to this, and the squire has never held up his head. He will be pretty well out of his mind with joy."

"I am very glad to hear what you say, John," Mrs. Walsham said. "I could hardly fancy the squire, who always has borne such a name for kindness, being so hard that he would not listen to his dying son's entreaties."

"No, ma'am. The squire was hard for a bit. Master Herbert's marriage was a sad disappointment to him. He had made up his mind he was going to do so well, and to cut such a figure in the world; but he would have come round. Lord bless you, he only meant to hold out for a bit. When he was ill at Athens, he was talking all the time about forgiving his son, and I could see how hard it had been to him to keep separated from him. On the voyage home he fidgeted ever so at the delay, and I knew that the first thing he did, when he got back, would be to write to Master Herbert and tell him to bring his wife down to the Hall. There's not a hard corner in the squire's heart.

"I thank the good God for the news you have told me, ma'am; it's the best I ever heard in all my life."

Mrs. Walsham now told him how the child had been brought up, and then the sergeant himself, who was waiting in the next room, was brought in; and to him John Petersham related the story of the squire's illness, the reason of the letters not reaching him for months after they had been written, and his intense sorrow and self reproach at having arrived too late, and told him of the efforts that had been made to find the child. The sergeant listened in grave silence.

"I am glad it is so," he said, after a pause. "I have misjudged the squire, and I am glad of it. It will be a blow to me to lose the child. I do not pretend that it won't; but it is for her good, and I must be content. He can hardly object to my seeing her sometimes, and if I know that she is well and happy, that is all I care for; and now the sooner it's over the better. Can she come up this evening?"

"Surely she can," John Petersham said. "The squire dines at five. If you will bring her up at six, I will take her in to him."

And so it was arranged, and in his walk with Aggie, afterwards, the sergeant told her the history of her parents, and that Squire Linthorne was her other grandfather, and that she was to go up and see him that evening.

Aggie had uttered her protest against fate. She did not wish to leave her grampa who had been so good to her, and Mrs. Walsham, and James. The description of the big house and its grandeurs, and the pleasures of a pony for herself, offered no enticement to her; and, weeping, she flung her arms round her grandfather's neck and implored him not to give her up.

"I must, my dear. It is my duty. I wish to God that it were not. You know how I love you, Aggie, and how hard it is for me to part with you; but it is for your good, my darling. You mayn't see it now, but when you get older you will know it. It will not be so hard now on me, dear, nor on you, as it would have been had I given you up two years ago; but we have learned to do a little without each other."

"But you will come and see me, just as you have here, won't you?" Aggie said, still weeping.

"I hope so, my dear. You see, the squire is your father's father, while I am only your mother's father, and somehow the law makes him nearer to you than I am, and he will have the right to say what you must do."

"I won't stay with him. I won't," Aggie said passionately, "if he won't let you come."

"You must not say that, dear," the sergeant said. "We must all do our duty, even when that duty is hard to do, and your duty will be to obey the squire's orders, and to do as he tells you. I have no doubt he will be very kind, and that you will be very happy with him, and I hope he will let you see me sometimes."

It was a long time before the child was at all reconciled. When her sobs began to cease, her grandfather told her what she was to do when she saw the squire.

"You will remember, my dear, that I have been more fortunate than he has. I have had you all these years, and he has had no one to love or care for him. You must remember that he was not to blame, because he objected to his son marrying my daughter. They were not in the same position of life, and it was only natural that he should not like it, at first; and, as I told you, he was coming home to make them both happy, when he found it was too late.

"You must think, dear, that while I have been happy all these years with you, he has been sorrowing and grieving, and you must try and love him, and make up to him for what he has suffered. I know you will not forget your old friends. You will love me whether you see me often or not; and Mrs. Walsham, who has been very kind to you; and James, you know, who saved your life."

"I shall never forget anyone, grampa. I shall always love you better than anyone," the child exclaimed, throwing her arms round his neck with a fresh burst of tears.

"There, there, my pet," the sergeant said soothingly. "You must not cry any more. I want you to look your best this evening, you know, and to do credit to us all. And now, I think we have settled everything, so we will be going back to tea."

That evening, the squire was sitting by himself in the great dining room, occasionally sipping the glass of port, which John Petersham had poured out before he left the room. The curtains were drawn, and the candles lighted; for it was late in September, and the evenings were closing in fast; and the squire was puzzling over John Petersham's behaviour at dinner.

Although the squire was not apt to observe closely what was passing around him, he had been struck with the old butler's demeanour. That something was wrong with him was clear. Usually he was the most quiet and methodical of servants, but he had blundered several times in the service. He had handed his master dishes when his plate was already supplied. He had spilled the wine in pouring it out. He had started nervously when spoken to. Mr. Linthorne even thought that he had seen tears in his eyes. Altogether, he was strangely unlike himself.

Mr. Linthorne had asked him if anything was the matter, but John had, with almost unnecessary earnestness, declared there was nothing. Altogether, the squire was puzzled. With any other servant, he would have thought he had been drinking, but such a supposition, in John's case, was altogether out of the question.

He could have had no bad news, so far as the squire knew, for the only children he had, had died young, and he had no near relatives or connections. It was ridiculous to suppose that John, at his age, had fallen in love. Altogether, the squire failed to suggest to himself any explanation of his old butler's conduct, and had just concluded, philosophically, by the reflection that he supposed he should know what it was sooner or later, when the door of the room quietly opened.

The squire did not look up. It closed again as quietly, and then he glanced towards it. He could hardly believe his eyes. A child was standing there–a girl with soft smooth hair, and large eyes, and a sensitive mouth, with an expression fearless but appealing. Her hands were clasped before her, and she was standing in doubt whether to advance. There was something so strange, in this apparition in the lonely room, that the squire did not speak for a moment. It flashed across him, vaguely, that there was something familiar to him in the face and expression, something which sent a thrill through him; and at the same instant, without knowing why, he felt that there was a connection between the appearance of the child, and the matter he had just been thinking of–John Petersham's strange conduct. He was still looking at her, when she advanced quietly towards him.

"Grandpapa," she said, "I am Aggie Linthorne."

A low cry of astonishment broke from the squire. He pushed his chair back.

"Can it be true?" he muttered. "Or am I dreaming?"

"Yes, grandpapa," the child said, close beside him now. "I am Aggie Linthorne, and I have come to see you. If you don't think it's me, grampa said I was to give you this, and then you would know;" and she held out a miniature, on ivory, of a boy some fourteen years old; and a watch and chain.

"I do not need them," the squire said, in low tones. "I see it in your face. You are Herbert's child, whom I looked for so long.

"Oh! my child! my child! have you come at last?" and he drew her towards him, and kissed her passionately, while the tears streamed down his cheeks.

"I couldn't come before, you know," the child said, "because I didn't know about you; and grampa, that's my other grandpapa," she nodded confidentially, "did not know you wanted me. But now he knows, he sent me to you. He told me I was to come because you were lonely.

"But you can't be more lonely than he is," she said, with a quiver in her voice. "Oh! he will be lonely, now!"

"But where do you come from, my dear? and how did you get here? and what have you been doing, all these years?"

"Grampa brought me here," the child said. "I call him grampa, you know, because I did when I was little, and I have always kept to it; but I know, of course, it ought to be grandpapa. He brought me here, and John–at least he called him John–brought me in. And I have been living, for two years, with Mrs. Walsham down in the town, and I used to see you in church, but I did not know that you were my grandpapa."

The squire, who was holding her close to him while she spoke, got up and rang the bell; and John opened the door, with a quickness that showed that he had been waiting close to it, anxiously waiting a summons.

"John Petersham," the squire said, "give me your hand. This is the happiest day of my life."

The two men wrung each other's hands. They had been friends ever since John Petersham, who was twelve years the senior of the two, first came to the house, a young fellow of eighteen, to assist his father, who had held the same post before him.

"God be thanked, squire!" he said huskily.

"God be thanked, indeed, John!" the squire rejoined, reverently. "So this was the reason, old friend, why your hand shook as you poured out my wine. How could you keep the secret from me?"

"I did not know how to begin to tell you, but I was pretty nigh letting it out, and only the thought that it was better the little lady should tell you herself, as we had agreed, kept it in. Only to think, squire, after all these years! But I never quite gave her up. I always thought, somehow, as she would come just like this."

"Did you, John? I gave up hope years ago. How did it come about, John?"

"Mrs. Walsham told me, as I came out of church today, as she wanted to speak to me. So I went down, and she told me all about it, and then I saw him—" John hesitated at the name, for he knew that, perhaps, the only man in the world against whom his master cherished a bitter resentment, was the father of his son's wife. "It seems he never saw your advertisements, never knew as you wanted to hear anything of the child, so he took her away and kept her. He has been here, off and on, all these years. I heard tell of him, often and often, when I had been down into Sidmouth, but never dreamt as it was him. He went about the country with a box on wheels with glasses—a peep show as they calls it."

The squire winced.

"He is well spoken of, squire," John said, "and I am bound to say as he doesn't seem the sort of man we took him for, at all, not by no means. He did not know you wanted to have her, but he thought it his duty to give her the chance, and so he put her with Mrs. Walsham, and never told her, till yesterday, who she was. Mrs. Walsham was quite grieved at parting with her, for she says she is wonderfully quick at her lessons, and has been like a daughter with her, for the last two years."

The child had sat quietly down in a chair, and was looking into the fire while the two men were speaking. She had done what she was told to do, and was waiting quietly for what was to come next. Her quick ear, however, caught, in the tones of John Petersham, an apologetic tone when speaking of her grandfather, and she was moved to instant anger.

"Why do you speak like that of my grampa?" she said, rising to her feet, and standing indignantly before him. "He is the best man in the world, and the kindest and the nicest, and if you don't like him, I can go away to him again. I don't want to stay here, not one minute.

"You may be my grandpapa," she went on, turning to the squire, "and you may be lonely, but he is lonely, too, and you have got a great house, and all sorts of nice things; and you can do better without me than he can, for he has got nothing to love but me, poor grampa!"

And her eyes filled with sudden tears, as she thought of him tramping on his lonely walks over the hills.

"We do not mean to speak unkindly of your grandfather, my dear," the squire said gently. "I have never seen him, you know, and John has never seen him but once. I have thought, all these years, bitterly of him; but perhaps I have been mistaken. He has ever been kind and good to you, and, above all, he has given you back to me, and that will make me think differently of him, in future. We all make mistakes, you know, and I have made terrible mistakes, and have been terribly punished for them. I daresay I have made a mistake here; but whether or no, you shall never hear a word, from me, against the man who has been so kind to you."

"And you will let me see him sometimes, grandpapa?" the child said, taking his hand pleadingly. "He said, if you said no, I must do as you told me; because somehow you are nearer to me than he is, though I don't know how that can be. But you won't say that, will you? For, oh! I know he is so lonely without me, and I should never be happy, thinking of him all alone, not if you were to be ever so kind to me, and to give me all sorts of grand things."

"No, my dear, I certainly shall not say so. You shall see him as often as you like."

"Oh, thank you, grandpapa!" she exclaimed joyfully, and she held up her face to kiss him.

The squire lifted her in his arms, and held her closely to him.

"John," he said, "you must tell Mrs. Morcombe to get a room ready for my granddaughter, at once, and you had better bring the tea in here, and then we will think of other things. I feel quite bewildered, at present."

When John returned with the tea, Aggie was sitting on the squire's knee. She was perfectly at home, now, and had been chattering to him of her life with her grandfather, and had just related the incident of her narrow escape from drowning.

"Do you hear that, John?" the squire said. "She was nearly drowned here, within sight of our home, and I might never have known anything about it. It seems that lad of Dr. Walsham's saved her life. He is a fine lad. He was her champion, you know, in that affair with my nephew. How strange that the two boys should have quarrelled over my granddaughter!"

"Yes, squire, and young Walsham came well out of it!" John said heartily; for to him, only, did the squire mention the circumstances of the case, and he chuckled now to himself, as he thought that Richard Horton had made an even greater mistake in that matter than he thought of, for John detested the boy with all his heart, and had only abstained from reporting his conduct, to the squire, from fear of giving his master pain.

The squire's brow clouded a little at the allusion.

"It will make a difference to him, John," he said, "for, of course, now my granddaughter will take his place."

"And a good thing, too!" John said heartily. "I have never said a word before, squire, because, as you had chosen him as your heir, there was no use in setting you against him; but a more hatefuller lad than Richard Horton I never comed across, and so said everyone here. You did not see much of him, squire, and natural thought well of him, for he was a good-looking boy, and could speak fair enough when he liked. I thought well of him, myself, when he first came, but I larned better, afterwards."

"There are many excuses to be made for him, John," the squire said, "and I have had good reports of him, since. Of course, I shall see that, although he can no longer be regarded as my heir here, he shall be well provided for. But there will be plenty of time to think of this."

"Mr. Wilks asked me to say, sir," the butler said as he prepared to leave them, "that he shall be staying in Sidmouth tomorrow, and that, if you wish to see him, he will come up here."

"Certainly I wish to see him," the squire replied. "I have many things to ask him. Let the boy go down, the first thing in the morning, or--no, if you don't mind, John, would you go down yourself tonight? He will naturally be anxious to know how his grandchild is getting on. Tell him with what joy I have received her, and take any message she may give you.

"Is there anything you would like to say to your grandfather, child?"

"Oh, yes. Please tell him that I think I shall like it, and that he is to come and see me when he likes, and that, of course, he is to see me when he comes in the morning, and then I can tell him all about it."

"And say, I shall be glad to see him the first thing after breakfast," the squire added.

The housekeeper soon entered, and Aggie, very sleepy after the excitements of the day, was taken off to bed. Her sleepiness, however, disappeared in her wonder at the size of the house, and at the vastness of her bedroom.

"Why, you have got a fire!" she exclaimed in astonishment. "I never saw a fire in a bedroom, before."

"I didn't light it for the cold, miss," the housekeeper said; "but because it is a long time since the room was slept in before, and because I thought it would be cheerful for you. I shall sleep in the next room, till things are settled, so that, if you want anything, you will only have to run in."

"Thank you," Aggie said gratefully. "It does all seem so big; but I am sure not to want anything. Thank you."

"Here is your box, miss. Would you like me to help undress you?"

"Oh, no!" Aggie laughed. "Why, of course I can undress myself;" and she laughed at the idea of assistance being required in such a matter.

"Then, good night!" the housekeeper said. "I shall leave the door ajar, between the two rooms, when I come to bed."

The next morning, soon after breakfast, Sergeant Wilks was ushered into the study, where the squire was expecting him. The two men had had hard thoughts of each other, for many years. The squire regarded the sergeant as a man who had inveigled his son into marrying his daughter, while the sergeant regarded the squire as a heartless and unnatural father, who had left his son to die alone among strangers. The conversation with John Petersham had taught the sergeant that he had wronged the squire, by his estimate of him, and that he was to be pitied rather than blamed in the matter. The squire, on his part, was grateful to the sergeant for the care he had bestowed upon the child, and for restoring her to him, and was inclined, indeed, at the moment, to a universal goodwill to all men.

The sergeant was pale, but self possessed and quiet; while the squire, moved, by the events of the night before, out of the silent reserve in which he had, for years, enveloped himself, was agitated and nervous. He was the first to speak.

"Mr. Wilks," he said. "I have to give you my heartfelt thanks, for having restored my granddaughter to me–the more so as I know, from what she has said, how great a sacrifice you must be making. John has been telling me of his conversation with you, and you have learned, from him, that I was not so wholly heartless and unnatural a father as you must have thought me; deeply as I blame myself, and shall always blame myself, in the matter."

"Yes," the sergeant said. "I have learned that I have misread you. Had it not been so, I should have brought the child to you long ago–should never have taken her away, indeed. Perhaps we have both misjudged each other."

"I fear that we have," the squire said, remembering the letters he wrote to his son, in his anger, denouncing the sergeant in violent language.

"It does not matter, now," the sergeant went on quietly; "but, as I do not wish Aggie ever to come to think ill of me, in the future, it is better to set it right.

"When I left the army, I had saved enough money to furnish a house, and I took one at Southampton, and set up taking lodgers there. I had my pension, and lived well until my wife died–a year before your son came down, from London, with another gentleman, and took my rooms. My daughter was seventeen when her mother died, and she took to managing the house. I was careful of her, and gave her orders that, on no account, was she ever to go into the lodgers' rooms. I waited on them, myself.

"How your son first saw her, and got to speak to her, I don't know; but I am not surprised that, when he did, he loved her, for there was no prettier or sweeter girl in Hampshire. They took the rooms, first, only for a fortnight, then the other gentleman went away, and your son stayed on.

"One day–it came upon me like a thunderbolt–your son told me he wanted to marry my Agnes. I was angry, at first. Angry, because it had been done behind my back, and because I had been deceived. I said as much; but your son assured me that he had never spoken to her in the house, but had met her when she went out for her walks. Still, it was wrong, and I told him so, and I told her so, though, in my heart, I did not altogether blame them; for young people will be young people, and, as he had acted honourably in coming to me at once, I let that pass.

"But, squire, though but a sergeant in His Majesty's service, I had my pride as you had yours, and I told him, at once, that I would not give my consent to my daughter's marrying him, until you had given yours; and that he must leave the house at once, and not see Agnes again, until he came with your written consent to show me.

"He went away at once. After a time, he began to write to me, urging me to change my decision; and from this, although he never said so, I was sure that you had refused to sanction his marriage. However, I stuck to what I had said, though it was hard for me to do so, with my child growing thin and pale before my eyes, with all her bright happiness gone.

"So it went on, for three months, and then one morning she was gone, and I found a letter on her table for me, saying that she had been married to him a week before, when she went out, as I thought, to spend the day with a friend. She begged and prayed me to forgive her, and said how miserable she had been, and that she could not say no to her lover's pleadings.

"I wrote to the address she had given me, saying that she had well nigh broken my heart. She knew that I had only refused my consent because it would have seemed a dishonourable action, to allow your son to marry her without your consent. She knew how hard it had been for me to do my duty, when I saw her pining before my eyes, but I forgave her wholly, and did not altogether blame her, seeing that it was the way of Nature that young women, when they once took to loving, should put their father altogether in the second place;

"It was hard to me to write that letter, for I longed to see her bonny face again. But I thought it was my duty. I thought so then; but I think, now, it was pride.

"From time to time she wrote to me. I learned that you still refused to see your son, and I gathered, though she did not say much of this, that things were going badly with them. At last, she wrote that her husband was ill--very ill, she feared. He had, in vain, tried to get employment. I don't think he was naturally strong, and the anxiety had broken him down. Then I went up to London at once, and found them, in a little room, without the necessaries of life. I brought them down home, and nursed him for three months, till he died.

"A week later, Aggie was born. Ten days afterwards, I laid her mother by the side of her father. No answer had come to the letters he had written to you, while he had been ill, though in the later ones he had told you that he was dying. So, I looked upon the child as mine.

"Things had gone badly with me. I had been able to take no lodgers, while they were with me. I had got into debt, and even could I have cleared myself, I could not well have kept the house on, without a woman to look after it. I was restless, too, and longed to be moving about. So I sold off the furniture, paid my debts, and laid by the money that remained, for the child's use in the future.

"I had, some time before, met an old comrade travelling the country with a show. I happened to meet him again, just as I was leaving, and he told me the name of a man, in London, who sold such things. I left the child, for a year, with some people I knew, a few miles out of Southampton; came up to London, bought a show, and started. It was lonely work, at first; but, after a year, I fetched the child away, and took her round the country with me, and for four years had a happy time of it.

"I had chosen this part of the country, and, after a time, I became uneasy in my mind, as to whether I was doing right; and whether, for the child's sake, I ought not to tell you that she was alive, and offer to give her up, if you were willing to take her. I heard how your son's death had changed you, and thought that, maybe, you would like to take his daughter; but, before bringing her to you, I thought she should have a better education than I had time to give her, and that she should be placed with a lady, so that, if you took her, you need not be ashamed of her manners.

"I hoped you would not take her. I wanted to keep her for myself; but my duty to her was clear.

"And now, squire, you know all about it. I have been wrong to keep her so long from you, I grant; but I can only say that I have done my duty, as far as I could, and that, though I have made many mistakes, my conscience is clear, that I did the best, as far as it seemed to me at the time."

Chapter 5: A Quiet Time.

As the sergeant was telling the story, the squire had sat with his face shaded by his hand, but more than one tear had dropped heavily on the table.

"I wish I could say as much," he said sadly, when the other ended. "I wish that I could say that my conscience is clear, Mr. Wilks. I have misjudged you cruelly, and that without a tithe of the reason, which you had, for thinking me utterly heartless and cruel. You will have heard that I never got those letters my son wrote me, after he was ill, and that, when I returned home and received them, I posted to Southampton, only to find that I was too late; and that, for a year, I did all in my power to find the child. Still, all this is no excuse. I refused to forgive him, returned his letters unanswered, and left him, as it seemed, to his fate.

"It is no excuse to say that I had made up my mind to forgive him, when he was, as I thought, sufficiently punished. He did not know that. As to the poverty in which you found him, I can only plead that I did not dream that he would come to that. He had, I knew, some money, for I had just sent him his half-year's allowance before he wrote to me about this business. Then there was the furniture of his rooms in London, his horses, jewels, and other matters. I had thought he could go on very well for a year.

"Of course, I was mistaken. Herbert was always careless about money, and, no doubt, he spent it freely after he was first married. He would naturally wish to have everything pretty and nice for his young wife, and, no doubt, he counted upon my forgiving him long before the money was spent.

"I am not excusing myself. God knows how bitterly I have condemned myself, all these years. I only want to show you that I had no idea of condemning him to starvation. He was my only son, and I loved him. I felt, perhaps, his rebellion all the more, because he had never before given me a day's trouble. I was harsh, obstinate, and cruel.

"I have only the one old excuse. I never thought it would turn out as it did. What would I give, if I could say, as you can, that you have a clear conscience, and that you acted always as it seemed to be your duty!

"And now, Mr. Wilks, now that I have heard your story, I trust that you will forgive my past suspicions of you, and let me say how much I honour and esteem you for your conduct. No words can tell you how I thank you, for your goodness and kindness to my little granddaughter; our little granddaughter, I should say. You have the better right, a thousand-fold, to her than I have; and, had I been in your place, I could never have made such a sacrifice.

"We must be friends, sir, great friends. Our past has been saddened by the same blow. All our hopes, in the future, are centred on the same object."

The two men rose to their feet together, and their hands met in a firm clasp, and tears stood in both their eyes.

Then the squire put his hand on the other's shoulder, and said, "We will talk again, presently. Let us go into the next room. The little one is longing to see you, and we must not keep her."

For the next hour, the two men devoted themselves to the child. Now that she had her old friend with her, she felt no further misgivings, and was able to enter into the full delight of her new home.

The house and its wonders were explored, and, much as she was delighted with these, the gardens and park were an even greater excitement and pleasure. Dancing, chattering, asking questions of one or the other, she was half wild with pleasure, and the squire was no less delighted. A new light and joy had come into his life, and with it the ten years, which sorrow and regret had laid upon him, had fallen off; for, although his habits of seclusion and quiet had caused him to be regarded as quite an old man by his neighbours, he was still three years short of sixty, while the sergeant was two years younger.

It was a happy morning for them, all three; and when John Petersham went in, after lunch, to the kitchen, he assured his fellow servants that it was as much as he could do to keep from crying with joy, at the sight of the squire's happy face, and to hear him laugh and joke, as he had not done for eight years now.

The sergeant had stopped to that meal, for he saw, by the manner in which the squire asked him, that he should give pain if he refused; and there was a simple dignity about the old soldier, which would have prevented his appearing out of place at the table of the highest in the land.

"Now, pussy," the squire said, when they had finished, "you must amuse yourself for a bit. You can go in the garden again, or sit with Mrs. Morcombe in her room. She will look you out some picture books from the library. I am afraid there is nothing very suited to your reading, but we will soon put all that right. Your grandfather and I want to have another quiet chat together."

"Now I want your advice," he said when they were both comfortably seated in the study. "You see, you have been thinking and planning about the child for years, while it has all come new upon me, so I must rely upon you entirely. Of course, the child must have a governess, that is the first thing; not so much for the sake of teaching her, though, of course, she must be taught, but as a companion for her."

"Yes," the sergeant assented, "she must have a governess."

"It will be a troublesome matter to find one to suit," the squire said thoughtfully. "I don't want a harsh sort of Gorgon, to repress her spirits and bother her life out with rules and regulations; and I won't have a giddy young thing, because I should like to have the child with me at breakfast and lunch, and I don't want a fly-away young woman who will expect all sorts of attention. Now, what is your idea? I have no doubt you have, pictured in your mind, the exact sort of woman you would like to have over her."

"I have," the sergeant answered quietly. "I don't know whether it would suit you, squire, or whether it could be managed; but it does seem, to me, that you have got the very woman close at hand. Aggie has been for two years with Mrs. Walsham, who is a lady in every way. She is very fond of the child, and the child is very fond of her. Everyone says she is an excellent teacher. She would be the very woman to take charge of her."

"The very thing!" the squire exclaimed, with great satisfaction. "But she has a school," he went on, his face falling a little, "and there is a son."

"I have thought of that," the sergeant said. "The school enables them to live, but it cannot do much more, so that I should think she would feel no reluctance at giving that up."

"Money would be no object," the squire said. "I am a wealthy man, Mr. Wilks, and have been laying by the best part of my income for the last eight years. I would pay any salary she chose, for the comfort of such an arrangement would be immense, to say nothing of the advantage and pleasure it would be to the child. But how about the boy?"

"We both owe a good deal to the boy, squire," the sergeant said gravely, "for if it had not been for him, the child would have been lost to us."

"So she was telling me last night," the squire said. "And he really saved her life?"

"He did," the sergeant replied. "But for his pluck and promptitude she must have been drowned. A moment's hesitation on his part, and nothing could have saved her."

"I made up my mind last night," the squire said, "to do something for him. I have seen him before, and was much struck with him."

"Then, in that case, squire, I think the thing could be managed. If the lad were sent to a good school, his mother might undertake the management of Aggie. She could either go home of an evening, or sleep here and shut up her house, as you might arrange with her; living, of course, at home, when the boy was home for his holidays, and only coming up for a portion of the day."

"That would be a capital plan," the squire agreed warmly. "The very thing. I should get off all the bother with strange women, and the child would have a lady she is already fond of, and who, I have no doubt, is thoroughly qualified for the work. Nothing could be better. I will walk down this afternoon and see her myself, and I have no doubt I shall be able to arrange it.

"And now about yourself--what are your plans?"

"I shall start tomorrow morning on my tramp, as usual," the sergeant answered quietly; "but I shall take care, in future, that I do not come with my box within thirty miles or so of Sidmouth. I do not want Aggie's future to be, in any way, associated with a showman's box. I shall come here, sometimes, to see her, as you have kindly said I may, but I will not abuse the privilege by coming too often. Perhaps you won't think a day, once every three months, to be too much?"

"I should think it altogether wrong and monstrous!" the squire exclaimed hotly. "You have been virtually the child's father, for the last seven years. You have cared for her, and loved her, and worked for her. She is everything to you, and I feel how vast are your claims to her, compared to mine; and now you talk about going away, and coming to see her once every three months. The idea is unnatural. It is downright monstrous!

"No, you and I understand each other at last; would to Heaven we had done so eight years back! I feel how much more nobly you acted in that unhappy matter than I did, and I esteem and honour you. We are both getting on in life, we have one common love and interest, we stand in the same relation to the child, and I say, emphatically, that you have a right, and more than a right, to a half share in her. You must go away no more, but remain here as my friend, and as joint guardian of the child.

"I will have no refusal, man," he went on, as the sergeant shook his head. "Your presence here will be almost as great a comfort, to me, as to the child. I am a lonely man. For years, I have cut myself loose from the world. I have neither associates nor friends. But now that this great load is off my mind, my first want is a friend; and who could be so great a friend, who could enter into my plans and hopes for the future so well, as yourself, who would have an interest in them equal to my own?"

The sergeant was much moved by the squire's earnestness. He saw that the latter had really at heart the proposal he made.

"You are very good, squire," he said in a low voice; "but even if I could bring myself to eat another man's bread, as long as I can work for my own, it would not do. I am neither by birth nor education fitted for such a position as that you offer to me."

"Pooh, nonsense!" the squire said hotly. "You have seen the world. You have travelled and mixed with men. You are fit to associate as an equal with anyone. Don't you deceive yourself; you certainly do not deceive me.

"It is pride that stands in your way. For that you are going to risk the happiness of your granddaughter, to say nothing of mine; for you don't suppose that either of us is going to feel comfortable and happy, when the snow is whirling round, and the wind sweeping the moors, to think of you trudging along about the country, while we are sitting snugly here by a warm fire.

"You are wanting to spoil everything, now that it has all come right at last, by just the same obstinate pride which wrecked the lives of our children. I won't have it, man. I won't hear of it.

"Come, say no more. I want a friend badly, and I am sure we shall suit each other. I want a companion. Why, man, if I were a rich old lady, and you were a poor old lady, and I asked you to come as my companion, you would see nothing derogatory in the offer. You shall come as my companion, now, or if you like as joint guardian to the child. You shall have your own rooms in the house; and when you feel inclined to be grumpy, and don't care to take your meals with the child and me, you can take them apart.

"At any rate, try it for a month, and if you are not comfortable then I will let you go, though your rooms shall always be in readiness for you, whenever you are disposed to come back.

"Come, give me your hand on the bargain."

Sergeant Wilks could resist no longer. The last two years work, without the child, had indeed been heavy, and especially in winter, when the wind blew strong across the uplands, he began to feel that he was no longer as strong as he used to be. The prospect of having Aggie always near him was, however, a far greater temptation than that of ending his days in quiet and comfort.

His hand and that of the squire met in a cordial grip, and the matter was settled. Fortunately, as the sergeant reflected, he had still his pension of ten shillings a week, which would suffice to supply clothes and other little necessaries which he might require, and would thus save him from being altogether dependent on the squire.

Aggie was wild with delight, when she was called in and informed of the arrangement. The thought of her grandfather tramping the country, alone, had been the one drawback to the pleasure of her life at Mrs. Walsham's, and many a time she had cried herself to sleep, as she pictured to herself his loneliness. That he was to be with her always, was to give up his work to settle down in comfort, was indeed a delight to her.

Greatly pleased was she, also, to hear that Mrs. Walsham was to be asked to come up to be her governess.

"Oh, it will be nice!" she exclaimed, clapping her hands. "Just like the fairy stories you used to tell me, grampa, when everyone was made happy at the end by the good fairy. Grandpapa is the good fairy, and you and I are the prince and princess; and James–and what is to be done with James? Is he to come up, too?"

"No, my dear," the squire said, smiling. "James is to go to a good school, but you will see him when he comes home for his holidays. But that part of it is not arranged yet, you know; but if you will put on your hat, you can walk down with us to the town, and introduce me to Mrs. Walsham."

Mrs. Walsham had just dismissed her pupils, when the party arrived, and was thinking how quiet and dull the house was without Aggie, when the door opened, and the child rushed in and threw her arms round her neck.

"Oh, I have such good news to tell you! Grandpapa is so good and kind, and grampa is going to live with us, and you are to come up, too, and James is to go to school. Isn't it all splendid?"

"What are you talking about, Aggie?" Mrs. Walsham asked, bewildered, as the child poured out her news.

"Aggie is too fast, madam," the squire said, entering the room accompanied by the sergeant. "She is taking it all for granted, while it has yet to be arranged. I must apologize for coming in without knocking; but the child opened the door and rushed in, and the best thing to do was, we thought, to follow her.

"I have come, in the first place, to thank you for your great kindness to my little granddaughter, and to tell your son how deeply I feel indebted to him, for having saved her life two years ago.

"Now, Aggie, you run away and look for your friend, while I talk matters over with Mrs. Walsham."

Aggie scampered away to find James, who was at work at his books, and to tell him the news, while the squire unfolded his plans to Mrs. Walsham.

His offers were so handsome that Mrs. Walsham accepted them, without an instant's hesitation. She was to have the entire charge of the child during the day, with the option of either returning home in the evening, when Aggie went in to dessert after dinner, or of living entirely at the Hall. The squire explained his intention of sending James to a good school at Exeter, as an instalment of the debt he owed him for saving the child's life, and he pointed out that, when he was at home for his holidays, Aggie could have her holidays, too, and Mrs. Walsham need only come up to the Hall when she felt inclined.

Mrs. Walsham was delighted with the offer, even more for James's sake than her own, although the prospect for herself was most pleasant. To have only Aggie to teach, and walk with, would be delightful after the monotony of drilling successive batches of girls, often inordinately tiresome and stupid. She said, at once, that she should prefer returning home at night–a decision which pleased the squire, for he had wondered what he should do with her in the evening.

The arrangement was at once carried into effect. The school was broken up, and, as the parents of the children were almost all tenants of the squire, they offered no objection to the girls being suddenly left on their hands, when they heard that their teacher was going to live as governess at the Hall. Indeed, the surprise of Sidmouth and the neighbourhood, at learning that the little girl at Mrs. Walsham's was the squire's granddaughter, and that the showman was therefore a connection of the squire, and was going also to live at the Hall, was so great, that there was no room for any other emotion. Save for wrecks, or the arrival of shoals of fish off the coast, or of troubles between the smugglers and the revenue officers, Sidmouth had few excitements, and the present news afforded food for endless talk and conjecture.

On comparing notes, it appeared that there was not a woman in the place who had not been, all along, convinced that the little girl at Mrs. Walsham's was something more than she seemed to be, and that the showman was a man quite out of the ordinary way. And when, on the following Sunday, the sergeant, who had in the meantime been to Exeter, walked quietly into church with the squire, all agreed that the well-dressed military-looking man was a gentleman, and that he had only been masquerading under the name of Sergeant Wilks until, somehow or other, the quarrel between him and the squire was arranged, and the little heiress restored to her position; and Sidmouth remained in that belief to the end.

The sergeant's military title was henceforth dropped. Mr. Linthorne introduced him to his acquaintances–who soon began to flock in, when it was known that the squire's granddaughter had come home, and that he was willing to see his friends and join in society again–as "My friend Mr. Wilks, the father of my poor boy's wife."

And the impression made was generally favourable.

None had ever known the exact story of Herbert's marriage. It was generally supposed that he had married beneath him; but the opinion now was that this must have been a mistake, for there was nothing in any way vulgar about the quiet, military-looking gentleman, with whom the squire was evidently on terms of warm friendship.

The only person somewhat dissatisfied with the arrangement was James Walsham. He loved his mother so much, that he had never offered the slightest dissent to her plan, that he should follow in his father's footsteps. She was so much set on the matter, that he could never bring himself to utter a word in opposition. At heart, however, he longed for a more stirring and more adventurous life, such as that of a soldier or sailor, and he had all along cherished a secret hope, that something might occur to prevent his preparing for the medical profession, and so enable him to carry out his secret wishes. But the present arrangement seemed to put an end to all such hopes, and, although grateful to the squire for sending him to a good school, he wished, with all his heart, that he had chosen some other way of manifesting his gratitude.

Four years passed quietly. James Walsham worked hard when at school, and, during his holidays, spent his time for the most part on board the fishermen's boats. Sometimes he went up to the Hall, generally at the invitation of Mr. Wilks.

"Why don't you come oftener, Jim?" the latter asked him one day. "Aggie was saying, only yesterday, that you used to be such friends with her, and now you hardly ever come near her. The squire is as pleased as I am to see you."

"I don't know," Jim replied. "You see, I am always comfortable with you. I can chat with you, and tell you about school, and about fishing, and so on. The squire is very kind, but I know it is only because of that picking Aggie out of the water, and I never seem to know what to talk about with him. And then, you see, Aggie is growing a young lady, and can't go rambling about at my heels as she used to do, when she was a little girl. I like her, you know, Mr. Wilks, just as I used to do; but I can't carry her on my shoulder now, and make a playfellow of her."

"I suppose that's all natural enough, Jim," Aggie's grandfather said; "but I do think it is a pity you don't come up more often. You know we are all fond of you, and it will give us a pleasure to have you here."

Jim was, in fact, getting to the awkward age with boys. When younger, they tyrannize over their little sisters, when older they may again take pleasure in girls' society; but there is an age, in every boy's life, when he is inclined to think girls a nuisance, as creatures incapable of joining in games, and as being apt to get in the way.

Still, Jim was very fond of his former playmate, and had she been still living down in Sidmouth with his mother, they would have been as great friends as ever.

At the end of the fourth year, Richard Horton came back, after an absence of five years. He was now nearly twenty, and had just passed as lieutenant. He was bronzed with the Eastern sun, and had grown from a good-looking boy into a handsome young man, and was perfectly conscious of his good looks. Among his comrades, he had gained the nickname of "The Dandy"–a name which he accepted in good part, although it had not been intended as complimentary, for Richard Horton was by no means a popular member of his mess.

Boys are quick to detect each other's failings, and several sharp thrashings, when he first joined, had taught Richard that it was very inexpedient to tell a lie on board a ship, if there was any chance of its being detected. As he had become one of the senior midshipmen, his natural haughtiness made him disliked by the younger lads; while, among those of his own standing, he had not one sincere friend, for there was a general feeling, among them, that although Richard Horton was a pleasant companion, and a very agreeable fellow when he liked, he was not somehow straight, not the sort of fellow to be depended upon in all emergencies.

By the captain and lieutenants, he was considered a smart young officer. He was always careful to do his duty, quiet, and gentlemanly in manner, and in point of appearance, and dress, a credit to the ship. Accordingly, all the reports that his captain had sent home of him had been favourable.

Great as was the rage and disappointment which Richard had felt, when he received the letter from his uncle telling him of the discovery of his long-lost granddaughter, he had the tact to prevent any signs of his feelings being visible, in the letter in which he replied. The squire had told him that, although the discovery would, of course, make a considerable difference in his prospects, he should still, if the reports of his conduct continued satisfactory, feel it his duty to make a handsome provision for him.

"Thanks to my quiet life during the last ten years," the squire had written, "I have plenty for both of you. The estate will, of course, go to her; but, always supposing that your conduct will be satisfactory, I shall continue, during my lifetime, the allowance you at present receive, and you will find yourself set down, in my will, for the sum of twenty thousand pounds."

Richard had replied in terms which delighted the squire.

"You see, the boy has a good heart," he said, as he handed the letter to Mr. Wilks. "No one could express himself better."

His companion read the letter over in silence.

"Charmingly expressed," he said as he returned it. "Almost too charmingly, it seems to me."

"Come, come, Wilks, you are prejudiced against the young fellow, for that business with Aggie and young Walsham."

"I hope I am not prejudiced, squire," his friend replied; "but when I know that a lad is a liar, and that he will bring false accusations to shield himself, and when I know that he was detested by all who came in contact with him–John Petersham, the gardener, and the grooms–I require a good deal more than a few satisfactory reports from his captain, who can know very little of his private character, and a soft-soldering letter like that, to reinstate him in my good opinion. I will wager that, if you and I had been standing behind him when he opened your letter, you would have heard an expression of very different sentiments from those he writes you here.

"Look at this: 'I regret, indeed, my dear uncle, that my new cousin must have such a bad opinion of me, owing to my roughness in that unfortunate affair, which I have never ceased to regret; but I hope that, when we meet, I shall be able to overcome the dislike which she must feel for me.'

"Bah!" the old soldier said scornfully. "I would lay all my pension, to a shilling, that boy has already made up his mind that someday he will marry Aggie, and so contrive to get the estates after all."

The squire burst into a good-humoured laugh.

"It's well I don't take up your wager. Such ideas as that might occur to you and me, but hardly to a lad not yet seventeen."

"Well, we shall see," the other said, cooling down. "I hope I may be mistaken in him. We shall see when he comes home."

When he did come home, the old soldier could find but little fault with the young man. He had a frank and open manner, such as is common to men of his profession. He was full of life and anecdote. His manner to the squire was admirable, affectionate, and quietly respectful, without any air of endeavouring especially to ingratiate himself with him. Nor could the ex-sergeant find anything to complain of in the young man's manner towards himself. He took the first opportunity, when they were alone, to say how glad he had been, to hear that his grandfather had met with a friend and companion in his lonely life, and to express a hope that the bad opinion, which he had doubtless formed of him from his conduct when a boy, would not be allowed to operate against him now.

But, though there was nothing he could find fault with, the old soldier's prejudices were in no way shaken, and, indeed, his antipathy was increased, rather than diminished, by the young officer's conduct towards Aggie. It might be, of course, that he was only striving to overcome the prejudiced feeling against him; but every time the old soldier saw him with his granddaughter, he felt angry.

In point of fact, Aggie was disposed to like Richard, even before his arrival. Six years had eradicated every tinge of animosity for that shove on the sand. His letters had been long, bright, and amusing, and with the mementos of travel which he picked up in the ports of India and China, and from time to time sent home to his uncle, there was always a little box with some pretty trinket "for my cousin." She found him now a delightful companion. He treated her as if she had been seventeen, instead of eleven; was ready to ride or walk with her, or to tell her stories of the countries he had seen, as she might choose; and to humour all her whims and fancies.

"Confound him and his pleasant manners!" the ex-sergeant would mutter to himself, as he watched them together, and saw, as he believed, in the distance, the overthrow of the scheme he had at heart. "He is turning the child's head; and that foolish boy, James, is throwing away his chances."

James, indeed, came home from school for the last time, two or three weeks after Richard Horton's return. He was now nearly eighteen, and, although a broad and powerful fellow, was still a boy at heart. He did not show to advantage by the side of Richard Horton. The first time he went up to the Hall, after his return, the latter had met him with outstretched hand.

"I am glad to meet you again," he said. "I behaved like a blackguard, last time we met, and you gave me the thrashing which I deserved. I hope we shall get on better, in the future."

Aggie and her two grandfathers were present, and James Walsham certainly did not show to advantage, by the side of the easy and self-possessed young officer. He muttered something about its being all right, and then found nothing else to say, being uncomfortable, and ill at ease. He made some excuse about being wanted at home, and took his leave; nor did he again go up to call. Several times, the old soldier went down to Sidmouth to see him, and on one occasion remonstrated with him for not coming up to the Hall.

"What's the use?" James said, roughly. "I have got lots of reading to do, for in two months, you know, I am to go up to London, to walk the hospitals. No one wants me up there. Aggie has got that cousin of hers to amuse her, and I should feel only in the way, if I went."

Mr. Wilks was fairly out of temper at the way things were going. He was angry with James; angry with the squire, who evidently viewed with satisfaction the good understanding between his granddaughter and nephew; angry, for the first time in his life, with Aggie herself.

"You are growing a downright little flirt, Miss Aggie," he said one day, when the girl came in from the garden, where she had been laughing and chatting with her cousin.

He had intended to speak playfully, but there was an earnestness in his tone which the girl, at once, detected.

"Are you really in earnest, grampa?" she asked, for she still retained the childish name for her grandfather—so distinguishing him from the squire, whom she always called grandpapa.

"No; I don't know that I am in earnest, Aggie," he said, trying to speak lightly; "and yet, perhaps, to some extent I am."

"I am sure you are," the girl said. "Oh, grampa! You are not really cross with me, are you?" and the tears at once sprang into her eyes. "I have not been doing anything wrong, have I?"

"No, my dear, not in the least wrong," her grandfather said hastily. "Still, you know, I don't like seeing Jim, who has always been so good and kind to you, quite neglected, now this young fellow, who is not fit to hold a candle to him, has turned up."

"Well, I haven't neglected him, grampa. He has neglected me. He has never been near since that first day, and you know I can't very well go round to Sidmouth, and say to him, 'Please come up to the Hall.'"

"No, my dear, I know you can't, and he is behaving like a young fool."

"Why is he?" Aggie asked, surprised. "If he likes sailing about better than coming up here, why shouldn't he?"

"I don't think it's for that he stays away, Aggie. In fact, you see, Jim has only just left school, and he feels he can't laugh, and talk, and tell you stories about foreign countries, as this young fellow can, and having been so long accustomed to have you to himself, he naturally would not like the playing second fiddle to Richard Horton."

"But he hasn't been here much," the girl said, "ever since I came here. He used to be so nice, and so kind, in the old days when I lived down there, that I can't make out why he has changed so."

"My dear, I don't think he has changed. He has been only a boy, and the fact is, he is only a boy still. He is fond of sailing, and of the amusements boys take to, and he doesn't feel at home, and comfortable here, as he did with you when you were a little girl at his mother's. But mind, Aggie, James is true as steel. He is an honourable and upright young fellow. He is worth fifty of this self-satisfied, pleasant-spoken young sailor."

"I know James is good and kind, grampa," the girl said earnestly; "but you see, he is not very amusing, and Richard is very nice."

"Nice! Yes," the old soldier said; "a fair weather sort of niceness, Aggie. Richard Horton is the squire's nephew, and I don't wish to say anything against him; but mark my words, and remember them, there's more goodness in James's little finger, than there is in his whole body. But there, I am a fool to be talking about it. There is your cousin calling you, in the garden. Go along with you."

The girl went off slowly, wondering at her grandfather's earnestness. She knew she liked her old playmate far better than Richard Horton, although the latter's attentions pleased and flattered her. The old soldier went straight off to the squire's study.

"Squire," he said, "you remember that talk we had, three years ago, when your nephew's answer came to your letter, telling him that Aggie was found. I told you that I would wager he had made up his mind to marry her. You laughed at me; but I was right. Child though she still is, he is already paving the way for the future."

"Master Richard certainly is carrying on a sort of flirtation with the little witch," the squire said, smiling; "but as she is such a mere child as you say, what does it matter?"

"I think it matters a great deal," the old soldier said seriously. "I see, squire, the young fellow has quite regained your good opinion; and unless I am mistaken, you have already thought, to yourself, that it would not be a bad thing if they were to come together someday.

"I have thought it over, and have made up my mind that, in spite of your four years' continued kindness to me, and of the warm friendship between us, I must go away for a time. My box is still lying at Exeter, and I would rather tramp the country again, and live on it and my pension, than stay here and see my darling growing up a woman with that future before her. I am sorry to say, squire, that what you call my prejudice is as strong as ever. I doubt that young fellow as strongly as I did before he came home. Then, I only had his past conduct and his letter to go by. Now I have the evidence of my own senses. You may ask me what I have against him. I tell you–nothing; but I misdoubt him from my heart. I feel that he is false, that what he was when a boy, he is now. There is no true ring about him."

The squire was silent for a minute or two. He had a very sincere friendship and liking for his companion, a thorough confidence in his judgment and principles. He knew his self-sacrificing nature, and that he was only speaking from his love for his grandchild.

"Do not let us talk about it now, old friend," he said quietly. "You and I put, before all other things, Aggie's happiness. Disagreement between us there can be none on the subject. Give me tonight to think over what you have said, and we will talk about it again tomorrow."

Chapter 6: A Storm.
After breakfast next morning, the squire asked his friend to go with him into his study.

"I have been thinking this matter over," he said, "very seriously, and, upon reflection, I agree with you that it is undesirable that Aggie should see much of Richard, until she is of an age to form a fair opinion for herself, and to compare him with other young men. I agree with you, also, that we have not yet sufficient proofs that he is completely changed. I hope that he is. You think he is not. At any rate, he must have a longer trial, and until it is proved to your satisfaction, as well as mine, that he is in every way a desirable husband for Aggie, the less they see of each other, the better. I therefore propose to write at once to my friend Admiral Hewson, to ask him to use his influence, at the admiralty, to get the young fellow appointed to a ship. Does that meet your approval, my friend?"

"Quite so," the other said cordially. "Nothing could be better. In the meantime, as you say, should Richard turn out well, and the young people take a liking for each other, no match could be more satisfactory. What I want is that she should take no girlish fancy for him, at present."

"So be it, then," the squire said. "I think, you know, that we are a couple of old fools, to be troubling ourselves about Aggie's future, at present. Still, in a matter which concerns us both so nearly, we cannot be too careful. If we had a woman with us, we could safely leave the matter in her hands; as it is, we must blunder on, as best we may."

And so it was settled, and a week later, Richard Horton received an official letter from the admiralty, ordering him to proceed at once to Portsmouth to join the Thetis, to which he was appointed as fourth lieutenant. The order gave Richard extreme satisfaction. He was beginning to find his life desperately dull, and he was heartily sick of playing the attentive nephew. He was well content with the progress he had made; nothing had gone wrong since he returned, his uncle had clearly taken him back into his favour, and he had no doubt that Aggie quite appreciated the pains he had bestowed to gain her liking.

He detested the squire's companion, for he felt that the latter disliked and distrusted him, and that his projects would meet with a warm opposition on his part. Still, with the squire and Aggie herself on his side, he did not fear the result. As to James Walsham, whom he had come home prepared to regard as a possible rival, from his early intimacy with the child, and the fact that his mother was her governess, he now regarded him with contempt, mingled with a revengeful determination to pay off the old score, should a chance ever present itself.

He therefore started next day in high spirits, assuming, however, a great reluctance to tear himself away. A few days later a letter came from him, saying that he hoped that he should be able to come back, sometimes, for a day or two, as the Thetis was at present to be attached to the Channel squadron, and it was not expected that she would, for some time, proceed on foreign service.

Early in October, James Walsham was to go up to London, to commence his medical course. A week before he was to start, Mr. Wilks went down in the morning, intending to insist on his returning with him to the Hall. As he went down towards Sidmouth, the old soldier noticed how strongly the wind was blowing, the trees were swaying and thrashing in the wind, the clouds were flying past overhead. Everything portended a severe gale.

Finding, at Mrs. Walsham's, that James was down on the beach, he continued his course until he joined him there. James was standing with a group of fishermen, who were looking seaward. Now that he was exposed to the full force of the wind, Mr. Wilks felt that, not only was it going to blow a gale, but that it was blowing one already. The heavy clouds on the horizon seemed to lie upon the water, the waves were breaking with great force upon the beach, and the fishermen had hauled their boats up across the road.

"It's blowing hard, Jim," he said, laying his hand on the young fellow's shoulder.

"It is blowing hard, and it will blow a great deal harder before nightfall. The fishermen all think it is going to be an exceptional gale. It is blowing dead on shore. It will be bad work for any ships that happen to be coming up Channel today. Eight or ten of our boats are out. We thought we had made out three of them just before you came, but the cloud closed down on them. The fishermen are just going to get lifelines ready. I am afraid we are going to have a terrible night of it."

"I came down to ask you if you will come up to lunch, Jim, but I suppose you will not be able to tear yourself away from here."

"I shouldn't like to leave now, indeed. There is no saying what may happen. Besides, so many of the fishermen are away, that I may be useful here if a vessel comes ashore, and there may be half a dozen before the morning. Every hand will be wanted to give assistance."

"But you could not get a boat out through those breakers, could you, Jim?"

"Yes," Jim replied, "we might get one of the big boats through it now; but it's going to be worse, presently. When I went out, last year, with a boat to the brig which was driven ashore, it was worse than this.

"I shall be very glad to come up tomorrow, if you will let me. I hear that fellow Horton went away last week."

"Yes, he went away, Jim. But why his being there should have kept you from going up is beyond me."

"I don't like the fellow, Mr. Wilks. He may mean very well, but I don't like him. I have been in one row about him with the squire, and I don't want another; but I am quite sure, if I had gone up much while he was there, it would have ended in my trying to punch his head again."

"In that case, perhaps," the old soldier said, smiling, "you were wise to stay away, Jim. I don't like the lad myself. Still, punching his head would not have been a desirable thing."

"I am glad you don't like him," James said, warmly. "Somehow I made up my mind that you were all sure to like him, and I don't suppose the idea made me like him any the better. He was just the free-and-easy sort of fellow to get along well, and I was quite sure that Aggie would not want me, when she had him to go about with her. I saw him drive through in the pony carriage with her, two or three times, and it was easy to see how thoroughly she was enjoying herself."

"Well, it was your own fault, my boy. If you choose to sulk down here, and never to go up to the Hall, you can't blame Aggie for letting herself be amused by someone else."

"Oh! I don't blame her," James said hastily. "Of course, it is all right that she should enjoy herself with her cousin. Only somehow, you know, after being great friends with anyone, one doesn't like to see someone else stepping into your place."

"But as I have told you, over and over again, during the last three years, Jim, you have willfully stepped out of your place. You know how often I have asked you to come up, and how seldom you have come. You have never shown Aggie that you have any wish to continue on the footing of friendship, on which you stood towards each other when she was at your mother's, and as you have chosen to throw her over, I don't see why she shouldn't take to anyone else who takes pains to make himself pleasant to her."

"Oh! I don't blame her a bit, Mr. Wilks. How could you think such a thing! I was very fond of little Aggie when she was at my mother's; but of course, I was not ass enough to suppose that she was going trotting about the country with me, when she once went up to the Hall as the squire's granddaughter. Of course, the whole thing was changed."

"Ah! Here comes the rain."

As he spoke, a sudden splash of rain struck them. It might have been noticed coming across the water in a white line. With it came a gust of wind, to which that which had already been blowing was a trifle. There was no more talking, for nothing less than a shout could have been heard above the roaring of the wind. It was scarcely possible to stand against the fury of the squall, and they were driven across the road, and took shelter at the corner of some houses, where the fishermen had already retired.

The squall lasted but a few minutes, but was soon succeeded by another, almost equally furious, and this seemed to increase in strength, until the wind was blowing a perfect hurricane; but the fishermen now struggled across the road again, for, between the rain squalls, a glimpse had been caught of two of the fishing boats, and these were now approaching the shore. A mere rag of sail was set on each, and yet they tore over the waves at tremendous speed.

One was some two hundred yards ahead of the other, and by the course they were making, they would come ashore nearly at the same spot. The news that two boats were in sight spread rapidly, and many of the fishermen's wives, with shawls over their heads, ran down and stood peering out from behind shelter, for it was well-nigh impossible to stand exposed to the fury of the gale.

An old fisherman stood, with a coil of rope in his hand, close to the water's edge. Several of the others stood close to him, and four of them had hold of the other end of the rope. When the boat was within fifty yards of shore, the sail was lowered; but she still drove straight on before the wind, with scarce an abatement in her speed. A man stood in her bow, also with a coil of rope in his hand, and, as he approached, threw it far ahead. The fisherman rushed waist deep into the water and caught the end of it, which in a moment was knotted to the one in his hand.

"Run along with her," he shouted.

For a moment, the boat towered on the top of a wave, which raced in towards the shore. The next, as it came, took her stern, and she was in the act of swinging round, when the strain of the rope came upon her, and brought her straight again. Higher and higher the wave rose, and then crashed down, and the boat shot forward, like an arrow, in the foam. The fishermen rushed forward and caught it, those on board leapt out waist-deep; all were taken off their feet by the backward rush, but they clung to the sides of the boat, while the men at the head rope, with their heels dug deeply into the sand, withstood the strain, and kept her from being swept out again.

A few seconds, and the boat was left dry, and the next wave carried it high up on the beach, amid a loud cheer from the fishermen and lookers on; but there was no time to waste, for the next boat was close at hand. Again, the rope was thrown to the shore, but this time the strain came a moment too late, the following wave turned the boat round, the next struck it broadside and rolled it, over and over, towards the shore. The fishermen, in an instant, joined hands, and rushing down into the water, strove to grasp the men.

Several times, those in front were knocked down and rolled up on the beach, but three of the crew were brought in with them. There was one still missing, and there was a shout as he was seen, clinging to an oar, just outside the line of breakers. James Walsham had been working with the fishermen in saving those already brought to shore. He now fastened the end of a line round his body.

"You can never get through those rollers—they will break you up like an eggshell," the old fisherman shouted.

"I will dive through them," Jim shouted back. "Give me plenty of slack, and don't pull, till you see I have got him."

The lad waited for his opportunity, and then, rushing down after the sheet of white foam, he stood, waist deep, as a great wave, some twelve feet high, towered up like a wall towards him. It was just going to break, when James plunged, head foremost, into it. There was a crash which shook the earth, a mass of wildly rushing foam, and then, some ten yards beyond the spot where the wave had broken, Jim's head appeared above the surface. It was but for a moment, for he immediately dived again, under the next wave, and then came up within a few yards of the floating oar. A stroke or two, and he was alongside. He seized the man, and held up one arm as a signal. In a moment the rope tightened, and they moved towards shore. When they were close to the edge of the breaking waves, Jim held up his hand, and the strain stopped.

"Now," he said to the man, "the moment they begin to pull, leave go of the oar, and throw your arms round me."

He waited until a wave, bigger than ordinary, approached, and, just as it began to pass under him, gave the signal. Higher and higher they seemed to rise, then they were dashed down with a tremendous shock. There was a moment's confusion as they were swept along in the white water. Jim felt a terrific strain, and it seemed to him that the rope would cut him in sunder. Then he was seized by a dozen strong arms, and carried high and dry, before the next wave could reach him.

For a minute or two he was scarce conscious. The breath had been almost knocked out of his body, with the break of the wave, and the rushing water seemed still singing in his ears.

"Are you hurt, my boy? Are you hurt, James?" were the first words he clearly heard.

"No, I think I am all right," he said, trying to sit up. "Is the other fellow all right?"

"He has broke his arm," one of the fishermen, who had just helped the man to his feet, replied. "He may be thankful it's no worse."

James was now helped to his feet.

"I am all right," he repeated to Mr. Wilks, "except that I feel as if I had a hot iron round my body. That rope has taken the skin off all round me, I fancy, and doesn't it smart, just, with the salt water!"

"Oh, James, how could you do it?" a girl's voice said suddenly.

The fishermen drew aside, and Aggie Linthorne pressed forward.

The squire had gone into her schoolroom and had said:

"Mrs. Walsham, I think you had better give up your lessons for the morning, and get home. It is blowing a gale now, and we shall probably have the rain down before long. I will walk down with you. The wind is dead on the shore, and it will be a grand sight."

Aggie at once set her mind on going, too; but the squire refused, until Mrs. Walsham suggested that, if it came on wet, Aggie could stop at her house until it cleared up, or, if necessary, till morning. Whereupon, the squire had given way, and the three had started together for Sidmouth, leaving Mrs. Walsham at her house as they passed. The others had struggled down, against the wind, until they came within sight of the sea. The first boat had just been run safely on shore when they arrived, and Aggie gave a cry, and put her hands over her face, as the second boat was seen to capsize.

"Cling to me, Aggie," the squire said. "See, they are rushing in the water to save them. They will have them, yet!"

At the cheer which broke out from the spectators, clustering thickly now, as the first of the shipwrecked crew was brought to shore, Aggie looked out again. It was a sight she never forgot. With the great waves crashing down on the shore, and the line of straggling figures, waist deep in the white foam, in which were scattered, here and there, portions of the boat, oars, sails, and nets.

"Well done, well done!" the squire exclaimed. "They have dragged up three of them. I don't know whether there are any more."

"Yes, yes, look!" Aggie cried; "there, out in the waves–there, I can see a head. That's just about where I was nearly drowned. Oh, grandpapa, take me away, I can't look at it."

"There's someone going out to save him, Aggie. Listen to the cheer."

Aggie looked again.

"Oh, grandpapa, stop him, stop him!" she cried, "it's James."

But at the same moment the plunge was made, and the figure lost to sight.

Aggie threw her arms round her grandfather, and hid her face.

"I can't look, I can't look," she cried. "Tell me about it."

"There, he is up; bravo!" the squire exclaimed, almost as excited as she was. "He has dived again, dear,"–then, after a pause–"there he is close to him. He has got him, Aggie! Now he is waving his hand; now they are tightening the rope; now he is waving his hand again, and they are waiting. There!"

There was a pause, which seemed to the girl to be endless, then the squire cried:

"They have got them out, both of them;" and a loud cheer broke from all standing round.

"Come along, grandpapa, let us go down to them."

"Stay a moment, my dear. They may be hurt. It's better you should not go."

The girl stood, with her hands clasped, gazing at the fishermen grouped on the shore, stooping over the prostrate figures. Then one of them stood up and waved his hand, and the spectators knew that all was well. Then the girl ran down to join them.

"Why, Aggie!" James exclaimed in astonishment, as she pressed forward. "Why, my dear, what brings you here in this storm? Whatever will the squire say?"

"The squire has brought her down himself," Mr. Linthorne said, following closely behind his granddaughter; "and he is glad he did, James, for she has seen a grand sight.

"You are a fine fellow;" and he wrung the lad's hand.

"A grand fellow, Wilks, isn't he?"

"I always said so, squire," the old soldier said, his face beaming with satisfaction; "but now, let us get him home, and Aggie, too. The child will be blown away."

But, for a minute or two, they could not carry James off, so closely did the men and women press round him, and shake him by the hand. At last they got him away, and, escorted by a crowd of cheering boys, led him back to his mother's.

"Your son is a hero, Mrs. Walsham!" the squire exclaimed as they entered; "but don't talk to him now, but mix him a glass of hot grog.

"Wilks, you get him between the blankets directly. I will tell his mother all about it, while she is mixing the grog.

"Hallo, Aggie! Why, bless the child, she's fainted."

The girl had borne up till they reached the house, towards which the wind had blown her along, as she clung to her grandfather's arm; but the excitement had been too much for her, and, the instant they entered the room, she had dropped into an armchair, and at once lost consciousness.

Mrs. Walsham kept her presence of mind, in spite of her bewilderment at these sudden occurrences. She at once laid the girl on the sofa, removed her dripping bonnet and cloak, and poured a few drops of brandy between her lips, while she set the squire to work, to chafe her hands. Aggie soon opened her eyes, and recovered her consciousness.

"Don't try to get up, Aggie," Mrs. Walsham said. "You are faint and shaken with all this excitement. Your grandpapa and I were two very foolish people, to let you come out.

"Now, Mr. Wilks, the best thing you can do, is to find a boy outside, and send him up to the Hall, with a message that the carriage is to come down directly.

"I think, Mr. Linthorne, she had better get back home. I should be glad enough, as you know, to keep her here for the night; but this house is rocking with the wind, now, and she would not be likely to get any sleep here. I will run up and see how James is, and if he is all right, I will come up with her and stop the night. She is very much shaken, and had better not be alone."

Mrs. Walsham soon came downstairs again, and said that James said he never felt better in his life, and that, by all means, she was to go up to the Hall. She then set about and prepared a cup of tea, which greatly restored Aggie, and, by the time the carriage arrived, the girl was able to walk to the gate.

Mr. Wilks had offered to remain with James, but the latter would not hear of it. The lad was, indeed, well pleased to hear that they were all going up to the Hall, as thereby he escaped hearing any more of his own praises. Besides, he was most anxious to get down to the beach again, for no one could say what might take place there before morning.

As soon, therefore, as he heard the door close, he jumped out of bed, and when, peeping through the blinds, he saw the carriage drive off with its four occupants, he at once began to dress. He felt bruised and sore from the blows he had received, and a red wheal round his chest, beneath the arms, showed where the rope had almost cut into the flesh. However, he soon dressed himself, and descended the stairs, went into the kitchen, and told the astonished girl that he was going out; then, having made a hasty meal of bread and cold meat, he put on his oilskins again, and started for the shore.

He did not, however, wait long. So heavy was the sea, now, that nothing whatever could be done should any vessel drive ashore, and, as for the fisher boats, the sailors shook their heads as they spoke of them.

"They were farther away to the west, so the chaps as got ashore tells us. They may have got in, somewhere, before it got to the worst. If not, it must have gone hard with them."

Finding that there was nothing to be done, and that he was much more stiff and bruised than he had believed, Jim made his way back again, and turned into bed; where he soon fell asleep, and did not wake until the following morning.

One of the grooms had come down from the Hall, at six o'clock, to inquire how he was, and the message given by the girl, that he had been out, but that he had come back and was now sound asleep, satisfied Mrs. Walsham, and enabled her to devote her undivided attention to her charge, who needed her care more than her son. Before night, indeed, the squire had sent down to Sidmouth for Dr. Walsham's successor, who said that Aggie was very feverish, and must be kept perfectly quiet for some days.

He sent her up a soothing draught, and Mrs. Walsham sat up with her all night. She slept but little, and talked almost incessantly, sometimes rambling a little.

The first thing in the morning, the doctor was again sent for, and on his recommendation the squire at once sent off a man, on horseback, to Exeter, for the leading physician of that town. When he arrived, late in the afternoon, Aggie was somewhat quieter, and his report was more cheering.

"Her pulse is very high," he said; "but Mr. Langford tells me that it is not so rapid as it was in the morning, and that he thinks the symptoms are abating. Undoubtedly, it is a sharp feverish attack, brought on by excitement and exposure. A very little more, and it would have been a case of brain fever, but I trust now that it will soon pass off. The sedatives that have been administered are taking effect, and I trust she will soon fall asleep.

"As you requested, I have made my arrangements for staying here tonight, and I trust that, by the morning, we shall have her convalescent."

Mr. Wilks had gone down, the first thing in the morning, to see James, and found him up and about as usual. He was very greatly concerned, at hearing that Aggie had passed a bad night, and came four times up to the Hall, during the day, to inquire about her; and on his last visit, late in the evening, he was told that she was sleeping quietly, and that the doctor had every hope that she would wake, in the morning, free from fever. This proved to be the case; but she was ordered to keep her bed for a day or two.

On the morning after the storm, the wind had gone down much, although a tremendous sea was still breaking on the shore. Messages arrived, in the course of the day, to say that all the missing boats, with one exception, had succeeded in gaining the shore before the storm was full on. The missing boat was never heard of again.

Two days later, James Walsham had strolled up the hill to the east of the town, and was lying, with a book before him, in a favourite nook of his looking over the sea. It was one of the lovely days which sometimes come late in autumn, as if the summer were determined to show itself at its best, before leaving. It could not be said that James was studying, for he was watching the vessels passing far out at sea, and inwardly moaning over the fact that he was destined for a profession for which he had no real liking, instead of being free to choose one of travel and adventure.

Presently, he heard voices behind him. The position, in which he was lying, was a little distance down on the slopes, on the seaward side of the path, and, as a screen of bushes grew behind it, he could not be seen by anyone passing along.

"All the men, with their pistols and cutlasses, are to assemble here at ten o'clock tonight, Johnson. But do not give them orders till late, and let them come up, one by one, so as not to attract attention. Lipscombe's men are to assemble at the same hour, and march to meet us. This time, I think, there is no mistake. The cargo is to be landed where I told you. It will be high tide at twelve o'clock, and they are sure to choose that hour, so that the cutter can run close in. I have sent off a man on horseback to Weymouth, for the revenue cutter to come round. If she's in time, we shall catch that troublesome lugger, as well as her cargo. She has been a thorn in our side for the last year. This time, I do hope we shall have her."

The speakers then moved on out of hearing, but James Walsham recognized the voice, as that of the revenue officer commanding the force at Sidmouth.

Smuggling was, at that time, carried on on a large scale along the coast, and there were frequent collisions between those engaged in it and the revenue officers. The sympathies of the population were wholly with the smugglers, and the cheating of the revenue was not at all considered in the light of a crime.

Many of the fishermen, from time to time, took a hand in smuggling cruises, and the country people were always ready to lend assistance in landing and carrying the cargoes.

When out in their boats at night, James had often heard the fishermen tell stories of their smuggling adventures, and more than once he had been with them, when they had boarded a lugger laden with contraband, to warn them that the revenue cutter was on the cruising ground, and it would not be safe to attempt to run cargo at present. He now determined, at once, that he would warn the smugglers of their danger. The question was, where was the cargo to be run? The officer had not mentioned the spot, but, as the force from the next station to the east was to cooperate, it must be somewhere between the two.

Waiting till the speakers must have gone well along the cliff, he rose to his feet, and returned to Sidmouth. He thought, at first, of telling some of the fishermen what he had heard, but as, in the event of an affray, it might come out how the smugglers had been warned of the intention of the revenue officers, he thought there would be less risk in giving them warning himself. He knew every path down the cliff for miles, and trusted that he should be able to make his way down, and give the boats notice of their danger, before the revenue men reached the shore.

At nine o'clock he dressed himself, in the rough sailor's suit he wore when he went out with the fishermen, and started along the cliff. For some distance he kept well inland, as the officer might have placed a man on the lookout, to stop anyone going towards the scene of action. The spot he thought the most likely was a mile and a half along the shore. There was a good landing place, and an easy path up the cliff, and he knew that cargoes had been more than once run here. Accordingly, when he reached this spot, he sat down among some bushes on the edge of the cliff, and waited for some sort of signal. Half an hour later, he heard the tramp of a number of men, passing along behind him.

"There go the revenue men," he thought to himself. "I suppose they are going to meet those coming the other way."

An hour passed without further sound, and James began to get uneasy. If this was the spot fixed for the landing, some of the country people ought to be arriving, by this time, to help to carry off the cargo. They might, for aught he knew, be already near, waiting for the signal before they descended the path. No doubt the revenue men would be lying in wait, a short distance off, and would allow the friends of the smugglers to go down to the water, without letting them know of their presence.

He kept his eyes fixed on the water to the east, watching anxiously for the appearance of a light. Presently he started. Immediately in front of him, about a mile at sea, a bright light was shown. In a second, it disappeared. Three times it flashed out, and then all was dark. The night was a very dark one. There was no moon, and the stars were obscured, and although he strained his eyes to the utmost, he could not make out the vessel from which the light had been shown.

"How foolish to show such a bright light!" he said to himself. "It would have been almost sure to attract the attention of anyone on the watch."

He made his way to the path, and descended to the edge of the water, and waited, expecting momentarily to be joined by people from above. But no one came. He strained his ears listening for the fall of approaching oars; but all was silent.

Half an hour passed, and then it flashed across him that the signal must have been made to deceive the revenue men, and to cause them to assemble at that spot, and so leave the point really determined upon free for operations.

With an exclamation of disgust at his own stupidity, in having been deceived, James ran up the path again at the top of his speed, and then took the road along the cliff. For two miles, he ran without interruption, and then saw a dark mass in front of him. He turned off, instantly, to the left. Doubtless he had been heard approaching, for two or three men detached themselves from the rest, and started to cut him off. James ran straight inland, and in the darkness soon lost sight of his pursuers. Then he turned, and made for the cliff again. Two or three hundred yards farther along, there was another path to the shore, and this he had no doubt, now, was the one the smugglers were about to use. He struck the cliff within a few yards of the spot. In an instant, two men jumped up and seized him.

"Who are you?"

For an instant, James thought that his assailants were revenue men, but, even in the darkness, he saw that they were countrymen.

"Quick!" he said. "The revenue men are close at hand. They are watching, two or three hundred yards along. Listen! Here they come."

A tramping of feet coming rapidly along the cliff was clearly heard, and the men, with an oath, released their hold and ran off, giving a loud whistle, and made for their carts, which were stationed a few hundred yards inland. James dashed down the path, shouting at the top of his voice. He had not gone many yards before he met a number of men, coming up with tubs of spirits on their shoulders.

"Throw them down," he cried, "and make along the shore. The revenue men are close behind."

His advice was taken at once. The tubs were thrown down, and went leaping and bounding down to the shore, while the men followed James, at full speed, down the path.

Their pursuers were close behind. There was no longer any use in concealment. Their officer shouted to them to press forward at full speed, while, from the beach below, a hubbub of voices suddenly broke out, and, at the same moment, a blue light was lit on the cliff above.

"Beat them back, my lads," one of the smugglers was shouting, as James ran down to the little crowd of men standing near two boats. "We are five to one against them. Come on."

"Surrender in the king's name," the revenue officer shouted, as he rushed forward, followed by his men.

The answer was a pistol shot, and, in a moment, a furious melee began. The advantage in numbers was all on the side of the smugglers. Those who had landed with the kegs were all armed with pistol and cutlass, and the countrymen had heavy sticks and bludgeons. The ten revenue men would have been overpowered, but suddenly a shout was heard, and another party of sailors ran up along the shore, and joined in the fray. It was the detachment from the other station, which had been waiting, at some little distance along the shore, for the signal from above.

"To the boats, lads," the leader of the smugglers shouted. "We are caught in a trap."

The smugglers rushed to the boats, and James, who was standing by the water's edge, leaped on board with them. Most of the country people fled at once along the shore, pursued by some of the revenue men, while the others made a rush for the boats. These had been kept afloat a few yards from the shore. Grapnels had been dropped over their sterns, and, as the men in charge hauled out the moment the fight began, they were in water shoulder deep when the smugglers scrambled on board.

The revenue men dashed in after them, and strove to hold the boats; but they were beaten off with oars and cutlasses, and the boats were soon hauled out into deep water. The grapnels were lifted, and the men, many of whom were wounded more or less severely in the fray, got out their oars and pulled to the lugger, amid a dropping fire of pistol shots from shore.

Chapter 7: Pressed.

Many and deep were the maledictions uttered, as the smugglers climbed on board their vessel; but their captain said cheerily:

"Never mind, lads, it might have been worse. It was only the first cargo of tubs, and half of those weren't ashore. The lace and silk are all right, so no great harm is done. Set to work, and get up sail as soon as you can. Likely enough there is a cutter in the offing; that blue light must have been a signal. They seem to have got news of our landing, somehow."

The crew at once set to work to get up sail. Three or four of the countrymen, who had, like James, got on board the boats, stood in a group looking on, confused and helpless; but James lent his assistance, until the sails were hoisted and the craft began to move through the water.

"Now, then," the captain said, "let us go below and look at the wounds. We daren't show a light, here on deck."

The wounds were, for the most part, slashes and blows with cutlasses; for in the darkness and confusion of the fight, only two of the bullets had taken effect. One of the smugglers had fallen, shot through the head, while one of those on board had his arm broken by a pistol ball.

"Now for our passengers," the captain said, after the wounds had been bandaged.

"Who are you?" and he lifted a lantern to James's face.

"Why, it is young Mr. Walsham!" he exclaimed in surprise.

James knew the man now, for the lugger had several times put in at Sidmouth, where, coming in as a peaceable trader, the revenue officers, although well aware of the nature of her vocation, were unable to touch her, as vessels could only be seized when they had contraband on board.

"Why, what brings you into this affair, young master?"

James related the conversation he had overheard, and his determination to warn the smugglers of their danger.

"I should have managed it, in plenty of time, if I had known the exact spot on which you were going to land; but I saw a signal light, two miles down the coast, and that kept me there for half an hour. It struck me, then, it was a ruse to attract the officers from the real spot of landing, but though I ran as hard as I could, I was only just before them."

"Thank you heartily," the smuggler said. "I expect you saved us from a much worse mess than we got into. I have no doubt they meant to capture the tubs, as they were loaded, without raising an alarm; and the fellows on the shore would have come up quietly, and taken us by surprise as we were landing the last boat loads. Thanks to you, we have got well out of it, and have only lost one of our hands, and a score or so of tubs."

"You can't put me ashore, I suppose?" James said.

"That I can't," the smuggler replied. "I have no doubt that cutter from Weymouth is somewhere outside us, and we must get well off the coast before morning. If we give her the slip, I will send you off in a boat sometime tomorrow. I must go ashore, myself, to make fresh arrangements for getting my cargo landed."

James went on deck again. The breeze was light, and the lugger was slipping along quietly through the water. He could faintly see the loom of the cliffs on his right, and knew that the lugger was running west, keeping as close inshore as she could, to avoid the cutter watching for her outside. He wondered what they would say at home, when it was found that he was missing; but consoled himself by thinking that his mother, who was still up at the Hall, would no doubt suppose that he had gone out for a night's fishing, as he had often done before, and that, as she was away, he had forgotten to leave word with the servant.

Suddenly, a blue light burned out on the top of the cliff. An angry exclamation broke from the captain, who was standing at the helm.

"Confound it!" he exclaimed. "They have caught sight of us from the cliff, and are signalling our whereabouts to the cutter."

As he spoke, he turned the vessel's head seaward, and, for a quarter of an hour, sailed straight out.

"Now," he said quietly, "I think we must be out of sight of those fellows on shore. Get her on the other tack, lads, but be as quiet as you can about it. There's no saying how close the cutter may be to us."

The great sails were lowered, as the boat's head paid off to the east. The yards were shifted to the other sides of the masts, and the sails hoisted again, and the lugger began to retrace her way back along the coast.

"It's just a chance, now," the captain said to James, who was standing close by him, "whether the commander of the cutter guesses, or not, that we shall change our course. He will know we are likely enough to do it."

"What should you do if you were in his place?" James said.

"I should run straight out to sea, and lay to, eight or ten miles off. He would be able to make us out then at daylight, whichever course we take; whereas, by trying to follow in the dark, he would run the chance of missing us altogether. I wish the wind would get up a bit. We are not moving through the water more than three knots an hour, and it's dying away. However, I fancy it will blow up again in the morning."

"Do you know whether she is faster than you are?" James asked.

"There is not much difference," the captain replied. "If the wind is strong, we have the legs of her; but in a light breeze, she is the fastest. She has chased us half a dozen times already, but we have always given her the slip."

"Then, even if she does run out to sea, as you say," James said, "we ought to be safe, as we should be a dozen miles or so along the coast."

"Yes, but not that ahead of her," the captain answered, "for she would be so much to the seaward. Still, that would be far enough; but she will begin to fire long before we are in range, and will bring any other king's ship within hearing down on us. However, I daresay we shall give her the slip, as we have done before."

The hours passed slowly. The wind continued to drop, until the vessel scarcely moved through the water, and, after a while, the sweeps were got out, and were worked until the day broke. All eyes were on the lookout for the cutter, as the day dawn began to steal over the sky.

"There she is, sure enough," the captain exclaimed at length, "lying to on the watch, some eight miles to the west. She must have seen us, for we are against the light sky; but, like, ourselves, she is becalmed."

It was a quarter of an hour, however, before the position of the cutter was seen to change. Then her head was suddenly turned east.

"She has got the wind," the captain said. "Now we only want a good breeze, and you'll have a lively day of it, lads."

From the time when she had turned, the lugger had made only about eight miles along the coast to the east, and an equal distance seaward, for the tide had set against her. The morning was bright and clear, the sea was perfectly smooth. As yet, the sails hung idly down, but there were dark lines on the water that showed that a breeze was coming.

"We shall have plenty of wind presently," the skipper said. "See how light the sky is to the south. There will be white tops on the waves in an hour or two.

"Here comes a flaw. Haul in your sheets, lads, now she begins to move."

The puff did not last long, dying away to nothing in a few minutes, and then the lugger lay immovable again. The men whistled, stamped the deck impatiently, and cast anxious glances back at the cutter.

"She is walking along fast," the skipper said, as he examined her through a glass. "She has got the wind steady, and must be slipping along at six knots an hour. This is hard luck on us. If we don't get the breeze soon, it will be a close thing of it."

Another quarter of an hour passed without a breath of wind ruffling the water. The cutter was fully two miles nearer to them than when she had first been seen, and was holding the wind steadily.

"Here it comes, lads," the skipper said cheerfully. "Another ten minutes, and we shall have our share."

The time seemed long, indeed, before the dark line on the water reached the lugger, and there was something like a cheer, from the crew, as the craft heeled slightly over, and then began to move through the water. It was the true breeze this time, and increased every moment in force, till the lugger was lying well over, with a white wave at her bow.

But the cutter had first gained by the freshening breeze, and James Walsham, looking back at her, judged that there were not more than four miles of water between the boats. The breeze was nearly due west, and, as the lugger was headed as close as she would lie to it, the cutter had hauled in her sheets and lay up on the same course, so that they were now sailing almost parallel to each other.

"If we could change places," the skipper said, "we should be safe. We can sail nearer the wind than she can, but she can edge away now, and has all the advantage of us."

James had already perceived this, and wondered that the lugger did not pay off before the wind, so as to make a stern chase of it.

"I want to get a few miles farther out," the skipper said. "Likely enough there is another cutter somewhere inshore. It is quite enough to have one of these fellows at one's heels."

Another half hour and the cutter, edging in, was little over three miles distant. Then the skipper gave the word, the helm was put down, the sheets slackened off, and, in a minute, the lugger was running dead before the wind with her sails boomed out, one on either side. The cutter followed her example, and hoisted a large square sail.

The wind was blowing fresh now, and the sea was getting up. Not a cloud was to be seen in the sky, and the sun shone brightly on the white heads which were beginning to show on the water. The lugger was tearing along, occasionally throwing a cloud of spray over her bows, and leaving a track of white water behind her.

"I think she still gains on us," the captain said to the mate, who had taken the helm.

"Ay, she is gaining," the sailor agreed, "but the wind is freshening every minute. She can't carry that topsail much longer. It's pressing her bows under now."

"She will go almost as fast without it," the skipper said.

The commander of the cutter seemed to be of the same opinion, for, just as he spoke, the topsail was seen to flutter, and then descended to the deck. It was a quarter of an hour before the skipper spoke again.

"I think we just about hold our own," he said. "I didn't think the Polly could have held her running."

"She couldn't, in a light wind," the mate replied; "but with this wind, it will want a fast boat to beat her."

The hands were now set to work, shifting the kegs further aft.

"That's better," the skipper said presently. "I am sure we are gaining ground, and our masts will stand it, if the cutter's will."

With her stern low in the water, the lugger was now tearing along at a tremendous pace. Stout as were her masts, and strong the stays, James Walsham wondered at their standing the strain of the great brown sails, as they seemed, at times, almost to lift her bodily out of the water. Buoyant as the craft was, the waves broke over her bows and flooded her decks, and sheets of spray flew over her.

The cutter, with her sharper bows and all her sail forward, was feeling it still more severely, and the spirits of all on board the lugger rose rapidly, as it was evident that they were dropping their pursuers. Suddenly, the gaff of the cutter's mainsail was seen to droop, and the boom was hauled on board.

"I thought it would be too much for them," the skipper said exultantly. "They are going to reef."

"We had better reef down too, I think," the mate said. "She has had as much as she could bear for some time."

"I'll hold on ten minutes longer," the skipper said. "Every half mile counts."

But before that time was up, the sails were one after another reefed, for the wind continued to freshen. The sky was still cloudless, but there was a misty light in the air, and a heavy sea was beginning to run.

Suddenly, a gun flashed out from the cutter. The skipper uttered an oath. Their pursuer was more than three miles astern, and he knew that she could only be firing as a signal.

There were several large ships in sight on their way up or down the Channel. To these, little attention had been paid. The skipper shaded his eyes with a hand, and gazed earnestly at a large ship on the weather beam, some four miles away.

"That is a frigate, sure enough," he exclaimed. "We are fairly caught between them."

"Haul in the sheets, lads, we will have a try for it yet."

The lugger was brought sharp up into the wind, and was soon staggering along seaward, with the lee bulwark almost under water. The cutter instantly lowered her square sail, and followed her example, continuing to fire a gun every minute. All eyes were turned towards the frigate, which was now on the port beam.

"We shall cross two miles to windward of her," the skipper said. "If she keeps on her course, a quarter of an hour will do it, but she is sure to notice the guns. The wind will take them down to her.

"Ah, there she goes."

As he spoke, a puff of smoke darted out from the frigate's bow. Her sails fluttered, and her head bore round, until she was on the same tack as the lugger.

The latter was now about equidistant from her two pursuers. The cutter and the lugger were nearly abreast, but the former, being to windward, could edge down. The frigate was three miles to leeward, but she was fully a mile ahead.

"There is no way out of it," the skipper said bitterly. "In a light wind we could run away from the frigate, but with this breeze we have no chance with her. Look how she is piling on sail!"

The crew shared the captain's opinion. Some shook their fists and cursed vainly at their pursuers, some stood sullenly scowling, while the French portion of the crew gave way to wild outbursts of rage. Rapidly the three vessels closed in towards each other, for the cutter edged in so rapidly that the lugger was obliged to bear off towards the frigate again. As a last hope, the lugger's course was changed, and she again tried running, but the superior weight and power of the frigate brought her rapidly down. Presently a heavy gun boomed out, and a shot came dancing along the water, a hundred yards away.

"Lower the sails," the skipper said. "It is no use going farther. The inside of a prison is better than the bottom of the sea, anyhow."

Down came the sails, and the lugger lay rolling heavily in the waves, as the frigate bore down upon her with a white roll of water on her stem.

"Get ready, lads," the skipper said. "There is just one chance yet. She will run by us. The instant she is past, up sail again. We shall be a mile away before they can get her round into the wind again. If she doesn't cripple us with her shot, we may weather her yet. We needn't mind the cutter."

The frigate came foaming along, the crew busy in taking sail off her. The instant she had passed, and was preparing to round to, the sails of the lugger flew up like magic, and she was soon tearing along almost in the eye of the wind, as if to meet the cutter, which was running down towards her.

"Down below, lads, every man of you," the captain shouted. "We shall have a broadside in a minute."

In a moment, the deck was clear of all save the skipper and his mate, who stood at the tiller. The frigate swept slowly round, and then, as her guns came to bear, shot after shot was fired at the lugger, already three-quarters of a mile to the windward. The shot hummed overhead, one struck the water alongside, a yard or two away, but still she was untouched.

"Some of her shots went as near the cutter as they did to us," the skipper said. "She won't fire again."

They were now fast approaching the cutter, which, when she was within a quarter of a mile, changed her course and was brought up again into the wind, firing the four guns she carried on her broadside as she came round. The lugger's head was paid off, and this placed the cutter on her starboard quarter, both going free. The former was travelling the faster, but a gun was fired from the cutter's bow, and the shot struck splinters from the lugger's quarter. The crew were on deck again now.

"Train that gun over the stern," the skipper said. "If we can knock her mast out of her, we are saved. If not, they will have us yet."

He had scarcely spoken when there was a crash. A shot from the cutter had struck the mizzen mast, a few feet above the deck, and the mast and sail fell over to leeward. There was a cry of rage and dismay.

"Luck's against us," the skipper said bitterly. "Down with the sail, lads. This time it is all up with us."

The sail was lowered, and the lugger lay motionless in the water, until the cutter came up and lay within fifty yards of her. A boat was at once lowered, and an officer was rowed to the lugger.

"So we have caught you, my friends, at last," he said, as he sprang on board.

"You wouldn't have done it, if it had not been for the frigate," the skipper said.

"No; I will say your craft sails like a witch," the officer replied. "I wish we could have done it without her. It will make all the difference to us. The frigate will get the lion's share of the prize. What is the value of your cargo?"

"Two hundred kegs of brandy," the skipper replied, "and fifteen hundred pounds' worth of lace and silks."

"A good prize," the officer said. "Not your own, I hope, for you have made a brave chase of it."

"No," the skipper answered. "Fortunately, I only took a very small share this time. It's bad enough to lose my boat; I own two-thirds of her."

"I am sorry for you," the officer said, for he was in high spirits at the success of the chase, and could afford to be pleasant. "Here comes a boat from the frigate. You played them a rare trick, and might have got off, if it hadn't been for that lucky shot of ours.

"I see you were just getting out a stern chaser," and he pointed to the gun. "It is well for you that you didn't fire it, as you can't be charged with armed resistance."

"I wish I had fired it, for all that. It might have been my luck to cripple you."

"It would have made no difference if you had," the officer replied. "The frigate would have overhauled you. With this wind she would sail five feet to your four."

The boat from the frigate now came alongside.

"How are you, Cotterel?" the officer said, as he stepped on board. "That was a lucky shot of yours; but I think it's lucky for the lugger that you hit her, for the captain was so savage, at that trick they played him, that I believe he would have sunk her when he came up to her again. I heard him say to the first lieutenant, 'I won't give her a chance to play me such a trick again.'"

"What orders have you brought?" the other asked.

"We are outward bound, so you are to put a crew on board and take her into port; but, as we are very short of hands, we will relieve you of the prisoners."

All on board the lugger were at once ordered into the frigate's boat, and were rowed off to the ship. On gaining the deck, they were drawn up in line, and the captain and first lieutenant came up. The good humour of the former had been restored by the capture of the lugger.

"Hallo!" he said, looking at the bandaged heads and arms of some of the men, "so you have been having a fight trying to run your cargo, I suppose. That will make it all the worse for you, when you get on shore. Now, I might press you all without giving you a choice, but I don't want unwilling hands, so I will leave it to you. Which is it to be--an English prison for two or three years, or a cruise on board the Thetis?"

The greater part of the men at once stepped forward, and announced their willingness to volunteer.

"Who have we here," the captain asked, looking at the three countrymen.

"They are passengers, sir," the skipper of the lugger said, with a half smile.

A few questions brought to light the facts of the surprise while the cargo was being landed.

"Well, my lads," the captain said, "you are in the same boat with the rest. You were engaged in an unlawful enterprise, and in resisting his majesty's officers. You will get some months in prison anyhow, if you go back. You had better stay on board, and let me make men of you."

The countrymen, however, preferred a prison to a man o' war.

James Walsham had been turning over the matter in his mind. He had certainly taken no part in the fray, but that would be difficult to prove, and he could not account for his presence except by acknowledging that he was there to warn them. It would certainly be a case of imprisonment. Surely, it would be better to volunteer than this. He had been longing for the sea, and here an opportunity opened for him for abandoning the career his mother intended for him, without setting himself in opposition to her wishes. Surely she would prefer that he should be at sea for a year or two to his being disgraced by imprisonment. He therefore now stepped forward.

"I do not belong to the lugger's crew, sir, and had nothing to do with running their cargo, though I own I was on the spot at the time. I am not a sailor, though I have spent a good deal of time on board fishing boats. Mr. Horton, whom I see there, knows me, and will tell you that I am a son of a doctor in Sidmouth. But, as I have got into a scrape, I would rather serve than go back and stand a trial."

"Very well, my lad," the captain said. "I like your spirit, and will keep my eye on you."

The three countrymen and four of the French sailors, who declined to join the Thetis, were taken back to the cutter, and the Thetis at once proceeded on her way down channel. James had given a hastily scribbled line, on the back of an old letter which he happened to have in his pocket, to the men who were to be taken ashore, but he had very little hope that it would ever reach his mother. Nor, indeed, did it ever do so. When the cutter reached Weymouth with the lugger, the men captured in her were at once sent to prison, where they remained until they were tried at assizes three months afterwards; and, although all were acquitted of the charge of unlawful resistance to the king's officers, as there was no proof against any of the six men individually, they were sentenced to a year's imprisonment for smuggling.

Whether Jim's hurriedly written letter was thrown overboard, or whether it was carried in the pocket of the man to whom he gave it until worn into fragments, James never knew, but it never reached his mother.

The news that James was missing was brought to her upon the day after the event by Mr. Wilks. He had, as usual, gone down after breakfast to report how Aggie was getting on, with a message from his mother that her charge was now so completely restored that it was unnecessary for her to stay longer at the Hall, and that she should come home that evening at her usual time. Hearing from the girl that James had not returned since he went out at nine o'clock on the previous evening, the old soldier sauntered down to the beach, to inquire of the fishermen in whose boat James had gone out.

To his surprise, he found that none of the boats had put to sea the evening before. The men seemed less chatty and communicative than usual. Most of them were preparing to go out with their boats, and none seemed inclined to enter into a conversation. Rather wondering at their unusual reticence, Mr. Wilks strolled along to where the officer of the revenue men was standing, with his boatswain, watching the fishermen.

"A fine morning, lieutenant."

"Yes," the latter assented. "There will be wind presently. Have you heard of the doings of last night?"

"No," Mr. Wilks said in surprise, "I have heard nothing. I was just speaking to the fishermen, but they don't seem in as communicative a mood as usual this morning."

"The scamps know it is safest for them to keep their mouths shut, just at present," the officer said grimly. "I have no doubt a good many of them were concerned in that affair last night. We had a fight with the smugglers. Two of my men were shot and one of theirs, and there were a good many cutlass wounds on each side. We have taken a score of prisoners, but they are all country people who were assisting in the landing; the smugglers themselves all got off. We made a mess of the affair altogether, thanks to some fellow who rushed down and gave the alarm, and upset all the plans we had laid.

"It is too provoking. I had got news of the exact spot and hour at which the landing was to take place. I had my men all up on the cliff, and, as the fellows came up with kegs, they were to have been allowed to get a hundred yards or so inland and would there have been seized, and any shout they made would not have been heard below. Lieutenant Fisher, with his party from the next station, was to be a little way along at the foot of the cliffs, and when the boats came with the second batch, he was to rush forward and capture them, while we came down from above. Then we intended to row off and take the lugger. There was not wind enough for her to get away.

"All was going well, and the men were just coming up the cliff with the tubs, when someone who had passed us on the cliff ran down shouting the alarm. We rushed down at once, but arrived too late. They showed fight, and kept us back till Fisher's party came up; but by that time the boats were afloat, and the smugglers managed to get in and carry them off, in spite of us. We caught, as I tell you, some of the countrymen, and Fisher has taken them off to Weymouth, but most of them got away. There are several places where the cliff can be climbed by men who know it, and I have no doubt half those fishermen you see there were engaged in the business."

"Then the smuggler got away?" Mr. Wilks asked.

"I don't know," the lieutenant said shortly. "I had sent word to Weymouth, and I hope they will catch her in the offing. The lugger came down this way first, but we made her out, and showed a blue light. She must have turned and gone back again, for this morning at daylight we made her out to the east. The cutter was giving chase, and at first ran down fast towards her. Then the smugglers got the wind, and the last we saw of them they were running up the Channel, the cutter some three miles astern.

"I would give a couple of months' pay to know who it was that gave the alarm. I expect it was one of those fishermen. As far as my men could make out in the darkness, the fellow was dressed as a sailor. But I must say good morning, for I am just going to turn in."

Mr. Wilks had been on the point of mentioning that James was missing, but a vague idea that he might, in some way, be mixed up with the events of the previous night, checked the question on his lips; and yet he thought, as the officer walked away, it was not probable. Had James been foolish enough to take part in such a business, he would either have been taken prisoner, or would, after he escaped, have returned home. He had evidently not been taken prisoner, or the officer would have been sure to mention it.

Much puzzled, he walked slowly back to the fishermen. Some of the boats had already pushed off. He went up to three of the men, whose boat, being higher up than the rest, would not be afloat for another quarter of an hour.

"Look here, lads," he said. "My young friend Jim Walsham is missing this morning, and hasn't been at home all night. As none of the fishing boats put out in the evening he cannot have gone to sea. Can any of you tell me anything about him?"

The men gave no answer.

"You need not be afraid of speaking to me, you know," he went on, "and it's no business of mine whether any of the men on the shore were concerned in that affair. The lieutenant has just been telling me of last night; but hearing of that, and finding Jim is missing, I can't help thinking there is some connection between the two things. Nothing you say to me will go further, that I can promise you; but the lad's mother will be in a terrible way. I can't make it out, for I know that, if he had anything to do with this smuggling business, he would have told me. Again, if he was there and got away, he would naturally have come straight home, for his absence would only throw suspicion upon him."

"Well, Mr. Wilks," the youngest of the sailors said, "I don't know nothing about it myself. No one does, so far as I know, but I have heard say this morning as how he was there or thereabouts; but don't you let out as I told you, 'cause they would want to know who I heard it from."

"You can rely upon my silence, my lad, and here's half a guinea to drink my health between you. But can't you tell me a little more?"

"Well, sir, they do say as how it war Mr. Jim as came running down into the middle of them on the beach, shouting the alarm, with the revenue men close at his heels. I don't say as it were he–likely enough it weren't–but that's the talk, and that's all I have heared about the matter. How he came for to know of it, or how he got there, no one knows, for sartin he has had nought to do with any landings afore. He was a lot among us, but I know as he never was told about it; for, though everyone would have trusted Jim, still, seeing how he was placed, with his mother up at the Hall, and the squire a magistrate, it was thought better as he shouldn't be let into it. Everyone on the shore here likes Jim."

"But if he was there, and he hasn't been taken prisoner–and I am sure the lieutenant would have told me if he was–why shouldn't he have got home?"

"We didn't know as he hadn't got home, did us, Bill?" the fisherman appealed to one of his comrades.

"No," the other said. "We thought likely he had got safely away with the rest. It war a dark night, and I expect as everyone was too busy looking after himself to notice about others."

"He may have been wounded," the old soldier said anxiously, "and may be in hiding in some house near the place."

The fisherman was silent. Such a thing was, of course, possible.

"He might that," one of the sailors said doubtfully, "and yet I don't think it. The chase was a hot one, and I don't think anyone, wounded so bad as he couldn't make his way home, would have got away. I should say as it wur more likely as he got on board one of the boats. It seems to me as though he might have come to warn us–that is to say, to warn them, I mean–just to do em a good turn, as he was always ready to do if he had the chance. But he wouldn't have had anything to do with the scrimmage, and might have been standing, quiet like, near the boats, when the other lot came along the shore, and then, seeing as the game was up, he might, likely enough, have jumped on board and gone off to the lugger."

"That is possible," Mr. Wilks said. "Anyhow, I will go off at once, and make inquiries at all the houses within a mile or so of the landing place."

Chapter 8: Discharged.

Contrary to his usual habits of punctuality, Mr. Wilks did not return to luncheon at the Hall, and it was two hours later before he came in, looking fagged and anxious. He had been to all the farm houses within two miles of the scene of the fight, and had ascertained, for certain, that Jim was not lying wounded at any of them. At first, his inquiries had everywhere been coldly received. There was scarce a farm house near the coast, but the occupants had relations with the smugglers, assisting with their carts and men at the landings, or having hiding places where goods could be stowed away. At first, therefore, all professed entire ignorance of the events of the previous night; but, when persuaded by the earnestness of the old soldier's manner that his mission was a friendly one, they became more communicative, and even owned that some of their men had been taken prisoners and marched to Weymouth; but none of them had heard of any wounded man being in hiding.

Convinced, at last, that James must have gone off to the lugger, Mr. Wilks returned to Sidmouth, a prey to great anxiety. Everything depended now on whether the lugger was captured. If so, James would have to stand his trial for being concerned in the fight on the beach, and, as two of the revenue men had been killed, his sentence might be a heavy one.

If she got away, all would be well. They would doubtless hear by letter from Jim, and it would be better that he should not return at present to Sidmouth, but should at once take up his residence in London, and commence his studies there.

He met the squire just as the latter was starting for Sidmouth.

"Well, Wilks, we began to think that you were lost," he said, cheerfully. "Aggie was downstairs to lunch, and was mightily offended that you should not be there at her first appearance.

"But you look tired and fagged. Has anything gone wrong?"

"Things have gone very wrong, squire."

And he related to his friend all the news that he had gathered, and his conviction that James Walsham was on board the lugger.

"This is a pretty kettle of fish," the squire said irritably. "What on earth did the boy mean by getting himself mixed up with such an affair as that?"

"It is a foolish business, squire," the old soldier agreed. "But we can't expect wise heads on young shoulders, I suppose. He, somehow or other, learnt the surprise which the revenue men intended, and as most of his friends, the fishermen, would probably be concerned in it, he went to give them notice, intending, no doubt, to go quietly back again before the revenue men arrived. I don't know that he's altogether to be blamed in the matter. Most young fellows would do the same."

"Well, I suppose they would," the squire agreed reluctantly; "but it is a most awkward business. If the lad gets caught, and gets two or three years' imprisonment, it will ruin his prospects in life. His mother will be broken hearted over the business, and I am sure Aggie will take it terribly to heart. They were great friends of old, though she hasn't seen much of him for the last two or three years, and, of course, that affair of the other day has made quite a hero of him."

"We must hope the lugger will get safely over to France," his companion said. "Then no great harm will have been done."

"We must hope so," the squire assented moodily. "Confound the young jackanapes, turning everything upside down, and upsetting us all with his mad-brain freaks."

Mrs. Walsham was greatly distressed, when the news was broken to her by Mr. Wilks, and Aggie cried so that the squire, at last, said she must go straight up to bed unless she stopped, for she would be making herself ill again. When she was somewhat pacified, the matter was discussed in every light, but the only conclusion to be arrived at was, that their sole hope rested in the hugger getting safely off.

"Of course, my dear madam," the squire said, "if they are taken I will do my best to get a pardon for your son. I am afraid he will have to stand his trial with the rest; but I think that, with the representations I will make as to his good character, I may get a mitigation, anyhow, of a sentence. If they find out that it was he who gave the alarm, there will be no hope of a pardon; but if that doesn't come out, one would represent his being there as a mere boyish freak of adventure, and, in that case, I might get him a free pardon. You must not take the matter too seriously to heart. It was a foolish business, and that is the worst that can be said of it."

"I think it was a grand thing," Aggie said indignantly, "for him to risk being shot, and imprisoned, and all sorts of dreadful things, just to save other people."

"And I think you are a goose, Aggie," the squire said. "If everyone were to go and mix themselves up in other people's business, there would be no end of trouble. I suppose next you will say that, if you heard me arranging with the constable to make a capture of some burglars, you would think it a grand thing to put on your hat to run off to warn them."

"Oh, grandpapa, how can you say such a thing!" the girl said. "Burglars and smugglers are quite different. Burglars are wicked men, and thieves and robbers. Smugglers are not, they are only trying to get goods in without paying duty."

"They try to rob the king, my dear, and in the eyes of the law are just as criminal as burglars. Both of them are leagued to break the law, and both will resist and take life if they are interfered with. I allow that, in general estimation, the smugglers are looked upon in a more favourable light, and that a great many people, who ought to know better, are in league with them, but that does not alter the facts of the case."

The girl did not argue the question, but the squire was perfectly aware that he had in no way convinced her, and that her feeling, that James Walsham's action was a highly meritorious one, was in no way shaken. It was agreed that nothing was to be said about James's absence, and, after taking some refreshment, Mr. Wilks went down into Sidmouth again, to tell the girl at Mrs. Walsham's that she was not to gossip about James being away.

Three days later, a letter was received by the squire from Richard Horton.

"I am taking the opportunity of writing a few lines to you, my dear uncle, as I have a chance of sending it ashore by the revenue cutter Thistle, which is lying alongside of us. Between us, we have just captured a rascally smuggling lugger, with a cargo of lace, silk, and spirits. You will, I am sure, be surprised and grieved to hear that among the crew of the lugger was James Walsham. I could hardly believe my eyes, when I saw him in such disreputable company. It will be a sad blow for his poor mother. As we were short of hands, our captain offered the crew of the lugger the choice of shipping with us, or being sent on shore for trial. Most of them chose the former alternative, among them James Walsham, of which I was glad, as his mother will be spared the disgrace of his being placed in the dock with his associates. I need not say that if I could have obtained his release, I should have done so, knowing that you had a high opinion of him; but it was, of course, out of my power to interfere."

The squire was alone in his study when he received the letter, for it was midday before the post arrived at Sidmouth, when a man from the Hall went down each day, with a bag, to fetch the letters. He rang the bell, and ordered the servant to tell Mr. Wilks he should be glad if he would step in to him. When his friend came, he handed him the letter without a word.

"That settles the matter," he said, as he threw the letter angrily down upon the table. "A malicious young viper! I wish I had him here."

"It is not nicely worded," the squire said gravely; "but it was an unpleasant story to have to tell."

"It was not an unpleasant story for him to tell," the old soldier said hotly. "There is malice in every line of it. He speaks of the men as James's associates, talks about the disgrace he would bring on his mother. There's malice, squire, in every line of it."

"I'm afraid it's a bad letter," the squire assented gravely.

"It's a natural letter," Mr. Wilks said savagely. "It is written in a hurry, and he's had no time to pick and choose his words, and round off his sentences, as he generally does in his letters to you. He was so full of malicious exultation that he did not think how much he was showing his feeling, as he wrote."

"It's a bad letter and a nasty letter," the squire assented; "but let that pass, now. The first question is—How are we to tell Jim's mother? Do you think it will be a relief to her, or otherwise?"

"It will be a blow to know that the lugger has been captured," Mr. Wilks said—"a severe blow, no doubt, for her escape is what we have been building our hopes upon. It will be a heavy blow, too, for her to know that James is a seaman before the mast; that it will be years before she will see him again, and that all her plans for his future are upset. But I think this will be much better for her than if she knew he was a prisoner, and would have to stand a trial.

"Between ourselves, squire, as far as the lad himself is concerned, I am not sure that he will be altogether sorry that events have turned out as they have. In our talks together, he has often confided to me that his own inclinations were altogether for a life of activity and adventure; but that, as his mother's heart was so set upon his following his father's profession, he had resolved upon never saying a word, to her, which would lead her to suppose that his own wishes lay in any other direction. This business will give him the opportunity he has longed for, to see the world, without his appearing in any way to thwart his mother's plans."

"At any rate," the squire said, "I am heartily glad he has got off being tried. Even if I had got a free pardon for him, it would have been a serious slur upon him that he had been imprisoned, and would have been awkward for us all in the future. I think, Wilks, I will leave it to you to break it to his mother."

"Very well," the other agreed. "It is an unpleasant business, squire; but perhaps I had better do it. It may console her if I tell her that, at heart, he always wanted to go to sea, and that, accustomed as he is to knock about in the fishermen's boats, he will find it no hardship on board a man o' war, and will come back, in the course of two or three years, none the worse for his cruise. She may think he will take up doctoring again after that, though I have my doubts whether he will do that. However, there is no use in telling her so. Shall I show her that letter, squire?"

"No," the squire replied, "of course you can tell her what's in it; but I will keep the letter myself. I would give a good deal if he had not written it. It is certainly badly worded, though why he should feel any malice, towards the other, is more than I can tell."

His companion was about to speak, but thought better of it, and, without another word, went to break the news to Mrs. Walsham.

Mrs. Walsham was terribly upset. After suffering her to cry for some time in silence, Mr. Wilks said:

"My dear madam, I know that this news must distress you terribly; but it may be that in this, as in all things, a providence has overruled your plans for your son, for his own good. I will tell you now what you would never have known had this affair never occurred. Jim, at heart, hates his father's profession. He is a dutiful son and, rather than give you pain, he was prepared to sacrifice all his own feelings and wishes. But the lad is full of life and energy. The dull existence of a country surgeon, in a little town like this, is the last he would adopt as his own choice; and I own that I am not surprised that a lad of spirit should long for a more adventurous life. I should have told you this long ago, and advised you that it would be well for you both to put it frankly to him that, although you would naturally like to see him following his father's profession, still that you felt that he should choose for himself; and that, should he select any other mode of life, you would not set your wishes against his. But the lad would not hear of my doing so. He said that, rather than upset your cherished plans, he would gladly consent to settle down in Sidmouth for life. I honoured him for his filial spirit; but, frankly, I think he was wrong. An eagle is not made to live in a hen coop, nor a spirited lad to settle down in a humdrum village; and I own that, although I regret the manner of his going, I cannot look upon it as an unmixed evil, that the force of circumstances has taken him out of the course marked out for him, and that he will have an opportunity of seeing life and adventure."

Mrs. Walsham had listened, with a surprise too great to admit of her interrupting the old soldier's remarks.

"I never dreamed of this," she said at last, when he ceased. "I cannot remember, now, that I ever asked him, but I took it for granted that he would like nothing better than to follow in his father's steps. Had I known that he objected to it, I would not for a moment have forced him against his inclinations. Of course it is natural that, being alone in the world, I should like to have him with me still, but I would never have been so selfish as to have sacrificed his life to mine. Still, though it would be hard to have parted from him in any way, it is harder still to part like this. If he was to go, he need not have gone as a common sailor. The squire, who has done so much for him, would no doubt, instead of sending him to school, have obtained a midshipman's berth for him, or a commission in the army; but it is dreadful to think of him as a common sailor, liable to be flogged."

"Well, Mrs. Walsham, perhaps we may set the matter partly to rights. I will speak to the squire, and I am sure he will write to his friend at the admiralty, and have an order sent out, at once, for Jim's discharge. At the same time, it would be better that he should not return here just at present. His name may come out, at the trial of the smugglers, as being concerned in the affair, and it would be better that he should stay away, till that matter blows over. At any rate, if I were you I should write to him, telling him that you know now that he has no taste for the medical profession, and that, should he see anything that he thinks will suit him in America, you would not wish him to come home immediately, if he has a fancy for staying out there; but that, if he chooses to return, you are sure that the squire will exert himself, to give him a start in any other profession he may choose."

Mrs. Walsham agreed to carry out the suggestion and, that afternoon, the squire sent off a letter to his friend at the admiralty, and three letters were also posted to James himself.

The voyage of the Thetis was uneventful. Her destination was Hampton, at the opening of Chesapeake Bay, where the troops on board would join the expedition under General Braddock, which was advancing up the Potomac. When she arrived there, they found several ships of war under Commodore Keppel. Braddock's force had marched to Wills Creek, where a military post named Fort Cumberland had been formed. The soldiers on board were at once disembarked, and marched up the banks of the Potomac to join the force at Fort Cumberland. The sailors were employed in taking stores up the river in boats.

James Walsham had done his best, during the voyage, to acquire a knowledge of his duties. His experience in the fishing boats was useful to him now, and he was soon able to do his work as an able-bodied seaman. His good spirits and willingness rendered him a general favourite. He was glad that he was not put in the same watch with Richard Horton, as, after their first meeting, the young lieutenant showed no signs of recognition. He was not, James found, popular among the men. He was exacting and overbearing with them, and some on board, who had served with him on his previous voyage, had many tales to his disadvantage.

A fortnight after the arrival of the Thetis at Hampton, orders were issued among the ships of war for thirty volunteers for Braddock's expedition, of which the Thetis was to furnish ten. So many sent in their names, that the first lieutenant had difficulty in choosing ten, who were looked upon with envy by the rest of the ship's company; for there seemed little chance, at present, of fighting at sea, and the excitement of a march on shore, with adventures of all sorts, and encounters with the French and their Indian allies, seemed delightful to the tars.

Upon the following day a ship arrived from England and, an hour afterwards, an order was passed forward that the first lieutenant wanted James Walsham upon the quarterdeck.

"Walsham," he said, "an order has just come from the admiralty for your discharge, and you are to have a passage in the first ship returning, if you choose to take it. I am sorry you are leaving the ship, for I have noticed that you show great willingness and activity, and will make a first-rate sailor. Still, I suppose, your friends in England did not care about your remaining before the mast."

James touched his hat and walked forward. He was scarcely surprised, for he had thought that his mother would probably ask the squire to use his influence to obtain his discharge. He scarcely knew whether he was glad or sorry. He was in a false position, and could not hope for promotion except by some lucky chance, such as was not likely to occur, of distinguishing himself.

At the same time, he sighed as he thought that he must now return and take up the profession for which his mother had intended him. A quarter of an hour later, however, the ship's corporal came round and distributed the mails, and James, to his delight, found there were three letters for him. He tore open that from his mother. It began by gently upbraiding him for getting himself mixed up in the fight between the smugglers and the revenue men.

"In the next place, my dear boy," she said, "I must scold you, even more, for not confiding in your mother as to your wishes about your future profession. Mr. Wilks has opened my eyes to the fact that, while I have all along been taking it for granted, that your wishes agreed with mine as to your profession, you have really been sacrificing all your own inclinations in order to avoid giving me pain. I am very thankful to him for having opened my eyes, for I should have been grieved indeed had I found, when too late, that I had chained you down to a profession you dislike.

"Of course, I should have liked to have had you with me, but in no case would have had you sacrifice yourself; still less now, when I have met with such kind friends, and am happy and comfortable in my life. Therefore, my boy, let us set aside at once all idea of your becoming a doctor. There is no occasion for you to choose, immediately, what you will do. You are too old now to enter the royal navy, and it is well that, before you finally decide on a profession, you have the opportunity of seeing something of the world.

"I inclose bank notes for a hundred pounds so that, if you like, you can stay for a few weeks or months in the colonies, and then take your passage home from New York or Boston. By that time, too, all talk about this affair with the smugglers will have ceased; but, as your name is likely to come out at the trial of the men who were taken, so the squire thinks it will be better for you to keep away, for a time."

The rest of the letter was filled up with an account of the excitement and alarm which had been felt when he was first missed.

"We were glad, indeed," she said, "when a letter was received from Richard Horton, saying that you were on board the Thetis. Mr. Wilks tells me it was an abominably spiteful letter, and I am sure the squire thinks so, too, from the tone in which he spoke this afternoon about his nephew; but I can quite forgive him, for, if it had not been for his letter, we should not have known what had become of you, and many months might have passed before we might have heard from you in America. As it is, only four or five days have been lost, and the squire is writing tonight to obtain your discharge, which he assures me there will be no difficulty whatever about."

The squire's was a very cordial letter, and he, too, enclosed notes for a hundred pounds.

"Mr. Wilks tells me," he said, "that you do not like the thought of doctoring. I am not surprised, and I think that a young fellow, of such spirit and courage as you have shown, ought to be fitted for something better than administering pills and draughts to the old women of Sidmouth. Tell me frankly, when you write, what you would like. You are, of course, too old for the royal navy. If you like to enter the merchant service, I have no doubt I could arrange with some shipping firm in Bristol, and would take care that, by the time you get to be captain, you should also be part owner of the ship. If, on the other hand, you would like to enter the army–and it seems to me that there are stirring times approaching–I think that, through one or other of my friends in London, I could obtain a commission for you. If there is anything else you would like better than this, you may command my best services. I never forget how much I am indebted to you for my present happiness, and, whatever I can do for you, still shall feel myself deeply your debtor."

The old soldier wrote a characteristic letter. In the first place, he told James that he regarded him as a fool, for mixing up in an affair in which he had no concern whatever. Then he congratulated him on the fact that circumstances had broken the chain from which he would never otherwise have freed himself.

"You must not be angry with me," he said, "for having betrayed your confidence, and told the truth to your mother. I did it in order to console her, by showing her that things were, after all, for the best; and I must say that madam took my news in the very best spirit, and I am sure you will see this by her letter to you. There is no one I honour and esteem more than I do her, and I was sure, all along, that you were making a mistake in not telling her frankly what your wishes were. Now you have got a roving commission for a time, and it will be your own fault if you don't make the best of it. There is likely to be an exciting time in the colonies, and you are not the lad I take you for, if you dawdle away your time in the towns, instead of seeing what is going on in the forest."

These letters filled James with delight, and, without an hour's delay, he sat down to answer them. In his letter to the squire he thanked him most warmly for his kindness, and said that, above all things, he should like a commission in the army. He wrote a very tender and affectionate letter to his mother, telling her how much he felt her goodness in so promptly relinquishing her own plans, and in allowing him to choose the life he liked.

"Thank Aggie," he concluded, "for the message she sent by you. Give her my love, and don't let her forget me."

To the old soldier he wrote a gossipping account of his voyage.

"It was impossible," he said, "for the news of my discharge to have come at a better moment. Thirty sailors from the fleet are going with General Braddock's force, and everyone else is envying their good luck–I among them. Now I shall go up, at once, and join the Virginian regiment which is accompanying them. I shall join that, instead of either of the line regiments, as I can leave when I like. Besides, if the squire is able to get me a commission, it would have been pleasanter for me to have been fighting here as a volunteer, than as a private in the line.

"By the way, nobody thinks there will be much fighting, so don't let my mother worry herself about me; but, at any rate, a march through the great forests of this country, with a chance of a brush with the redskins, will be great fun. Perhaps, by the time it is over, I may get a letter from you saying that I have got my commission.

As I hear there is a chance of a regular war between the French and us out here, the commission may be for a regiment on this side."

After finishing his letters, and giving them to the ship's corporal to place in the next post bag, James said goodbye to his messmates, and prepared to go on shore. The ten men chosen for the expedition were also on the point of starting. Richard Horton was standing near, in a state of great discontent that he had not been chosen to accompany them in their expedition. James Walsham stepped up to him, and touched his hat respectfully.

"I wish to thank you, Lieutenant Horton, for your extremely kind letter, telling my friends that I was on board this ship. It has been the means of my obtaining my discharge at once, instead of having to serve, for many months, before I could send the news home and obtain an answer in return."

Without another word he turned and, walking to the gangway, took his place in a boat about starting with some sailors for the shore, leaving Richard Horton in a state of fury, with himself, for having been the means of obtaining James's discharge. He had already, more than once, felt uncomfortable as he thought of the wording of the letter; and that this indulgence of his spite had had the effect of restoring James's liberty, rendered him well-nigh mad with rage.

On landing, James Walsham at once disposed of his sailor's clothes, and purchased a suit similar to those worn by the colonists; then he obtained a passage up the river to Alexandria, where the transports which had brought the troops were still lying. Here, one of the companies of the Virginia corps was stationed, and James, finding that they were expecting, every day, to be ordered up to Wills Creek, determined to join them at once.

The scene was a busy one. Stores were being landed from the transports, teamsters were loading up their waggons, officers were superintending the operations, the men of the Virginia corps, who wore no uniform, but were attired in the costume used by hunters and backwoodsmen; namely, a loose hunting shirt, short trousers or breeches, and gaiters; were moving about unconcernedly, while a few of them, musket on shoulder, were on guard over the piles of stores.

Presently a tall, slightly-built young man, with a pleasant but resolute face, came riding along, and checked his horse close to where James was standing. James noticed that the men on sentry, who had, for the most part, been sitting down on fallen logs of wood, bales, or anything else which came handy; with their muskets across their knees, or leaning beside them; got up and began pacing to and fro, with some semblance of military position.

"Who is that young man?" he asked a teamster standing by.

"That is Colonel Washington," the man replied, "one of the smartest of the colonial officers."

"Why, he only looks two or three and twenty," James said in surprise.

"He is not more than that," the man said; "but age don't go for much here, and Colonel Washington is adjutant general of the Virginian militia. Only a few months back, he made a journey with despatches, right through the forests to the French station at Port de Beuf, and, since then, he has been in command of the party which went out to build a fort, at the forks of the Ohio, and had some sharp fighting with the

French. A wonderful smart young officer they say he is, just as cool, when the bullets are flying, as if sitting on horseback."

James resolved, at once, that he would speak to Colonel Washington, and ask him if he could join the Virginian militia. He accordingly went up to him, and touched his hat.

"If you please, sir, I am anxious to join the Virginian militia, and, as they tell me that you are adjutant general, I have come to ask you if I can do so."

"I see no difficulty in it, my lad," the colonel said; "but if you have run away from home, in search of adventure, I should advise you to go back again, for we are likely to have heavy work."

"I don't mind that, sir, and I have not run away. I am English. I was pressed on board a frigate, and was brought over here, but my friends in England procured my discharge, which came for me here, a fortnight after my arrival. They are, I believe, about to obtain for me a commission in a king's regiment; but, as I was here, I thought that I should like to see some service, as it may be some months before I hear that I have got my commission. I would rather if I could join as a volunteer, as I do not want pay, my friends having supplied me amply with money."

"You seem to be a lad of spirit," Colonel Washington said, "and I will at once put you in the way of doing what you desire. You shall join the Virginian corps as a volunteer. Have you money enough to buy a horse?"

"Yes, plenty," Jim said. "I have two hundred pounds."

"Then you had better leave a hundred and fifty, at least, behind you," the colonel said. "I will direct you to a trader here, with whom you can bank it. You can get an excellent horse for twenty pounds. I asked you because, if you like, I can attach you to myself. I often want a mounted messenger; and, of course, as a volunteer, you would mess with me."

"I should like it above all things," James said thankfully.

"Then we will at once go to the tent of the officer commanding this company," Washington said, "and enroll you as a volunteer."

On reaching the tent, Washington dismounted and led the way in.

"Captain Hall," he said, "this is a young English gentleman, who will shortly have a commission in the king's army, but, in the meantime, he wishes to see a little brisk fighting, so he is to be enrolled as a volunteer in your company; but he is going to obtain a horse, and will act as a sort of aide-de-camp to me."

Captain Hall at once entered James's name as a volunteer on the roll of his company.

"Do you know of anyone who has a good horse for sale?" Washington asked.

"Yes," the captain replied, "at least, there was a farmer here half an hour ago with a good-looking horse which he wants to sell. I have no doubt he is in the camp, still."

Captain Hall went to the door of the tent, and told two of the men there to find the farmer, and tell him he had a purchaser for his horse.

Ten minutes later the farmer came up, and James bought the horse, Captain Hall doing the bargaining for him.

"Now," Washington said, "we will go round to the storekeeper I spoke of, and deposit the best part of your money with him. I should only take a pound or two, if I were you, for you will find no means of spending money when you once set forward, and, should anything happen to you, the Indians would not appreciate the value of those English notes of yours. You will want a brace of pistols and a sword, a blanket, and cooking pot–that is about the extent of your camp equipment."

Chapter 9: The Defeat Of Braddock.

England and France were, at this time, at peace in Europe, although the troops of both nations were about to engage in conflict, in the forests of America. Their position there was an anomalous one. England owned the belt of colonies on the east coast. France was mistress of Canada in the north, of Louisiana in the south, and, moreover, claimed the whole of the vast country lying behind the British colonies, which were thus cooped up on the seaboard. Her hold, however, of this great territory was extremely slight. She had strong posts along the chain of lakes from the Saint Lawrence to Lake Superior, but between these and Louisiana, her supremacy was little more than nominal.

The Canadian population were frugal and hardy, but they were deficient in enterprise; and the priests, who ruled them with a rod of iron, for Canada was intensely Catholic, discouraged any movements which would take their flocks from under their charge. Upon the other hand, the colonists of New England, Pennsylvania, and Virginia were men of enterprise and energy, and their traders, pushing in large numbers across the Alleghenies, carried on an extensive trade with the Indians in the valley of the Ohio, thereby greatly exciting the jealousy of the French, who feared that the Indians would ally themselves with the British colonists, and that the connection between Canada and Louisiana would be thereby cut.

The English colonists were greatly superior to the French in number; but they laboured under the disadvantage that the colonies were wholly independent of each other, with strong mutual jealousies, which paralysed their action and prevented their embarking upon any concerted operations. Upon the other hand, Canada was governed by the French as a military colony. The governor was practically absolute, and every man capable of bearing arms could, if necessary, be called by him into the field. He had at his disposal not only the wealth of the colony, but large assistance from France, and the French agents were, therefore, able to outbid the agents of the British colonies with the Indians.

For years there had been occasional troubles between the New England States and the French, the latter employing the Indians in harassing the border; but, until the middle of the eighteenth century, there had been nothing like a general trouble. In 1749 the Marquis of Galissoniere was governor general of Canada. The treaty of Aix la Chapelle had been signed; but this had done nothing to settle the vexed question of the boundaries between the English and French colonies. Meanwhile, the English traders from Pennsylvania and Virginia were poaching on the domain which France claimed as hers, ruining the French fur trade, and making friends with the Indian allies of Canada. Worse still, farmers were pushing westward and settling in the valley of the Ohio.

In order to drive these back, to impress the natives with the power of France, and to bring them back to their allegiance, the governor of Canada, in the summer of 1749, sent Celoron de Bienville. He had with him fourteen officers, twenty French soldiers, a hundred and eighty Canadians, and a band of Indians. They embarked in twenty-three birch-bark canoes, and, pushing up the Saint Lawrence, reached Lake Ontario, stopping for a time at the French fort of Frontenac, and avoiding the rival English port of Oswego on the southern shore, where a trade in beaver skins, disastrous to French interests, was being carried on, for the English traders sold their goods at vastly lower prices than those which the French had charged.

On the 6th of July the party reached Niagara, where there was a small French fort, and thence, carrying their canoes round the cataract, launched them upon Lake Erie. Landing again on the southern shore of the lake, they carried their canoes nine miles through the forest to Chautauqua Lake, and then dropped down the stream running out of it until they reached the Ohio. The fertile country here was inhabited by the Delawares, Shawanoes, Wyandots, and Iroquois, or Indians of the Five Nations, who had migrated thither from their original territories in the colony of New York. Further west, on the banks of the Miami, the Wabash, and other streams, was a confederacy of the Miami and their kindred tribes. Still further west, in the country of the Illinois, near the Mississippi, the French had a strong stone fort called Fort Chartres, which formed one of the chief links of the chain of posts that connected Quebec with New Orleans.

The French missionaries and the French political agents had, for seventy years, laboured hard to bring these Indian tribes into close connection with France. The missionaries had failed signally; but the presents, so lavishly bestowed, had inclined the tribes to the side of their donors, until the English traders with their cheap goods came pushing west over the Alleghenies. They carried their goods on the backs of horses, and journeyed from village to village, selling powder, rum, calicoes, beads, and trinkets. No less than three hundred men were engaged in these enterprises, and some of them pushed as far west as the Mississippi.

As the party of Celoron proceeded they nailed plates of tin, stamped with the arms of France, to trees; and buried plates of lead near them, with inscriptions saying that they took possession of the land in the name of Louis the Fifteenth, King of France.

Many of the villages were found to be deserted by the natives, who fled at their approach. At some, however, they found English traders, who were warned at once to leave the country; and, by some of them, letters were sent to the governor of Pennsylvania, in which Celoron declared that he was greatly surprised to find Englishmen trespassing in the domain of France, and that his orders were precise, to leave no foreign traders within the limits of the government of Canada.

At Chiningue, called Logstown by the English, a large number of natives were gathered, most of the inhabitants of the deserted villages having sought refuge there. The French were received with a volley of balls from the shore; but they landed without replying to the fire, and hostilities were avoided. The French kept guard all night, and in the morning Celoron invited the chiefs to a council, when he told them he had come, by the order of the governor, to open their eyes to the designs of the English against their lands, and that they must be driven away at once. The reply of the chiefs was humble; but they begged that the English traders, of whom there were, at that moment, ten in the town, might stay a little longer, since the goods they brought were necessary to them.

After making presents to the chiefs, the party proceeded on their way, putting up the coats of arms and burying the lead inscriptions. At Scioto a large number of Indians were assembled, and the French were very apprehensive of an attack, which would doubtless have been disastrous to them, as the Canadians of the party were altogether unused to war. A council was held, however, at which Celoron could obtain no satisfaction whatever, for the interests of the Indians were bound up with the English.

There can be no doubt that, had they been able to look into the future, every Indian on the continent would have joined the French in their effort to crush the English colonies. Had France remained master of America the Indians might, even now, be roaming free and unmolested on the lands of their forefathers. France is not a colonizing nation. She would have traded with the Indians, would have endeavoured to Christianize them, and would have left them their land and freedom, well satisfied with the fact that the flag of France should wave over so vast an extent of country; but on England conquering the soil, her armies of emigrants pressed west, and the red man is fast becoming extinct on the continent of which he was once the lord.

Celoron's expedition sailed down the Ohio until it reached the mouth of the Miami, and toiled for thirteen days against its shallow current, until they reached a village of the Miami Indians, ruled over by a chief called, by the French, La Demoiselle, but whom the English, whose fast friend he was, called Old Britain. He was the great chief of the Miami confederation.

The English traders there withdrew at the approach of the French. The usual council was held, and Celoron urged the chief to remove from this location, which he had but newly adopted, and to take up his abode, with his band, near the French fort on the Maumee. The chief accepted the Frenchman's gifts, thanked him for his good advice, and promised to follow it at a more convenient time; but neither promises nor threats could induce him to stir at once.

No sooner, indeed, had the French departed, than the chief gathered the greater part of the members of the confederation on that spot; until, in less than two years after the visit of Celoron, its population had increased eightfold, and it became one of the greatest Indian towns of the west, and the centre of English trade and influence.

Celoron reached Miami, and then returned northward to Lake Erie, and thence back to Montreal, when he reported to the governor that English influence was supreme in the valley of the Ohio.

In the following year, a company was formed in Virginia for effecting a settlement in Ohio, and a party proceeded west to the village of the chief called Old Britain, by whom they were received with great friendship, and a treaty of peace was solemnly made between the English and the Indians. While the festivities, consequent on the affair, were going on, four Ottawa Indians arrived from the French, with the French flag and gifts, but they were dismissed with an answer of defiance. If, at this time, the colonists could have cemented their alliance with the Indians, with gifts similar to those with which the French endeavoured to purchase their friendship, a permanent peace with the Indians might have been established; but the mutual jealousies of the colonies, and the nature of the various colonial assemblies, rendered any common action impossible. Pennsylvania was jealous of the westward advance of Virginia, and desired to thwart rather than to assist her.

The governors of New York, Pennsylvania, and Virginia were fully conscious of the importance of the Indian alliance, but they could do nothing without their assemblies. Those of New York and Pennsylvania were largely composed of tradesmen and farmers, absorbed in local interests, and animated but by two motives; the cutting down of all expenditure, and bitter and continuous opposition to the governor, who represented the royal authority. Virginia and Pennsylvania quarrelled about their respective rights over the valley of the Ohio. The assembly of New York refused to join in any common action, saying, "We will take care of our Indians, and they may take care of theirs."

The states further removed from the fear of any danger, from the action of the Indians and French, were altogether lukewarm.

Thus, neither in the valley of the Ohio, nor on the boundaries of the New England states, did the Indians receive their promised gifts, and, as the French agents were liberal both in presents and promises, the Indians became discontented with their new friends, and again turned their eyes towards France. Old Britain, however, remained firm in his alliance; and the English traders, by constant presents, and by selling their goods at the lowest possible rates, kept him and his warriors highly satisfied and contented.

The French, in vain, tried to stir up the friendly tribes to attack Oswego on Lake Ontario, and the village of Old Britain, which were the two centres to which the Indians went to trade with the English; but they were unsuccessful until, in June, 1752, Charles Langlade, a young French trader, married to a squaw at Green Bay, and strong in influence with the tribes of that region, came down the lakes with a fleet of canoes, manned by two hundred and fifty Ottawa and Ojibwa warriors. They stopped awhile at the fort at Detroit, then paddled up the Maumee to the next fort, and thence marched through the forests against the Miamis.

They approached Old Britain's village in the morning. Most of the Indians were away on their summer hunt, and there were but eight English traders in the place. Three of these were caught outside the village, the remaining five took refuge in the fortified warehouse they had built, and there defended themselves.

Old Britain and the little band with him fought bravely, but against such overwhelming numbers could do nothing, and fourteen of them, including their chief, were killed. The five white men defended themselves till the afternoon, when two of them managed to make their escape, and the other three surrendered. One of them was already wounded, and was at once killed by the French Indians. Seventy years of the teaching of the French missionaries had not weaned the latter from cannibalism, and Old Britain was boiled and eaten.

The Marquis of Duquesne, who had succeeded Galissoniere as governor, highly praised Langlade for the enterprise, and recommended him to the minister at home for reward. This bold enterprise further shook the alliance of the Indians with the English, for it seemed to them that the French were enterprising and energetic, while the English were slothful and cowardly, and neglected to keep their agreements. The French continued to build forts, and Dinwiddie, governor of Virginia, sent George Washington to protest, in his name, against their building forts on land notoriously belonging to the English crown.

Washington performed the long and toilsome journey through the forests at no slight risks, and delivered his message at the forts, but nothing came of it. The governor of Virginia, seeing the approaching danger, made the greatest efforts to induce the other colonies to join in common action; but North Carolina, alone, answered the appeal, and gave money enough to raise three or four hundred men. Two independent companies maintained by England in New York, and one in South Carolina, received orders to march to Virginia. The governor had raised, with great difficulty, three hundred men. They were called the Virginia Regiment. An English gentleman named Joshua Fry was appointed the colonel, and Washington their major.

Fry was at Alexandria, on the Potomac, with half the regiment. Washington, with the other half, had pushed forward to the storehouse at Wills Creek, which was to form the base of operations. Besides these, Captain Trent, with a band of backwoodsmen, had crossed the mountain to build a fort at the forks of the Ohio, where Pittsburgh now stands.

Trent had gone back to Wills Creek, leaving Ensign Ward, with forty men, at work upon the fort, when, on the 17th of April, a swarm of canoes came down the Allegheny, with over five hundred Frenchmen, who planted cannon against the unfinished stockade, and summoned the ensign to surrender. He had no recourse but to submit, and was allowed to depart, with his men, across the mountains.

The French at once set to, to build a strong fort, which they named Fort Duquesne. While the governor of Virginia had been toiling, in vain, to get the colonists to move, the French had acted promptly, and the erection of their new fort at once covered their line of communication to the west, barred the advance of the English down the Ohio valley, and secured the allegiance of all the wavering Indian tribes.

Although war had not yet been declared between England and France, the colonists, after this seizure, by French soldiers, of a fort over which the English flag was flying, henceforth acted as if the two powers were at war. Washington moved forward from Wills Creek with his hundred and fifty men, and surprised a French force which had gone out scouting. Several of the French were killed, and the commander of Fort Duquesne sent despatches to France to say that he had sent this party out with a communication to Washington, and that they had been treacherously assassinated.

This obscure skirmish was the commencement of a war which set two continents on fire. Colonel Fry died a few days after this fight, and Washington succeeded to the command of the regiment, and collected his three hundred men at Green Meadow, where he was joined by a few Indians, and by a company from South Carolina.

The French at Duquesne were quickly reinforced, and the command was given to Coulon de Villiers, the brother of an officer who had been killed in the skirmish with Washington. He at once advanced against the English, who had fallen back to a rough breastwork which they called Fort Necessity, Washington having but four hundred men, against five hundred French and as many Indians.

For nine hours the French kept up a hot fire on the intrenchment, but without success, and at nightfall Villiers proposed a parley. The French ammunition was running short, the men were fatigued by their marches, and drenched by the rain which had been falling the whole day. The English were in a still worse plight. Their powder was nearly spent, their guns were foul, and among them they had but two cleaning rods.

After a parley, it was agreed that the English should march off with drums beating and the honours of war, carrying with them all their property; that the prisoners taken in the previous affair should be set free, two officers remaining with the French as hostages until they were handed over.

Washington and his men arrived, utterly worn out with fatigue and famine, at Wills Creek. This action left the French masters of the whole country beyond the Alleghenies.

The two mother nations were now preparing for war, and, in the middle of January, 1755, Major General Braddock, with the 44th and 48th Regiments, each five hundred strong, sailed from Cork for Virginia; while the French sent eighteen ships of war and six battalions to Canada.

Admiral Boscawen, with eleven ships of the line and one frigate, set out to intercept the French expedition. The greater part of the fleet evaded him, but he came up with three of the French men of war, opened fire upon them, and captured them. Up to this time a pretence of negotiations had been maintained between England and France, but the capture of the French ships brought the negotiations to a sudden end, and the war began.

A worse selection than that of Major General Braddock could hardly have been made. He was a brave officer and a good soldier, but he was rough, coarse, and obstinate. He utterly despised the colonial troops, and regarded all methods of fighting, save those pursued by regular armies in the field, with absolute contempt. To send such a man to command troops destined to fight in thick forests, against an enemy skilled in warfare of that kind, was to court defeat.

As might be expected, Braddock was very soon on the worst possible terms with the whole of the colonial authorities, and the delays caused by the indecision or obstinacy of the colonial assemblies chafed him to madness. At last, however, his force was assembled at Wills Creek. The two English regiments had been raised, by enlistment in Virginia, to 700 men each. There were nine Virginian companies of fifty men, and the thirty sailors lent by Commodore Keppel. General Braddock had three aides-de-camp–Captain Robert Orme, Captain Roger Morris, and Colonel George Washington.

It was the 1st of June, when James Walsham rode with Colonel Washington into the camp, and, three days later, the last companies of the Virginian corps marched in. During the next week, some of the English officers attempted to drill the Virginians in the manner of English troops.

"It is a waste of time," Colonel Washington said to James, one day, when he was watching them, "and worse. These men can fight their own way. Most of them are good shots, and have a fair idea of forest fighting; let them go their own way, and they can be trusted to hold their own against at least an equal number of French and Indians; but they would be hopelessly at sea if they were called upon to fight like English regulars. Most likely the enemy will attack us in the forest, and what good will forming in line, or wheeling on a flank, or any of the things which the general is trying to drum into their heads, do to them? If the French are foolish enough to wait at Fort Duquesne until we arrive, I have no doubt we shall beat them, but if they attack us in the woods it will go hard with us."

During the ten days which elapsed between his arrival and the start, James was kept hard at work, being for the most part employed galloping up and down the road, urging up the waggoners, and bringing back reports as to their position and progress. On the 10th of June the army started; 300 axemen led the way, cutting and clearing the road; the long train of pack horses, waggons, and cannon followed; the troops marched in the forest on either side, while men were thrown out on the flanks, and scouts ranged the woods to guard against surprise.

The road was cut but twelve feet wide, and the line of march often extended four miles. Thus, day by day they toiled on, crossing the Allegheny Mountains, range after range; now plunging down into a ravine, now ascending a ridge, but always in the deep shadow of the forest. A few of the enemy hovered round them, occasionally killing a straggler who fell behind.

On the 18th of June, the army reached a place called the Little Meadows. So weak were the horses, from want of forage, that the last marches had been but three miles a day, and, upon Washington's advice, Braddock determined to leave the heavy baggage here, with the sick men and a strong guard under Colonel Dunbar; while he advanced with 1200 men, besides officers and drivers.

But the progress was still no more than three miles a day, and it was not until the 7th of July that they arrived within eight miles of the French fort. Between them lay, however, an extremely difficult country with a narrow defile, and Braddock determined to ford the Monongahela, and then cross it again lower down.

The garrison of Fort Duquesne consisted of a few companies of regular troops, some hundreds of Canadians, and 800 Indian warriors. They were kept informed, by the scouts, of the progress of the English, and, when the latter approached the Monongahela, a party under Captain Beaujeu set out to meet them. His force consisted of 637 Indians, 100 French officers and soldiers, and 146 Canadians, in all about 900 men.

At one o'clock in the day, Braddock crossed the Monongahela for the second time. The troops had, all the day, been expecting the attack and had prepared for it. At the second ford the army marched in martial order, with music playing and flags flying. Once across the river they halted for a short time, and then again continued their advance.

Braddock made every disposition for preventing a surprise. Several guides, with six Virginian light horsemen, led the way. Then came the advanced column, consisting of 300 soldiers under Gage, and a large body of axemen, under Sir John Sinclair, with two cannon. The main body followed close behind. The artillery and waggons moved along the road, the troops marched through the woods on either hand, numerous flanking parties were thrown out a hundred yards or more right and left, and, in the space between them and the line of troops, the pack horses and cattle made their way, as they best could, among the trees.

Beaujeu had intended to place his men in ambuscade at the ford, but, owing to various delays caused by the Indians, he was still a mile away from the ford when the British crossed. He was marching forward when he came suddenly upon the little party of guides and Virginian light horsemen. These at once fell back. The Indians raised their war whoop, and, spreading right and left among the trees, opened a sharp fire upon the British.

Gage's column wheeled deliberately into line, and fired volley after volley, with great steadiness, at the invisible opponents. The greater part of the Canadians bolted at once, but the Indians kept up their fire from behind the shelter of the trees. Gage brought up his two cannon and opened fire, and the Indians, who had a horror of artillery, began also to fall back.

The English advanced in regular lines, cheering loudly. Beaujeu fell dead; but Captain Dumas, who succeeded him in command, advanced at the head of his small party of French soldiers, and opened a heavy fire.

The Indians, encouraged by the example, rallied and again came forward, and, while the French regulars and the few Canadians who had not fled held the ground in front of the column, the Indians swarmed through the forests along both flanks of the English, and from behind trees, bushes, and rocks opened a withering fire upon them. The troops, bewildered and amazed by the fire poured into them by an invisible foe, and by the wild war whoops of the Indians, ceased to advance, and, standing close together, poured fruitlessly volley after volley into the surrounding forest.

On hearing the firing, Braddock, leaving 400 men in the rear under Sir Peter Halket, to guard the baggage, advanced with the main body to support Gage; but, just as he came up, the soldiers, appalled by the fire which was mowing them down in scores, abandoned their cannon and fell back in confusion. This threw the advancing force into disorder, and the two regiments became mixed together, massed in several dense bodies within a small space of ground, facing some one way and some another, all alike exposed, without shelter, to the hail of bullets.

Men and officers were alike new to warfare like this. They had been taught to fight in line against solid masses of the enemy, and against an invisible foe like the present they were helpless. The Virginians alone were equal to the emergency. They at once adopted their familiar forest tactics, and, taking their post behind trees, began to fight the Indians in their own way.

Had Braddock been a man of judgment and temper, the fortunes of the day might yet have been retrieved, for the Virginians could have checked the Indians until the English troops were rallied and prepared to meet the difficulty; but, to Braddock, the idea of men fighting behind trees was at once cowardly and opposed to all military discipline, and he dashed forward on his horse, and with fierce oaths ordered the Virginians to form line. A body of them, however, under Captain Waggoner, made a dash for a huge fallen tree, far out towards the lurking places of the Indians, and, crouching behind it, opened fire upon them; but the regulars, seeing the smoke among the bushes, took them for the enemy and, firing, killed many and forced the rest to return.

A few of the soldiers tried to imitate the Indians, and fight behind the trees, but Braddock beat them back with the flat of his sword, and forced them to stand with the others, who were now huddled in a mass, forming a target for the enemy's bullets. Lieutenant Colonel Burton led 100 of them towards a knoll from which the puffs came thickest, but he fell wounded, and his men, on whom the enemy instantly concentrated their fire, fell back. The soldiers, powerless against the unseen foe, for afterwards some of the officers and men who escaped declared that, throughout the whole fight, they had not seen a single Indian, discharged their guns aimlessly among the trees.

They were half stupefied now with the terror and confusion of the scene, the rain of bullets, the wild yells which burst ceaselessly from their 600 savage foemen; while the horses, wild with terror and wounds, added to the confusion by dashing madly hither and thither. Braddock behaved with furious intrepidity. He dashed hither and thither, shouting and storming at the men, and striving to get them in order, and to lead them to attack the enemy. Four horses were, one after the other, shot under him. His officers behaved with equal courage and self devotion, and in vain attempted to lead on the men, sometimes advancing in parties towards the Indians, in hopes that the soldiers would follow them. Sir Peter Halket was killed, Horne and Morris, the two aides-de-camp, Sinclair the quartermaster general, Gates, Gage, and Gladwin were wounded. Of 86 officers, 63 were killed or disabled, while of non-commissioned officers and privates only 459 came off unharmed.

James Walsham had been riding by the side of Washington when the fight began, and followed him closely as he galloped among the troops, trying to rally and lead them forward. Washington's horse was pierced by a ball and, staggering, fell. James leaped from his horse and gave it to the colonel, and then, seeing that there was nothing for him to do, withdrew a short distance from the crowd of soldiers, and crouched down between the trunks of two great trees growing close to each other; one of which protected him, for the most part, from the fire of the Indians, and the other from the not less dangerous fire of the English. Presently, seeing a soldier fall at a short distance from him, he ran out and picked up his musket and cartridge box, and began to fire at the bushes where the puffs of smoke showed that men were in hiding.

After three hours' passive endurance of this terrible fire, Braddock, seeing that all was lost, commanded a retreat, and he and such officers as were left strove to draw off the soldiers in some semblance of order; but at this moment a bullet struck him, and, passing through his arm, penetrated his lungs, and he fell from his horse. He demanded to be left where he lay, but Captain Stewart of the Virginians, and one of his men, bore him between them to the rear.

The soldiers had now spent all their ammunition, and, no longer kept in their places by their general, broke away in a wild panic. Washington's second horse had now been shot, and as, trying to check the men, he passed the trees where James had taken up his position, the latter joined him.

In vain Washington and his other officers tried to rally the men at the ford. They dashed across it, wild with fear, leaving their wounded comrades, cannon, baggage, and military chest a prey to the Indians.

Fortunately, only about fifty of the Indians followed as far as the ford, the rest being occupied in killing the wounded and scalping the dead. Dumas, who had now but twenty Frenchmen left, fell back to the fort, and the remnants of Braddock's force continued the flight unmolested.

Chapter 10: The Fight At Lake George.
Fortunate was it, for the remnant of Braddock's force, that the Indians were too much occupied in gathering the abundant harvest of scalps, too anxious to return to the fort

to exhibit these trophies of their bravery, to press on in pursuit; for, had they done so, few indeed of the panic-stricken fugitives would ever have lived to tell the tale. All night these continued their flight, expecting every moment to hear the dreaded war whoop burst out again in the woods round them.

Colonel Washington had been ordered, by the dying general, to press on on horseback to the camp of Dunbar, and to tell him to forward waggons, provisions, and ammunition; but the panic, which had seized the main force, had already been spread by flying teamsters to Dunbar's camp. Many soldiers and waggoners at once took flight, and the panic was heightened when the remnants of Braddock's force arrived. There was no reason to suppose that they were pursued, and even had they been so, their force was ample to repel any attack that could be made upon it; but probably their commander saw that, in their present state of utter demoralization, they could not be trusted to fight, and that the first Indian war whoop would start them again in flight. Still, it was clear that a retreat would leave the whole border open to the ravages of the Indians, and Colonel Dunbar was greatly blamed for the course he took.

A hundred waggons were burned, the cannon and shells burst, and the barrels of powder emptied into the stream, the stores of provisions scattered through the woods, and then the force began its retreat over the mountains to Fort Cumberland, sixty miles away. General Braddock died the day that the retreat began. His last words were:

"We shall know better how to deal with them next time."

The news of the disaster came like a thunderbolt upon the colonists. Success had been regarded as certain, and the news that some fourteen hundred English troops had been utterly routed, by a body of French and Indians of half their strength, seemed almost incredible. The only consolation was that the hundred and fifty Virginians, who had accompanied the regulars, had all, as was acknowledged by the English officers themselves, fought with the greatest bravery, and had kept their coolness and presence of mind till the last, and that on them no shadow of the discredit of the affair rested. Indeed, it was said that the greater part were killed not by the fire of the Indians, but by that of the troops, who, standing in masses, fired in all directions, regardless of what was in front of them.

But Colonel Dunbar, not satisfied with retreating to the safe shelter of Fort Cumberland, to the amazement of the colonists, insisted upon withdrawing with his own force to Philadelphia, leaving the whole of the frontier open to the assaults of the hostile Indians. After waiting a short time at Philadelphia, he marched slowly on to join a force operating against the French in the region of Lake George, more than two hundred miles to the north. He took with him only the regulars, the provincial regiments being under the control of the governors of their own states.

Washington therefore remained behind in Virginia with the regiment of that colony. The blanks made in Braddock's fight were filled up, and the force raised to a thousand strong. With these he was to protect a frontier of three hundred and fifty miles long, against an active and enterprising foe more numerous than himself, and who, acting on the other side of the mountain, and in the shade of the deep forests, could choose their own time of attack, and launch themselves suddenly upon any village throughout the whole length of the frontier.

Nor were the troops at his disposal the material which a commander would wish to have in his hand. Individually they were brave, but being recruited among the poor whites, the most turbulent and troublesome part of the population, they were wholly unamenable to discipline, and Washington had no means whatever for enforcing it. He applied to the House of Assembly to pass a law enabling him to punish disobedience, but for months they hesitated to pass any such ordinance, on the excuse that it would trench on the liberty of free white men.

The service, indeed, was most unpopular, and Washington, whose headquarters were at Winchester, could do nothing whatever to assist the settlements on the border. His officers were as unruly as the men, and he was further hampered by having to comply with the orders of Governor Dinwiddie, at Williamsburg, two hundred miles away.

"What do you mean to do?" he had asked James Walsham, the day that the beaten army arrived at Fort Cumberland.

"I do not know," James said. "I certainly will not continue with Dunbar, who seems to me to be acting like a coward; nor do I wish to go into action with regulars again; not, at least, until they have been taught that, if they are to fight Indians successfully in the forests, they must abandon all their traditions of drill, and must fight in Indian fashion. I should like to stay with you, if you will allow me."

"I should be very glad to have you with me," Washington said; "but I do not think that you will see much action here. It will be a war of forays. The Indians will pounce upon a village or solitary farm house, murder and scalp the inhabitants, burn the buildings to the ground, and in an hour be far away beyond reach of pursuit. All that I can do is to occupy the chief roads, by which they can advance into the heart of the colony, and the people of the settlements lying west of that must, perforce, abandon their homesteads, and fly east until we are strong enough to again take up the offensive.

"Were I in your place, I would at once take horse and ride north. You will then be in plenty of time, if inclined, to join in the expedition against the French on Fort George, or in that which is going to march on Niagara. I fancy the former will be ready first. You will find things better managed there than here. The colonists in that part have, for many years, been accustomed to Indian fighting, and they will not be hampered by having regular troops with them, whose officers' only idea of warfare is to keep their men standing in line as targets for the enemy.

"There are many bodies of experienced scouts, to which you can attach yourself, and you will see that white men can beat the Indians at their own game."

Although sorry to leave the young Virginian officer, James Walsham thought that he could not do better than follow his advice, and accordingly, the next day, having procured another horse, he set off to join the column destined to operate on the lakes.

The prevision of Washington was shortly realized, and a cloud of red warriors descended on the border settlements, carrying murder, rapine, and ruin before them. Scores of quiet settlements were destroyed, hundreds of men, women, and children massacred, and in a short time the whole of the outlying farms were deserted, and crowds of weeping fugitives flocked eastward behind the line held by Washington's regiment.

But bad as affairs were in Virginia, those in Pennsylvania were infinitely worse. They had, for many years, been on such friendly terms with the Indians, that many of the settlers had no arms, nor had they the protection in the way of troops which the government of Virginia put upon the frontier. The government of the colony was at Philadelphia, far to the east, and sheltered from danger, and the Quaker assembly there refused to vote money for a single soldier to protect the unhappy colonists on the frontier. They held it a sin to fight, and above all to fight with Indians, and as long as they themselves were free from the danger, they turned a deaf ear to the tales of massacre, and to the pitiful cries for aid which came from the frontier. But even greater than their objection to war, was their passion of resistance to the representative of royalty, the governor.

Petition after petition came from the border for arms and ammunition, and for a militia law to enable the people to organize and defend themselves; but the Quakers resisted, declaring that Braddock's defeat was a just judgment upon him and his soldiers for molesting the French in their settlement in Ohio. They passed, indeed, a bill for raising fifty thousand pounds for the king's use, but affixed to it a condition, to which they knew well the governor could not assent; viz, that the proprietary lands were to pay their share of the tax.

To this condition the governor was unable to assent, for, according to the constitution of the colony, to which he was bound, the lands of William Penn and his descendants were free of all taxation. For weeks the deadlock continued. Every day brought news of massacres of tens, fifties, and even hundreds of persons, but the assembly remained obstinate; until the mayor, aldermen, and principal citizens clamoured against them, and four thousand frontiersmen started on their march to Philadelphia, to compel them to take measures for defence.

Bodies of massacred men were brought from the frontier villages and paraded through the town, and so threatening became the aspect of the population, that the Assembly of Quakers were at last obliged to pass a militia law. It was, however, an absolutely useless one. It specially excepted the Quakers from service, and constrained nobody, but declared it lawful for such as chose to form themselves into companies, and to elect officers by ballot. The company officers might, if they saw fit, elect, also by ballot, colonels, lieutenant colonels, and majors. These last might then, in conjunction with the governor, frame articles of war, to which, however, no officer or man was to be subjected, unless, after three days' consideration, he subscribed them in presence of a justice of the peace, and declared his willingness to be bound by them.

This mockery of a bill, drawn by Benjamin Franklin while the savages were raging in the colony and the smoke of a hundred villages was ascending to the skies, was received with indignation by the people, and this rose to such a height that the Assembly must have yielded unconditionally, had not a circumstance occurred which gave them a decent prbook for retreat.

The governor informed them that he had just received a letter from the proprietors, as Penn's heirs were called, giving to the province five thousand pounds to aid in its defence, on condition that the money should be accepted as a free gift, and not as their proportion of any tax that was or might be laid by the Assembly.

Thereupon, the Assembly struck out the clause taxing the proprietory estates, and the governor signed the bill. A small force was then raised, which enabled the Indians to be to some extent kept in check; but there was no safety for the unhappy settlers in the west of Pennsylvania during the next three years, while the French from Montreal were hounding on their savage allies, by gifts and rewards, to deeds of massacre and bloodshed.

The northern colonies had shown a better spirit. Massachusetts, which had always been the foremost of the northern colonies in resisting French and Indian aggression, had at once taken the lead in preparation for war. No less than 4500 men, being one in eight of her adult males, volunteered to fight the French, and enlisted for the various expeditions, some in the pay of the province, some in that of the king. Shirley, the governor of Massachusetts, himself a colonist, was requested by his Assembly to nominate the commander. He did not choose an officer of that province, as this would have excited the jealousy of the others, but nominated William Johnson of New York–a choice which not only pleased that important province, but had great influence in securing the alliance of the Indians of the Five Nations, among whom Johnson, who had held the post of Indian commissioner, was extremely popular.

Connecticut voted 1200 men, New Hampshire 500, Rhode Island 400, and New York 800, all at their own charge. Johnson, before assuming the command, invited the warriors of the Five Nations to assemble in council. Eleven hundred Indian warriors answered the invitation, and after four days' speech making agreed to join. Only 300 of them, however, took the field, for so many of their friends and relatives were fighting for the French, that the rest, when they sobered down after the excitement of the council, returned to their homes.

The object of the expedition was the attack of Crown Point–an important military post on Lake Champlain–and the colonists assembled near Albany; but there were great delays. The five colonial assemblies controlled their own troops and supplies. Connecticut had refused to send her men until Shirley promised that her commanding officer should rank next to Johnson, and the whole movement was for some time at a deadlock, because the five governments could not agree about their contributions of artillery and stores.

The troops were a rough-looking body. Only one of the corps had a blue uniform, faced with red. The rest wore their ordinary farm clothing. All had brought their own guns, of every description and fashion. They had no bayonets, but carried hatchets in their belts as a sort of substitute.

In point of morals the army, composed almost entirely of farmers and farmers' sons, was exemplary. It is recorded that not a chicken was stolen. In the camps of the Puritan soldiers of New England, sermons were preached twice a week, and there were daily prayers and much singing of psalms; but these good people were much shocked by the profane language of the troops from New York and Rhode Island, and some prophesied that disaster would be sure to fall upon the army from this cause.

Months were consumed in various delays; and, on the 21st of August, just as they were moving forward, four Mohawks, whom Johnson had sent into Canada, returned with the news that the French were making great preparations, and that 8000 men were marching to defend Crown Point. The papers of General Braddock, which fell, with all the baggage of the army, into the hands of the French, had informed them of the object of the gathering at Albany, and now that they had no fear of any further attempt against their posts in Ohio, they were able to concentrate all their force for the defence of their posts on Lake Champlain.

On the receipt of this alarming news, a council of war was held at Albany, and messages were sent to the colonies asking for reinforcements. In the meantime, the army moved up the Hudson to the spot called the Great Carrying Place, where Colonel Lyman, who was second in command, had gone forward and erected a fort, which his men called after him, but was afterwards named Fort Edward.

James Walsham joined the army a few days before it moved forward. He was received with great heartiness by General Johnson, to whom he brought a letter of introduction from Colonel Washington, and who at once offered him a position as one of his aides-de-camp. This he found exceedingly pleasant, for Johnson was one of the most jovial and open hearted of commanders. His hospitality was profuse, and, his private means being large, he was able to keep a capital table, which, on the line of march, all officers who happened to pass by were invited to share. This was a contrast, indeed, to the discipline which had prevailed in Braddock's columns, and James felt as if he were starting upon a great picnic, rather than upon an arduous march against a superior force.

After some hesitation as to the course the army should take, it was resolved to march for Lake George. Gangs of axemen were sent to hew a way, and, on the 26th, 2000 men marched for the lake, while Colonel Blanchard, of New Hampshire, remained with 500 to finish and defend Fort Lyman. The march was made in a leisurely manner, and the force took two days to traverse the fourteen miles between Fort Lyman and the lake. They were now in a country hitherto untrodden by white men save by solitary hunters.

They reached the southern end of the beautiful lake, which hitherto had received no English name, and was now first called Lake George in honour of the king. The men set to work, and felled trees until they had cleared a sufficient extent of ground for their camp, by the edge of the water, and posted themselves with their back to the lake. In their front was a forest of pitch pine, on their right a marsh covered with thick brush wood, on their left a low hill. Things went on in the same leisurely way which had marked the progress of the expedition.

No attempt was made to clear away the forest in front, although it would afford excellent cover for any enemy who might attack them, nor were any efforts made to discover the whereabouts or intention of the enemy. Every day waggons came up with provisions and boats.

On September 7th, an Indian scout arrived about sunset, and reported that he had found the trail of a body of men moving from South Bay, the southern extremity of Lake Champlain, towards Fort Lyman. Johnson called for a volunteer to carry a letter of warning to Colonel Blanchard. A waggoner named Adams offered to undertake the perilous service, and rode off with the letter. Sentries were posted, and the camp fell asleep.

While Johnson had been taking his leisure on Lake George, the commander of the French force, a German baron named Dieskau, was preparing a surprise for him.

He had reached Crown Point at the head of 3573 men–regulars, Canadians, and Indians–and he at once moved forward, with the greater portion of his command, on Cariolon, or, as it was afterwards called, Ticonderoga, a promontory at the junction of Lake George with Lake Champlain, where he would bar the advance of the English, whichever road they might take.

The Indians with the French caused great trouble to their commander, doing nothing but feast and sleep, but, on September 4th, a party of them came in bringing a scalp and an English prisoner, caught near Fort Lyman.

He was questioned, under the threat of being given over to the Indians to torture, if he did not tell the truth, but the brave fellow, thinking he should lead the enemy into a trap, told them that the English army had fallen back to Albany, leaving 500 men at Fort Lyman, which he represented as being entirely indefensible.

Dieskau at once determined to attack that place, and, with 216 regulars of the battalions of Languedoc and La Reine, 684 Canadians, and about 600 Indians, started in canoes and advanced up Lake Champlain, till they came to the end of South Bay. Each officer and man carried provisions for eight days in his knapsack.

Two days' march brought them to within three miles of Fort Lyman, and they encamped close to the road which led to Lake George. Just after they had encamped, a man rode by on horseback. It was Adams, Johnson's messenger. He was shot by the Indians, and the letter found upon him. Soon afterwards, ten or twelve waggons appeared, in charge of ammunition drivers who had left the English camp without orders.

Some of the drivers were shot, two taken prisoners, and the rest ran away. The two prisoners declared that, contrary to the assertion of the prisoner at Ticonderoga, a large force lay encamped by the lake. The Indians held a council, and presently informed Dieskau that they would not attack the fort, which they believed to be provided with cannon, but would join in an attempt on the camp by the lake. Dieskau judged, from the report of the prisoners, that the colonists considerably outnumbered him, although in fact there was no great difference in numerical strength, the French column numbering 1500 and the colonial force 2200, besides 300 Mohawk Indians. But Dieskau, emulous of repeating the defeat of Braddock, and believing the assertions of the Canadians that the colonial militia was contemptible, determined to attack, and early in the morning the column moved along the road towards the lake.

When within four miles of Johnson's camp, they entered a rugged valley. On their right was a gorge, hidden in bushes, beyond which rose the rocky height of French Mountain. On their left rose gradually the slopes of West Mountain. The ground was thickly covered with thicket and forest. The regulars marched along the road, the Canadians and Indians pushed their way through the woods as best they could. When within three miles of the lake, their scout brought in a prisoner, who told them that an English column was approaching. The regulars were halted on the road, the Canadians and Indians moved on ahead, and hid themselves in ambush among the trees and bushes on either side of the road.

The waggoners, who had escaped the evening before, had reached Johnson's camp about midnight, and reported that there was a war party on the road near Fort Lyman. A council of war was held, and under an entire misconception of the force of the enemy, and the belief that they would speedily fall back from Fort Lyman, it was determined to send out two detachments, each 500 strong, one towards Fort Lyman, the other to catch the enemy in their retreat. Hendrick, the chief of the Mohawks, expressed his strong disapproval of this plan, and accordingly it was resolved that the thousand men should go as one body. Hendrick still disapproved of the plan, but nevertheless resolved to accompany the column, and, mounting on a gun carriage, he harangued his warriors with passionate eloquence, and they at once prepared to accompany them. He was too old and fat to go on foot, and the general lent him a horse, which he mounted, and took his place at the head of the column.

Colonel Williams was in command, with Lieutenant Colonel Whiting as second. They had no idea of meeting the enemy near the camp, and moved forward so carelessly that not a single scout was thrown out in front or flank. The sharp eye of the old Indian chief was the first to detect a sign of the enemy, and, almost at the same moment, a gun was fired from the bushes. It is said that the Iroquois, seeing the Mohawks, who were an allied tribe, in the van, wished to warn them of danger. The warning came too late to save the column from disaster, but it saved it from destruction. From the thicket on the left a deadly fire blazed out, and the head of the column was almost swept away. Hendrick's horse was shot, and the chief killed with a bayonet as he tried to gain his feet.

Colonel Williams, seeing rising ground on his right, made for it, calling his men to follow; but, as he climbed the slope, the enemy's fire flashed out from behind every tree, and he fell dead. The men in the rear pressed forward to support their comrades, when the enemy in the bushes on the right flank also opened fire.

Then a panic began. Some fled at once for the camp, and the whole column recoiled in confusion, as from all sides the enemy burst out, shouting and yelling. Colonel Whiting, however, bravely rallied a portion of Williams' regiment, and, aided by some of the Mohawks, and by a detachment which Johnson sent out to his aid, covered the retreat, fighting behind the trees like the Indians, and falling back in good order with their faces to the enemy.

So stern and obstinate was their resistance that the French halted three-quarters of a mile from the camp. They had inflicted a heavy blow, but had altogether failed in obtaining the complete success they looked for. The obstinate defence of Whiting and his men had surprised and dispirited them, and Dieskau, when he collected his men, found the Indians sullen and unmanageable, and the Canadians unwilling to advance further, for they were greatly depressed by the loss of a veteran officer, Saint Pierre, who commanded them, and who had been killed in the fight. At length, however, he persuaded all to move forward, the regulars leading the way.

James Walsham had not accompanied the column, and was sitting at breakfast with General Johnson, on the stump of a tree in front of his tent, when, on the still air, a rattling sound broke out.

"Musketry!" was the general exclamation.

An instantaneous change came over the camp. The sound of laughing and talking was hushed, and every man stopped at his work. Louder and louder swelled the distant sound, until the shots could no longer be distinguished apart. The rattle had become a steady roll.

"It is a regular engagement!" the general exclaimed. "The enemy must be in force, and must have attacked Williams' column."

General Johnson ordered one of his orderlies to mount and ride out at full speed and see what was going on. A quarter of an hour passed. No one returned to his work. The men stood in groups, talking in low voices, and listening to the distant roar.

"It is clearer than it was," the general exclaimed.

Several of the officers standing round agreed that the sound was approaching.

"To work, lads!" the general said. "There is no time to be lost. Let all the axemen fell trees and lay them end to end to make a breastwork. The rest of you range the waggons in a line behind, and lay the boats up in the intervals. Carry the line from the swamp, on the right there, to the slope of the hill."

In an instant, the camp was a scene of animation, and the forest resounded with the strokes of the axe, and the shouts of the men as they dragged the waggons to their position.

"I was a fool," Johnson exclaimed, "not to fortify the camp before; but who could have supposed that the French would have come down from Crown Point to attack us here!"

In a few minutes terror-stricken men, whites and Indians, arrived at a run through the forest, and reported that they had been attacked and surprised by a great force in the forest, that Hendrick and Colonel Williams were killed, and numbers of the men shot down. They reported that all was lost; but the heavy roll of fire, in the distance, contradicted their words; and showed that a portion of the column, at least, was fighting sternly and steadily, though the sound indicated that they were falling back.

Two hundred men had already been despatched to their assistance, and the only effect of the news was to redouble the efforts of the rest. Soon parties arrived carrying wounded; but it was not until an hour and a half after the engagement began, that the main body of the column were seen marching, in good order, back through the forest.

By this time the hasty defences were well-nigh completed, and all the men were employed in cutting down the thick brushwood outside, so as to clear the ground as far as possible, and so prevent the enemy from stealing up, under shelter, to the felled trees.

Three cannon were planted, to sweep the road that descended through the pines. Another was dragged up to the ridge of the hill. Two hundred and fifty men were now placed on each flank of the camp, the main body stood behind the waggons or lay flat behind the logs and boats, the Massachusetts men on the right, the Connecticut men on the left.

"Now, my lads," Johnson shouted, in his cheery voice, "you have got to fight. Remember, if they get inside not one of you will ever go back to your families to tell the tale, while if you fight bravely you will beat them back sure enough."

In a few minutes, ranks of white-coated soldiers could be seen moving down the roads, with their bayonets showing between the boughs. At the same time, Indian war whoops rose loud in the forest, and then dark forms could be seen, bounding down the slope through the trees towards the camp in a throng.

There was a movement of uneasiness among the young rustics, few of whom ever heard a shot fired in anger before that morning; but the officers, standing pistol in hand, threatened to shoot any man who moved from his position.

Could Dieskau have launched his whole force at once upon the camp at that moment, he would probably have carried it, but this he was powerless to do. His regular troops were well in hand; but the mob of Canadians and Indians were scattered through the forest, shouting, yelling, and firing from behind trees.

He thought, however, that if he led the regulars to the attack, the others would come forward, and he therefore gave the word for the advance. The French soldiers advanced steadily, until the trees grew thinner. They were deployed into line, and opened fire in regular volleys. Scarcely had they done so, however, when Captain Eyre, who commanded the artillery, opened upon them with grape from his three guns, while from waggon, and boat, and fallen log, the musketry fire flashed out hot and bitter, and, reeling under the shower of iron and lead, the French line broke up, the soldiers took shelter behind trees, and thence returned the fire of the defenders.

Johnson received a flesh wound in the thigh, and retired to his tent, where he spent the rest of the day. Lyman took the command, and to him the credit of the victory is entirely due.

For four hours the combat raged. The young soldiers had soon got over their first uneasiness, and fought as steadily and coolly as veterans. The musketry fire was unbroken. From every tree, bush, and rock the rifles flashed out, and the leaden hail flew in a storm over the camp, and cut the leaves in a shower from the forest. Through this Lyman moved to and fro among the men, directing, encouraging, cheering them on, escaping as by a miracle the balls which whistled round him. Save the Indians on the English side, not a man but was engaged, the waggoners taking their guns and joining in the fight.

The Mohawks, however, held aloof, saying that they had come to see their English brothers fight, but, animated no doubt with the idea that, if they abstained from taking part in the fray, and the day went against the English, their friends the Iroquois would not harm them.

The French Indians worked round on to high ground, beyond the swamp on the left, and their fire thence took the defenders in the flank. Captain Eyre speedily turned his guns in that direction, and a few well-directed shells soon drove the Indians from their vantage ground. Dieskau directed his first attack against the left and centre; but the Connecticut men fought so stoutly, that he next tried to force the right, where the Massachusetts regiments of Titcomb, Ruggles, and Williams held the line. For an hour he strove hard to break his way through the intrenchments, but the Massachusetts men stood firm, although Titcomb was killed and their loss was heavy.

At length Dieskau, exposing himself within short range of the English lines, was hit in the leg. While his adjutant Montreuil was dressing the wound, the general was again hit in the knee and thigh. He had himself placed behind a tree, and ordered Montreuil to lead the regulars in a last effort against the camp.

But it was too late. The blood of the colonists was now up, and, singly or in small bodies, they were crossing their lines of barricade, and working up among the trees towards their assailants. The movement became general, and Lyman, seeing the spirit of his men, gave the word, and the whole of the troops, with a shout, leaped up and dashed through the wood against the enemy, falling upon them with their hatchets and the butts of their guns.

The French and their allies instantly fled. As the colonists passed the spot where Dieskau was sitting on the ground, one of them, singularly enough himself a Frenchman, who had ten years before left Canada, fired at him and shot him through both legs. Others came up and stripped him of his clothes, but, on learning who he was, they carried him to Johnson, who received him with the greatest kindness, and had every attention paid to him.

Chapter 11: Scouting.
It was near five o'clock before the final rout of the French took place; but, before that time, several hundreds of the Canadians and Indians had left the scene of action, and had returned to the scene of the fight in the wood, to plunder and scalp the dead. They were resting, after their bloody work, by a pool in the forest, when a scouting party from Fort Lyman, under Captains M'Ginnis and Folsom, came upon them and opened fire.

The Canadians and Indians, outnumbering their assailants greatly, fought for some time, but were finally defeated and fled. M'Ginnis was mortally wounded, but continued to give orders till the fight was over. The bodies of the slain were thrown into the pool, which to this day bears the name, "the bloody pool."

The various bands of French fugitives reunited in the forest, and made their way back to their canoes in South Bay, and reached Ticonderoga utterly exhausted and famished, for they had thrown away their knapsacks in their flight, and had nothing to eat from the morning of the fight until they rejoined their comrades.

Johnson had the greatest difficulty in protecting the wounded French general from the Mohawks, who, although they had done no fighting in defence of the camp, wanted to torture and burn Dieskau in revenge for the death of Hendrick and their warriors who had fallen in the ambush. He, however, succeeded in doing so, and sent him in a litter under a strong escort to Albany. Dieskau was afterwards taken to England, and remained for some years at Bath, after which he returned to Paris. He never, however, recovered from his numerous wounds, and died a few years later.

He always spoke in the highest terms of the kindness he had received from the colonial officers. Of the provincial soldiers he said that, in the morning they fought like boys, about noon like men, and in the afternoon like devils.

The English loss in killed, wounded, and missing was two hundred and sixty-two, for the most part killed in the ambush in the morning. The French, according to their own account, lost two hundred and twenty-eight, but it probably exceeded four hundred, the principal portion of whom were regulars, for the Indians and Canadians kept themselves so well under cover that they and the provincials, behind their logs, were able to inflict but little loss on each other.

Had Johnson followed up his success, he might have reached South Bay before the French, in which case the whole of Dieskau's column must have fallen into his hands; nor did he press forward against Ticonderoga, which he might easily have captured. For ten days nothing was done except to fortify the camp, and when, at the end of that time, he thought of advancing against Ticonderoga, the French had already fortified the place so strongly that they were able to defy attack. The colonists sent him large reinforcements, but the season was getting late, and, after keeping the army stationary until the end of November, the troops, having suffered terribly from the cold and exposure, became almost mutinous, and were finally marched back to Albany, a small detachment being left to hold the fort by the lake. This was now christened Fort William Henry.

The victory was due principally to the gallantry and coolness of Lyman; but Johnson, in his report of the battle, made no mention of that officer's name, and took all the credit to himself. He was rewarded by being made a baronet, and by being voted a pension, by parliament, of five thousand a year.

James Walsham, having no duties during the fight at the camp, had taken a musket and lain down behind the logs with the soldiers, and had, all the afternoon, kept up a fire at the trees and bushes behind which the enemy were hiding. After the battle, he had volunteered to assist the over-worked surgeons, whose labours lasted through the night. When he found that no forward movement was likely to take place, he determined to leave the camp. He therefore asked Captain Rogers, who was the leader of a band of scouts, and a man of extraordinary energy and enterprise, to allow him to accompany him on a scouting expedition towards Ticonderoga.

"I shall be glad to have you with me," Rogers replied; "but you know it is a service of danger. It is not like work with regular troops, where all march, fight, stand, or fall together. Here each man fights for himself. Mind, there is not a man among my band who would not risk his life for the rest; but, scattered through the woods as each man is, each must perforce rely principally on himself. The woods near Ticonderoga will be full of lurking redskins, and a man may be brained and scalped without his fellow, a few yards away, hearing a sound. I only say this that you may feel that you must take your chances. The men under me are, every one, old hunters and Indian fighters, and are a match for the redskin in every move of forest war. They are true grit to the backbone, but they are rough outspoken men, and, on a service when a foot carelessly placed on a dried twig, or a word spoken above a whisper, may bring a crowd of yelping redskins upon us, and cost every man his scalp, they would speak sharply to the king himself, if he were on the scout with them, and you must not take offence at any rough word that may be said."

James laughed, and said that he should not care how much he was blown up, and that he should thankfully receive any lessons from such masters of forest craft.

"Very well," Captain Rogers said. "In that case, it is settled. I will let you have a pair of moccasins. You cannot go walking about in the woods in those boots. You had better get a rifle. Your sword you had best leave behind. It will be of no use to you, and will only be in your way."

James had no difficulty in providing himself with a gun, for numbers of weapons, picked up in the woods after the rout of the enemy, were stored in camp. The rifles had, however, been all taken by the troops, who had exchanged their own firelocks for them. Captain Rogers went with him among the men, and selected a well-finished rifle of which one of them had possessed himself. Its owner readily agreed to accept five pounds for it, taking in its stead one of the guns in the store. Before choosing it,

Captain Rogers placed a bit of paper against a tree, and fired several shots at various distances at it.

"It is a beautiful rifle," he said. "Its only fault is that it is rather heavy, but it shoots all the better for it. It is evidently a French gun, I should say by a first-rate maker, built probably for some French officer who knew what he was about. It is a good workmanlike piece, and, when you learn to hold it straight, you can trust it to shoot."

That evening James, having made all his preparations, said goodbye to the general and to his other friends, and joined the scouts who were gathering by the shore of the lake. Ten canoes, each of which would carry three men, were lying by the shore.

"Nat, you and Jonathan will take this young fellow with you. He is a lad, and it is his first scout. You will find him of the right sort. He was with Braddock, and after that affair hurried up here to see fighting on the lakes. He can't have two better nurses than you are. He is going to be an officer in the king's army, and wants to learn as much as he can, so that, if he ever gets with his men into such a mess as Braddock tumbled into, he will know what to do with them."

"All right, captain! We will do our best for him. It's risky sort of business ours for a greenhorn, but if he is anyways teachable, we will soon make a man of him."

The speaker was a wiry, active man of some forty years old, with a weatherbeaten face, and a keen gray eye. Jonathan, his comrade, was a head taller, with broad shoulders, powerful limbs, and a quiet but good-tempered face.

"That's so, isn't it, Jonathan?" Nat asked.

Jonathan nodded. He was not a man of many words.

"Have you ever been in a canoe before?" Nat inquired.

"Never," James said; "but I am accustomed to boats of all sorts, and can handle an oar fairly."

"Oars ain't no good here," the scout said. "You will have to learn to paddle; but, first of all, you have got to learn to sit still. These here canoes are awkward things for a beginner. Now you hand in your traps, and I will stow them away, then you take your place in the middle of the boat. Here's a paddle for you, and when you begin to feel yourself comfortable, you can start to try with it, easy and gentle to begin with; but you must lay it in when we get near where we may expect that redskins may be in the woods, for the splash of a paddle might cost us all our scalps."

James took his seat in the middle of the boat. Jonathan was behind him. Nat handled the paddle in the bow. There was but a brief delay in starting, and the ten boats darted noiselessly out on to the lake. For a time, James did not attempt to use his paddle. The canoe was of birch bark, so thin that it seemed to him that an incautious movement would instantly knock a hole through her.

Once under weigh, she was steadier than he had expected, and James could feel her bound forward with each stroke of the paddles. When he became accustomed to the motion of the boat, he raised himself from a sitting position in the bottom, and, kneeling as the others were doing, he began to dip his paddle quietly in the water in time with their stroke. His familiarity with rowing rendered it easy for him to keep time and swing, and, ere long, he found himself putting a considerable amount of force into each stroke. Nat looked back over his shoulder.

"Well done, young 'un. That's first rate for a beginner, and it makes a deal of difference on our arms. The others are all paddling three, and, though Jonathan and I have beaten three before now, when our scalps depended on our doing so, it makes all the difference in the work whether you have a sitter to take along, or an extra paddle going."

It was falling dusk when the boat started, and was, by this time, quite dark. Scarce a word was heard in the ten canoes as, keeping near the right-hand shore of the lake, they glided rapidly along in a close body. So noiselessly were the paddles dipped into the water that the drip from them, as they were lifted, was the only sound heard.

Four hours' steady paddling took them to the narrows, about five-and-twenty miles from their starting point. Here, on the whispered order of Nat, James laid in his paddle; for, careful as he was, he occasionally made a slight splash as he put it in the water. The canoes now kept in single file, almost under the trees on the right bank, for the lake was here scarce a mile across, and watchful eyes might be on the lookout on the shore to the left. Another ten miles was passed, and then the canoes were steered in to the shore.

The guns, blankets, and bundles were lifted out; the canoes raised on the shoulders of the men, and carried a couple of hundred yards among the trees; then, with scarcely a word spoken, each man rolled himself in his blanket and lay down to sleep, four being sent out as scouts in various directions. Soon after daybreak, all were on foot again, although it had been arranged that no move should be made till night set in. No fires were lighted, for they had brought with them a supply of biscuit and dry deers' flesh sufficient for a week.

"How did you get on yesterday?" Captain Rogers asked, as he came up to the spot where James had just risen to his feet.

"First rate, captain!" Nat answered for him. "I hardly believed that a young fellow could have handled a paddle so well, at the first attempt. He rowed all the way, except just the narrows, and though I don't say as he was noiseless, he did wonderfully well, and we came along with the rest as easy as may be."

"I thought I heard a little splash, now and then," the captain said, smiling; "but it was very slight, and could do no harm where the lake is two or three miles wide, as it is here. But you will have to lay in your paddle when we get near the other end, for the sides narrow in there, and the redskins would hear a fish jump, half a mile away."

During the day the men passed their time in sleep, in mending their clothes, or in talking quietly together. The use of tea had not yet become general in America, and the meals were washed down with water drawn from the lake (where an over-hanging bush shaded the shore from the sight of anyone on the opposite bank), mixed with rum from the gourds which all the scouts carried.

Nat spent some time in pointing out, to James, the signs by which the hunters found their way through the forest; by the moss and lichens growing more thickly on the side of the trunks of the trees opposed to the course of the prevailing winds, or by a slight inclination of the upper boughs of the trees in the same direction.

"An old woodsman can tell," he said, "on the darkest night, on running his hand round the trunk of a tree, by the feel of the bark, which is north and south; but it would be long before you can get to such niceties as that; but, if you keep your eyes open as you go along, and look at the signs on the trunks, which are just as plain, when you once know them, as the marks on a man's face, you will be able to make your way through the woods in the daytime. Of course, when the sun is shining, you get its help, for, although it is not often a gleam comes down through the leaves, sometimes you come upon a little patch, and you are sure, now and then, to strike on a gap where a tree has fallen, and that gives you a line again. A great help to a young beginner is the sun, for a young hand in the woods gets confused, and doubts the signs of the trees; but, in course, when he comes on a patch of sunlight, he can't make a mistake nohow as to the direction."

James indulged in a silent hope that, if he were ever lost in the woods, the sun would be shining, for, look as earnestly as he would, he could not perceive the signs which appeared so plain and distinct to the scout. Occasionally, indeed, he fancied that there was some slight difference between one side of the trunk and the other; but he was by no means sure that, even in these cases, he should have noticed it unless it had been pointed out to him; while, in the greater part of the trees he could discern no difference whatever.

"It's just habit, my lad," Nat said encouragingly to him; "there's just as much difference between one side of the tree and the other, as there is between two men's faces. It comes of practice. Now, just look at the roots of this tree; don't you see, on one side they run pretty nigh straight out from the trunk, while from the other they go down deep into the ground. That speaks for itself. The tree has thrown out its roots, to claw into the ground and get a hold, on the side from which the wind comes; while, on the other side, having no such occasion, it has dipped its root down to look for moisture and food."

"Yes, I do see that," James said, "that is easy enough to make out; but the next tree, and the next, and, as far as I see, all the others, don't seem to have any difference in their roots one side or the other."

"That is so," the scout replied. "You see, those are younger trees than this, and it is like enough they did not grow under the same circumstances. When a few trees fall, or a small clearing is made by a gale, the young trees that grow up are well sheltered from the wind by the forest, and don't want to throw out roots to hold them up; but when a great clearing has been made, by a fire or other causes, the trees, as they grow up together, have no shelter, and must stretch out their roots to steady them.

"Sometimes, you will find all the trees, for a long distance, with their roots like this; sometimes only one tree among a number. Perhaps, when they started, that tree had more room, or a deeper soil, and grew faster than the rest, and got his head above them, so he felt the wind more, and had to throw out his roots to steady himself; while the others, all growing the same height, did not need to do so."

"Thank you," James said. "I understand now, and will bear it in mind. It is very interesting, and I should like, above all things, to be able to read the signs of the woods as you do."

"It will come, lad. It's a sort of second nature. These things are gifts. The redskin thinks it just as wonderful that the white man should be able to take up a piece of paper covered with black marks, and to read off sense out of them, as you do that he should be able to read every mark and sign of the wood. He can see, as plain as if the man was still standing on it, the mark of a footprint, and can tell you if it was made by a warrior or a squaw, and how long they have passed by, and whether they were walking fast or slow; while the ordinary white man might go down on his hands and knees, and stare at the ground, and wouldn't be able to see the slightest sign or mark. For a white man, my eyes are good, but they are not a patch on a redskin's. I have lived among the woods since I was a boy; but even now, a redskin lad can pick up a trail and follow it when, look as I will, I can't see as a blade of grass has been bruised. No; these things is partly natur and partly practice. Practice will do a lot for a white man; but it won't take him up to redskin natur."

Not until night had fallen did the party again launch their canoes on the lake. Then they paddled for several hours until, as James imagined, they had traversed a greater distance, by some miles, than that which they had made on the previous evening. He knew, from what he had learned during the day, that they were to land some six miles below the point where Lake George joins Lake Champlain, and where, on the opposite side, on a promontory stretching into the lake, the French were constructing their new fort.

The canoes were to be carried some seven or eight miles through the wood, across the neck of land between the two lakes, and were then to be launched again on Lake Champlain, so that, by following the east shore of that lake, they would pass Ticonderoga at a safe distance. The halt was made as noiselessly as before, and, having hauled up the canoes, the men slept till daybreak; and then, lifting the light craft on their shoulders, started for their journey through the woods. It was toilsome work, for the ground was rough and broken, often thickly covered with underwood. Ridges had to be crossed and deep ravines passed, and, although the canoes were not heavy, the greatest care had to be exercised, for a graze against a projecting bough, or the edge of a rock, would suffice to tear a hole in the thin bark.

It was not until late in the afternoon that they arrived on the shores of Lake Champlain. A fire was lighted now, the greatest care being taken to select perfectly dry sticks, for the Iroquois were likely to be scattered far and wide among the woods. The risk, however, was far less than when in sight of the French side of Lake George. After darkness fell, the canoes were again placed in the water, and, striking across the lake, they followed the right-hand shore. After paddling for about an hour and a half, the work suddenly ceased.

The lake seemed to widen on their left, for they had just passed the tongue of land between the two lakes, and on the opposite shore a number of fires were seen, burning brightly on the hillside. It was Ticonderoga they were now abreast of, the advanced post of the French. They lingered for some time before the paddles were again dipped in water, counting the fires and making a careful note of the position. They paddled on again until some twelve miles beyond the fort, and then crossed the lake and landed on the French shore.

But the canoes did not all approach the shore together, as they had done on the previous nights. They halted half a mile out, and Captain Rogers went forward with his own and another canoe and landed, and it was not for half an hour that the signal was given, by an imitation of the croaking of a frog, that a careful search had ascertained the forest to be untenanted, and the landing safe.

No sooner was the signal given than the canoes were set in motion, and were soon safely hauled up on shore. Five men went out, as usual, as scouts, and the rest, fatigued by their paddle and the hard day's work, were soon asleep.

In the morning they were about to start, and Rogers ordered the canoes to be hauled up and hidden among the bushes, where, having done their work, they would for the present be abandoned, to be recovered and made useful on some future occasion.

The men charged with the work gave a sudden exclamation when they reached the canoes.

"What is that?" Rogers said angrily. "Do you want to bring all the redskins in the forest upon us?"

"The canoes are all damaged," one of the scouts said, coming up to him.

There was a general movement to the canoes, which were lying on the bank a few yards' distance from the water's edge. Every one of them had been rendered useless. The thin birch bark had been gashed and slit, pieces had been cut out, and not one of them had escaped injury or was fit to take the water. Beyond a few low words, and exclamations of dismay, not a word was spoken as the band gathered round the canoes.

"Who were on the watch on this side?" Rogers asked.

"Nat and Jonathan took the first half of the night," one of the scouts said. "Williams and myself relieved them."

As all four were men of the greatest skill and experience, Rogers felt sure that no neglect or carelessness on their part could have led to the disaster.

"Did any of you see any passing boats, or hear any sound on the lake?"

The four men who had been on guard replied in the negative.

"I will swear no one landed near the canoes," Nat said. "There was a glimmer on the water all night; a canoe could not have possibly come near the bank, anywheres here, without our seeing it."

"Then he must have come from the land side," Rogers said. "Some skulking Indian must have seen us out on the lake, and have hidden up when we landed. He may have been in a tree overhead all the time, and, directly the canoes were hauled up, he may have damaged them and made off.

"There is no time to be lost, lads. It is five hours since we landed. If he started at once the redskins may be all round us now. It is no question now of our scouting round the French fort, it is one of saving our scalps."

"How could it have been done?" James Walsham asked Nat, in a low tone. "We were all sleeping within a few yards of the canoes, and some of the men were close to them. I should have thought we must have heard it."

"Heard it!" the hunter said contemptuously; "why, a redskin would make no more noise in cutting them holes and gashes, than you would in cutting a hunk of deer's flesh for your dinner. He would lie on the ground, and wriggle from one to another like an eel; but I reckon he didn't begin till the camp was still. The canoes wasn't hauled up till we had sarched the woods, as we thought, and then we was moving about close by them till we lay down.

"I was standing theer on the water's edge not six feet away from that canoe. I never moved for two hours, and, quiet as a redskin may be, he must have taken time to do that damage, so as I never heard a sound as loud as the falling of a leaf. No, I reckon as he was at the very least two hours over that job. He may have been gone four hours or a bit over, but not more; but that don't give us much of a start. It would take him an hour and a half to get to the fort, then he would have to report to the French chap in command, and then there might be some talk before he set out with the redskins, leaving the French to follow."

"It's no use thinking of mending the canoes, I suppose," James asked.

The hunter shook his head.

"It would take two or three hours to get fresh bark and mend those holes," he said, "and we haven't got as many minutes to spare. There, now, we are off."

While they had been speaking, Rogers had been holding a consultation with two or three of his most experienced followers, and they had arrived at pretty nearly the same conclusion as that of Rogers, namely, that the Indian had probably taken two or three hours in damaging the canoes and getting fairly away into the forest; but that, even if he had done so, the Iroquois would be up in the course of half an hour.

"Let each man pack his share of meat on his back," Rogers said. "Don't leave a scrap behind. Quick, lads, there's not a minute to be lost. It's a case of legs, now. There's no hiding the trail of thirty men from redskin eyes."

In a couple of minutes, all were ready for the start, and Rogers at once led the way, at a long slinging trot, straight back from the lake, first saying:

"Pick your way, lads, and don't tread on a fallen stick. There is just one chance of saving our scalps, and only one, and that depends upon silence."

As James ran along, at the heels of Nat, he was struck with the strangeness of the scene, and the noiselessness with which the band of moccasin-footed men flitted among the trees. Not a word was spoken. All had implicit confidence in their leader, the most experienced bush fighter on the frontier, and knew that, if anyone could lead them safe from the perils that surrounded them, it was Rogers.

James wondered what his plan could be. It seemed certain to him that the Indians must, sooner or later, overtake them. They would be aware of the strength of the band, and, confiding in their superior numbers, would be able to push forward in pursuit without pausing for many precautions. Once overtaken, the band must stand at bay, and, even could they hold the Indians in check, the sound of the firing would soon bring the French soldiers to the spot.

They had been gone some twenty minutes only, when a distant war whoop rose in the forest behind them.

"They have come down on the camp," Nat said, glancing round over his shoulder, "and find we have left it. I expect they hung about a little before they ventured in, knowing as we should be expecting them, when we found the canoes was useless. That war whoop tells 'em all as we have gone. They will gather there, and then be after us like a pack of hounds."

"Ah! That is what I thought the captain was up to."

Rogers had turned sharp to the left, the direction in which Ticonderoga stood. He slacked down his speed somewhat, for the perspiration was streaming down the faces even of his trained and hardy followers. From time to time, he looked round to see that all were keeping well together. Although, in such an emergency as this, none thought of questioning the judgment of their leader, many of them were wondering at the unusual speed at which he was leading them along. They had some two miles start of their pursuers, and, had evening been at hand, they would have understood the importance of keeping ahead until darkness came on to cover their trail; but, with the whole day before them, they felt that they must be overtaken sooner or later, and they could not see the object of exhausting their strength before the struggle began.

As they ran on, at a somewhat slower pace now, an idea as to their leader's intention dawned upon most of the scouts, who saw, by the direction they were taking, that they would again strike the lake shore near the French fort. Nat, who, light and wiry, was running easily, while many of his comrades were panting with their exertions, was now by the side of James Walsham.

"Give me your rifle, lad, for a bit. You are new to this work, and the weight of the gun takes it out of you. We have got another nine or ten miles before us, yet."

"I can hold on for a bit," James replied. "I am getting my wind better, now; but why only ten miles? We must be seventy away from the fort."

"We should never get there," Nat said. "A few of us might do it, but the redskins would be on us in an hour or two. I thought, when we started, as the captain would have told us to scatter, so as to give each of us some chance of getting off; but I see his plan now, and it's the only one as there is which gives us a real chance. He is making straight for the French fort. He reckons, no doubt, as the best part of the French troops will have marched out after the redskins."

"But there would surely be enough left," James said, "to hold the fort against us; and, even if we could take it, we could not hold it an hour when they all came up."

"He ain't thinking of the fort, boy, he's thinking of the boats. We know as they have lots of 'em there, and, if we can get there a few minutes before the redskins overtake us, we may get off safe. It's a chance, but I think it's a good one."

Others had caught their leader's idea and repeated it to their comrades, and the animating effect soon showed itself in the increased speed with which the party hurried through the forest. Before, almost every man had thought their case hopeless, had deemed that they had only to continue their flight until overtaken by the redskins, and that they must, sooner or later, succumb to the rifles of the Iroquois and their French allies. But the prospect that, after an hour's run, a means of escape might be found, animated each man to renewed efforts.

After running for some distance longer, Rogers suddenly halted and held up his hand, and the band simultaneously came to a halt. At first, nothing could be heard save their own quick breathing; then a confused noise was heard to their left front, a deep trampling and the sound of voices, and an occasional clash of arms.

"It is the French column coming out," Nat whispered, as Rogers, swerving somewhat to the right, and making a sign that all should run as silently as possible, continued his course.

Chapter 12: A Commission.

Presently the noise made by the column of French troops was heard abreast of the fugitives. Then it died away behind them, and they again directed their course to the left. Ten minutes later, they heard a loud succession of Indian whoops, and knew that the redskins pursuing them had also heard the French column on its march, and would be warning them of the course which the band were taking. The scouts were now but four miles from Ticonderoga, and each man knew that it was a mere question of speed.

"Throw away your meat," Rogers ordered, "you will not want it now, and every pound tells."

The men had already got rid of their blankets, and were now burdened only with their rifles and ammunition. The ground was rough and broken, for they were nearing the steep promontory on which the French fort had been erected. They were still a mile ahead of their pursuers, and although the latter had gained that distance upon them since the first start, the scouts knew that, now they were exerting themselves to the utmost, the redskins could be gaining but little upon them, for the trained white man is, in point of speed and endurance, fairly a match for the average Indian.

They had now descended to within a short distance of the edge of the lake, in order to avoid the valleys and ravines running down from the hills. The war whoops rose frequently in the forest behind them, the Indians yelling to give those at the fort notice that the chase was approaching.

"If there war any redskins left at the fort," Nat said to James, "they would guess what our game was; but I expect every redskin started out on the hunt, and the French soldiers, when they hear the yelling, won't know what to make of it, and, if they do anything, they will shut themselves up in their fort."

Great as were the exertions which the scouts were making, they could tell, by the sound of the war whoops, that some at least of the Indians were gaining upon them. Accustomed as every man of the party was to the fatigues of the forest, the strain was telling upon them all now. For twelve miles they had run almost at the top of their speed, and the short panting breath, the set faces, and the reeling steps showed that they were nearly at the end of their powers. Still they held on, with scarcely any diminishing of speed. Each man knew that if he fell, he must die, for his comrades could do nothing for him, and no pause was possible until the boats were gained.

They were passing now under the French works, for they could hear shouting on the high ground to the right, and knew that the troops left in the fort had taken the alarm; but they were still invisible, for it was only at the point of the promontory that the clearing had been carried down to the water's edge. A low cry of relief burst from the men, as they saw the forest open before them, and a minute later they were running along in the open, near the shore of the lake, at the extremity of the promontory, where, hauled up upon the shore, lay a number of canoes and flat-bottomed boats, used for the conveyance of troops. A number of boatmen were standing near, evidently alarmed by the war cries in the woods. When they saw the party approaching they at once made for the fort, a quarter of a mile away on the high ground, and, almost at the same moment, a dropping fire of musketry opened from the entrenchments.

"Smash the canoes," Rogers said, setting the example by administering a vigorous kick to one of them.

The others followed his example, and, in a few seconds, every one of the frail barks was stove in.

"Two of the boats will hold us well," Rogers said; "quick, into the water with them, and out with the oars. Ten row in each boat. Let the other five handle their rifles, and keep back the Indians as they come up. Never mind the soldiers."

For the white-coated troops, perceiving the scouts' intention, were now pouring out from the intrenchments.

A couple of minutes sufficed for the men to launch the boats and take their seats, and the oars dipped in the water just as three or four Indians dashed out from the edge of the forest.

"We have won the race by three minutes," Rogers said, exultantly. "Stretch to your oars, lads, and get out of range as soon as you can."

The Indians began to fire as soon as they perceived the boats. They were scarcely two hundred yards away, but they, like the white men, were panting with fatigue, and their bullets flew harmlessly by.

"Don't answer yet," Rogers ordered, as some of the scouts were preparing to fire. "Wait till your hands get steady, and then fire at the French. There won't be many of the redskins up, yet."

The boats were not two hundred yards from shore when the French soldiers reached the edge of the water and opened fire, but at this distance their weapons were of little avail, and, though the bullets splashed thickly around the boats, no one was injured, while several of the French were seen to drop from the fire of the scouts. Another hundred yards, and the boats were beyond any danger, save from a chance shot. The Indians still continued firing, and several of their shots struck the boats, one of the rowers being hit on the shoulder.

"Lay in your rifles, and man the other two oars in each boat," Rogers said. "The French are launching some of their bateaux, but we have got a fair start, and they won't overtake us before we reach the opposite point. They are fresher than we are, but soldiers are no good rowing; besides, they are sure to crowd the boats so that they won't have a chance."

Five or six boats, each crowded with men, started in pursuit, but they were fully half a mile behind when the two English boats reached the shore.

"Now it is our turn," Rogers said, as the men, leaping ashore, took their places behind trees. As soon as the French boats came within range, a steady fire was opened upon them. Confusion was at once apparent among them. Oars were seen to drop, and as the fire continued, the rowing ceased. Another minute and the boats were turned, and were soon rowing out again into the lake.

"There's the end of that," Rogers said, "and a close shave it has been."

"Well, youngster, what do you think of your first scout in the woods?"

"It has been sharper than I bargained for," James said, laughing, "and was pretty near being the last, as well as the first. If it hadn't been for your taking us to the boats, I don't think many of us would have got back to Fort Henry to tell the tale."

"There is generally some way out of a mess," Rogers said, "if one does but think of it. If I had not thought of the French boats, we should have scattered, and a few of us would have been overtaken, no doubt; but even an Indian cannot follow a single trail as fast as a man can run, and I reckon most of us would have carried our scalps back to camp. Still, with the woods full of Iroquois they must have had some of us, and I hate losing a man if it can be helped. We are well out of it.

"Now, lads, we had better be tramping. There are a lot more bateaux coming out, and I expect, by the rowing, they are manned by Indians. The redskin is a first-rate hand with the paddle, but is no good with an oar."

The man who had been hit in the shoulder had already had his wound bandaged. There was a minute's consultation as to whether they should continue their journey in the boats, some of the men pointing out that they had proved themselves faster than their pursuers.

"That may be," Rogers says; "but the Indians will land and follow along the shore, and will soon get ahead of us, for they can travel quicker than we can row, and, for aught we know, there may be a whole fleet of canoes higher up Lake George which would cut us off. No, lads, the safest way is to keep on through the woods."

The decision was received without question, and the party at once started at a swinging trot, which was kept up, with occasional intervals of walking, throughout the day. At nightfall their course was changed, and, after journeying another two or three miles, a halt was called, for Rogers was sure that the Indians would abandon pursuit, when night came on without their having overtaken the fugitives.

Before daybreak the march was continued, and, in the afternoon, the party arrived at Fort William Henry.

James now determined to leave the force, and return at once to New York, where his letters were to be addressed to him. He took with him a letter from General Johnson, speaking in the warmest tones of his conduct.

On arriving at New York he found, at the post office there, a great pile of letters awaiting him. They had been written after the receipt of his letter at the end of July, telling those at home of his share in Braddock's disaster.

"I little thought, my boy," his mother wrote, "when we received your letter, saying that you had got your discharge from the ship, and were going with an expedition against the French, that you were going to run into such terrible danger. Fortunately, the same vessel which brought the news of General Braddock's defeat also brought your letter, and we learned the news only a few hours before your letter reached us. It was, as you may imagine, a time of terrible anxiety to us, and the squire and Aggie were almost as anxious as I was. Mr. Wilks did his best to cheer us all, but I could see that he, too, felt it very greatly. However, when your letter came we were all made happy again, though, of course, we cannot be but anxious, as you say you are just going to join another expedition; still, we must hope that that will do better, as it won't be managed by regular soldiers. Mr. Wilks was quite angry at what you said about the folly of making men stand in a line to be shot at, he thinks so much of drill and discipline. The squire and he have been arguing quite fiercely about it; but the squire gets the best of the argument, for the dreadful way in which the soldiers were slaughtered shows that, though that sort of fighting may be good in other places, it is not suited for fighting these wicked Indians in the woods.

"The squire has himself been up to London about your commission, and has arranged it all. He has, as he will tell you in his letter, got you a commission in the regiment commanded by Colonel Otway, which is to go out next spring. He was introduced to the commander in chief by his friend, and told him that you had been acting as Colonel Washington's aide-de-camp with General Braddock, and that you have now gone to join General Johnson's army; so the duke said that, though you would be gazetted at once, and would belong to the regiment, you might as well stay out there and see service until it arrived; and that it would be a great advantage to the regiment to have an officer, with experience in Indian fighting, with it. I cried when he brought me back the news, for I had hoped to have you back again with us for a bit, before you went soldiering for good. However, the squire seems to think it is a capital thing for you. Mr. Wilks thinks so, too, so I suppose I must put up with it; but Aggie agrees with me, and says it is too bad that she should never have seen you, once, from the time when she saw you in that storm.

"She is a dear little girl, and is growing fast. I think she must have grown quite an inch in the five months you have been away. She sends her love to you, and says you must take care of yourself, for her sake."

The squire, in his letter, repeated the news Mrs. Walsham had given.

"You are now an ensign," he said, "and, if you go into any more fights before your regiment arrives, you must, Mr. Wilks said, get a proper uniform made for you, and fight as a king's officer. I send you a copy of the gazette, where you will see your name."

Mr. Wilks's letter was a long one.

"I felt horribly guilty, dear Jim," he said, "when the news came of Braddock's dreadful defeat. I could hardly look your dear mother in the face, and, though the kind lady would not, I know, say a word to hurt my feelings for the world, yet I could see that she regarded me as a monster, for it was on my advice that, instead of coming home when you got your discharge, you remained out there and took part in this unfortunate expedition. I could see Aggie felt the same, and, though I did my best to keep up their spirits, I had a terrible time of it until your letter arrived, saying you were safe. If it had not come, I do believe that I should have gone quietly off to Exeter, hunted up my box again, and hired a boy to push it for me, for I am not so strong as I was. But I would rather have tramped about, for the rest of my life, than remain there under your mother's reproachful eye. However, thank God you came through it all right, and, after such a lesson, I should hope that we shall never have repetition of such a disaster as that. As an old soldier, I cannot agree with what you say about the uselessness of drill, even for fighting in a forest. It must accustom men to listen to the voice of their officers, and to obey orders promptly and quickly, and I cannot but think that, if the troops had gone forward at a brisk double, they would have driven the Indians before them. As to the whooping and yells you talk so much about, I should think nothing of them; they are no more to be regarded than the shrieks of women, or the braying of donkeys."

James smiled as he read this, and thought that, if the old soldier had heard that chaos of blood-curdling cries break out, in the still depth of the forest, he would not write of them with such equanimity.

"You will have heard, from the squire, that you are gazetted to Otway's regiment which, with others, is to cross the Atlantic in a few weeks, when it is generally supposed war will be formally declared. Your experience will be of great use to you, and ought to get you a good staff appointment. I expect that, in the course of a year, there will be fighting on a large scale on your side of the water, and the English ought to get the best of it, for France seems, at present, to be thinking a great deal more of her affairs in Europe than of her colonies in America. So much the better, for, if we can take Canada, we shall strike a heavy blow to her trade, and some day North America is going to be an important place in the world."

The letters had been lying there several weeks, and James knew that Otway's regiment had, with the others, arrived a few days before, and had already marched for Albany. Thinking himself entitled to a little rest, after his labours, he remained for another week in New York, while his uniform was being made, and then took a passage in a trading boat up to Albany.

Scarcely had he landed, when a young officer in the same uniform met him. He looked surprised, hesitated, and then stopped.

"I see you belong to our regiment," he said. "Have you just arrived from England? What ship did you come in?"

"I have been out here some time," James replied. "My name is Walsham. I believe I was gazetted to your regiment some months ago, but I only heard the news on my arrival at New York last week."

"Oh, you are Walsham!" the young officer said. "My name is Edwards. I am glad to meet you. We have been wondering when you would join us, and envying your luck, in seeing so much of the fighting out here. Our regiment is encamped about half a mile from here. If you will let me, I will go back with you, and introduce you to our fellows."

James thanked him, and the two walked along talking together. James learned that there were already five ensigns junior to himself, his new acquaintance being one of them, as the regiment had been somewhat short of officers, and the vacancies had been filled up shortly before it sailed.

"Of course, we must call on the colonel first," Mr. Edwards said. "He is a capital fellow, and very much liked in the regiment."

Colonel Otway received James with great cordiality.

"We are very glad to get you with us, Mr. Walsham," he said, "and we consider it a credit to the regiment to have a young officer who has been, three times, mentioned in despatches. You will, too, be a great service to us, and will be able to give us a good many hints as to this Indian method of fighting, which Braddock's men found so terrible."

"It is not formidable, sir, when you are accustomed to it; but, unfortunately, General Braddock forced his men to fight in regular fashion, that is, to stand up and be shot at, and that mode of fighting, in the woods, is fatal. A hundred redskins would be more than a match, in the forest, for ten times their number of white troops, who persisted in fighting in such a ridiculous way; but, fighting in their own way, white men are a match for the redskins. Indeed, the frontiersmen can thrash the Indians, even if they are two or three to one against them."

"You have been in this last affair on the lake, have you not, Mr. Walsham? I heard you were with Johnson."

"Yes, sir, I was, and at the beginning it was very nearly a repetition of Braddock's disaster; but, after being surprised and, at first, beaten, the column that went out made such a stout fight of it, that it gave us time to put the camp in a state of defence. Had the Indians made a rush, I think they would have carried it; but, as they contented themselves with keeping up a distant fire, the provincials, who were all young troops, quite unaccustomed to fighting, and wholly without drill or discipline, gradually got steady, and at length sallied out and beat them decisively."

"I will not detain you, now," the colonel said; "but I hope, ere long, you will give us a full and detailed account of the fighting you have been in, with your idea of the best way of training regular troops for the sort of work we have before us. Mr. Edwards will take you over to the mess, and introduce you to your brother officers."

James was well received by the officers of his regiment, and soon found himself perfectly at home with them. He had to devote some hours, every day, to acquiring the mysteries of drill. It was, to him, somewhat funny to see the pains expended in assuring that each movement should be performed with mechanical accuracy; but he understood that, although useless for such warfare as that which they had before them, great accuracy in details was necessary, for ensuring uniformity of movement among large masses of men in an open country.

Otherwise, the time passed very pleasantly. James soon became a favourite in the regiment, and the young officers were never tired of questioning him concerning the redskins, and their manner of fighting. There were plenty of amusements. The snow was deep on the ground, now, and the officers skated, practised with snowshoes, and drove in sleighs. Occasionally they got up a dance, and the people of Albany, and the settlers round, vied with each other in their hospitality to the officers.

One day, in February, an orderly brought a message to James Walsham, that the colonel wished to speak to him.

"Walsham," he said, "I may tell you, privately, that the regiment is likely to form part of the expedition which is being fitted out, in England, against Louisbourg in Cape Breton, the key of Canada. A considerable number of the troops from the province will accompany it."

"But that will leave the frontier here altogether open to the enemy," James said in surprise.

"That is my own opinion, Walsham. Louisbourg is altogether outside the range of the present struggle, and it seems to me that the British force should be employed at striking at a vital point. However, that is not to the purpose. It is the Earl of Loudon's plan. However, it is manifest, as you say, that the frontier will be left terribly open, and therefore two companies of each of the regiments going will be left. Naturally, as you are the only officer in the regiment who has had any experience in this forest warfare, you would be one of those left here; but as an ensign you would not have much influence, and I think that it would be at once more useful to the service, and more pleasant for yourself, if I can obtain for you something like a roving commission. What do you think of that?"

"I should greatly prefer that, sir," James said gratefully.

"The general is a little vexed, I know," the colonel went on, "at the numerous successes, and daring feats, gained by Rogers and the other leaders of the companies of scouts, while the regulars have not had an opportunity to fire a shot: and I think that he would, at once, accept the proposal were I to make it to him, that a company, to be called the Royal Scouts, should be formed of volunteers taken from the various regiments, and that you should have the command."

"Thank you, sir," James said, "and I should like it above all things; but I fear that we should have no chance, whatever, of rivalling the work of Rogers and the other partisan leaders. These men are all trained to the work of the woods, accustomed to fight Indians, equally at home in a canoe or in the forest. I have had, as you are good enough to say, some experience in the work, but I am a mere child by their side, and were I to lead fifty English soldiers in the forest, I fear that none of us would ever return."

"Yes, but I should not propose that you should engage in enterprises of that sort, Walsham. My idea is that, although you would have an independent command, with very considerable freedom of action, you would act in connection with the regular troops. The scouts are often far away when wanted, leaving the posts open to surprise. They are so impatient of any discipline, that they are adverse to going near the forts, except to obtain fresh supplies. You, on the contrary, would act as the eyes of any post which you might think threatened by the enemy. At present, for instance, Fort William Henry is the most exposed to attack.

"You would take your command there, and would report yourself to Major Eyre, who is in command. As for service there, your letter of appointment would state that you are authorized to act independently, but that, while it would be your duty to obey the orders of the commanding officer, you will be authorized to offer such suggestions to him as your experience in Indian warfare would lead you to make. You would train your men as scouts. It would be their special duty to guard the fort against surprise, and, of course, in case of attack to take part in its defence. In the event of the provincial scouts making any concerted movement against a French post, you would be authorized to join them. You would then have the benefit of their skill and experience, and, in case of success, the army would get a share of the credit. What do you think of my plan?"

"I should like it above all things," James replied. "That would be precisely the duty which I should select had I the choice."

"I thought so," the colonel said. "I have formed a very high opinion of your judgment and discretion, from the talks which we have had together, and I have spoken strongly in your favour to the general, who had promised me that, in the event of the army moving forward, you should have an appointment on the quartermaster general's staff, as an intelligence officer.

"Since I heard that the main portion of the army is to sail to Louisbourg, I have been thinking this plan over, and it certainly seems to me that a corps, such as that that I have suggested, would be of great service. I should think that its strength should be fifty men. You will, of course, have another officer with you. Is there anyone you would like to choose, as I may as well take the whole scheme, cut and dried, to the general?"

"I should like Mr. Edwards, sir. He is junior to me in the regiment, and is very active and zealous in the service; and I should greatly like to be allowed to enlist, temporarily, two of the scouts I have served with in the force, with power for them to take their discharge when they wished. They would be of immense utility to me in instructing the men in their new duties, and would add greatly to our efficiency."

"So be it," the colonel said. "I will draw out the scheme on paper, and lay it before the general today."

In the afternoon, James was again sent for.

"The earl has approved of my scheme. You will have temporary rank as captain given you, in order to place your corps on an equal footing with the provincial corps of scouts. Mr. Edwards will also have temporary rank, as lieutenant. The men of the six companies, of the three regiments, will be paraded tomorrow, and asked for volunteers for the special service. If there are more than fifty offer, you can select your own men."

Accordingly, the next morning, the troops to be left behind were paraded, and an order was read out, saying that a corps of scouts for special service was to be raised, and that volunteers were requested. Upwards of a hundred men stepped forward, and, being formed in line, James selected from them fifty who appeared to him the most hardy, active, and intelligent looking. He himself had, that morning, been put in orders as captain of the new corps, and had assumed the insignia of his temporary rank. The colonel had placed at his disposal two intelligent young non-commissioned officers.

The next morning, he marched with his command for Fort William Henry. No sooner had he left the open country, and entered the woods, than he began to instruct the men in their new duties. The whole of them were thrown out as skirmishers, and taught to advance in Indian fashion, each man sheltering himself behind a tree, scanning the woods carefully ahead, and then, fixing his eyes on another tree ahead, to advance to it at a sharp run, and shelter there.

All this was new to the soldiers, hitherto drilled only in solid formation, or in skirmishing in the open, and when, at the end of ten miles skirmishing through the wood, they were halted and ordered to bivouac for the night, James felt that his men were beginning to have some idea of forest fighting. The men themselves were greatly pleased with their day's work. It was a welcome change after the long monotony of life in a standing camp, and the day's work had given them a high opinion of the fitness of their young officer for command.

But the work and instruction was not over for the day. Hitherto, none of the men had had any experience in camping in the open. James now showed them how to make comfortable shelters against the cold, with two forked sticks and one laid across them, and with a few boughs and a blanket laid over them, with dead leaves heaped round the bottom and ends; and how best to arrange their fires and cook their food.

During the following days, the same work was repeated, and when, after a week's marching, the force issued from the forest into the clearing around Fort William Henry, James felt confident that his men would be able to hold their own in a brush with the Indians. Major Eyre, to whom James reported himself, and showed his appointment defining his authority and duties, expressed much satisfaction at the arrival of the reinforcement.

"There are rumours, brought here by the scouts," he said, "that a strong force will, ere long, come down from Crown Point to Ticonderoga, and that we shall be attacked.

Now that the lake is frozen, regular troops could march without difficulty, and my force here is very inadequate, considering the strength with which the French will attack. None of my officers or men have any experience of the Indian methods of attack, and your experience will be very valuable. It is a pity that they do not give me one of these companies of scouts permanently. Sometimes one or other of them is here, but often I am without any of the provincials, and, although I have every confidence in my officers and men, one cannot but feel that it is a great disadvantage to be exposed to the attack of an enemy of whose tactics one is altogether ignorant.

"You will, of course, encamp your men inside the fort. I see you have brought no baggage with you, but I have some spare tents here, which are at your service."

"Thank you, sir," James replied; "I shall be glad to put the men under cover, while they are here, but I intend to practise them, as much as possible, in scouting and camping in the woods, and, although I shall always be in the neighbourhood of the fort, I do not propose always to return here at night. Are any of Captain Rogers's corps at present at the fort?"

"Some of them came in last night," Major Eyre replied.

"I have authority," James said, "to enlist two of them in my corps."

Major Eyre smiled.

"I do not think you will find any of them ready to submit to military discipline, or to put on a red coat."

"They are all accustomed to obey orders, promptly enough, when at work," James said, "though there is no attempt at discipline when off duty. You see them at their worst here. There is, of course, nothing like military order in the woods, but obedience is just as prompt as among our troops. As to the uniform, I agree with you, but on that head I should not be particular. I can hardly fancy any of the scouts buttoned tightly up with stiff collars; but as, after all, although they are to be enlisted, they will be attached to the corps, rather than be regular members of it, I do not think I need insist upon the uniform."

After leaving the major, James saw to the pitching of the tents, and the comforts of his men, and when he had done so strolled off towards a group of scouts, who were watching his proceedings, and among whom he recognized the two men for whom he was looking.

He received a cordial greeting from all who had taken part in his previous adventures with Captain Rogers's band.

"And so you are in command of this party?" Nat said. "I asked one of the men just now, and he said you were the captain. You are young to be a captain, but, at any rate, it's a good thing to have a king's officer here who knows something about the woods. The rest ain't no more idea of them than nothing."

"I want to chat to you, Nat, and also to Jonathan, if you will come across with me to my tent."

"I'm agreeable," Nat said; and the two scouts walked across to the tent with James.

Lieutenant Edwards, who shared the tent with him, was inside, arranging a few things which Major Eyre had sent down for their use.

"Edwards, these are the two scouts, Nat and Jonathan, of whom you have often heard me speak. Now, let us sit down and have a chat.

"There is some first-rate rum in that bottle, Nat. There are two tin pannikins, and there is water in that keg.

"Now, Nat," he went on, when the party were seated on blankets laid on the ground, "this corps of mine has been raised, specially, to act as scouts round this or any other fort which may be threatened, or to act as the advanced guard of a column of troops."

"But what do they know of scouting?" Nat said contemptuously. "They don't know no more than children."

"They don't know much, but they are active fellows, and ready to learn. I think you will find that, already, they have a pretty fair idea of fighting in Indian fashion in the woods, and, as I have authority to draw extra supplies of ball cartridge, I hope, in a few weeks, to make fair shots of them. You have taught me something of forest ways, and I shall teach them all I know; but we want better teachers, and I want to propose, to you and Jonathan, to join the corps."

"What, and put on a red coat, and choke ourselves up with a stiff collar!" Nat laughed. "Nice figures we should look! No, no, captain, that would never do."

"No, I don't propose that you should wear uniform, Nat. I have got a special authority to enlist you and Jonathan, with the understanding that you can take your discharge whenever you like. There will be no drilling in line, or anything of that sort. It will be just scouting work, the same as with Captain Rogers, except that we shall not make long expeditions, as he does, but keep in the neighbourhood of the fort. I should want you to act both as scouts and instructors, to teach the men, as you have taught me, something of woodcraft, how to find their way in a forest, and how to fight the Indians in their own way, and to be up to Indian devices. You will be guides on the line of march, will warn me of danger, and suggest the best plan of meeting it. You will, in fact, be scouts attached to the corps, only nominally you will be members of it. I know your ways, and should not exact any observance of discipline, more than that which you have with Rogers, and should treat you in the light of non-commissioned officers."

"Well, and what do you say, Jonathan?" Nat said, turning to his tall companion. "You and I have both taken a fancy to the captain here, and though he has picked up a lot for a young 'un, and will in time make a first-rate hand in the woods, I guess he won't make much hand of it, yet, if he hadn't got someone as knows the woods by his side. We have had a spell of hard work of it with Rogers lately, and I don't mind if I have a change, for a bit, with the redcoats."

"I will go, of course," Jonathan said briefly.

"Very well, then, that's settled, captain," Nat said. "Rogers will be in tonight, and I will tell him we are going to transfer ourselves over to you."

"He won't mind, I hope," James said.

"He won't mind," Nat replied. "We ain't very particular about times of service in our corps. We just comes and goes, pretty well as the fancy takes us. They would never get us to join, if they wanted to get us to bind down hard and fast. Sometimes they start on an expedition fifty strong, next time perhaps not more than thirty turns up.

"Is there anything to do to join the corps?"

"Not much, Nat. I give you each a shilling and attest you, that is to say, swear you in to serve the king, and, in your case, give you a paper saying that you are authorized to take your discharge, whensoever it pleases you."

"Very well, captain. Then on those terms we join, always understood as we don't have to put on red coats."

The two men were sworn in, and then Nat, standing up, said:

"And now, captain, discipline is discipline. What's your orders?"

James went to the door of the tent, and called the sergeant.

"Sergeant, these two men are enlisted as scouts in the corps. They will draw rations, and be a regular part of the company like the rest, but they will not wear uniform, acting only as scouts. They will have the rank and position of corporals, and will specially instruct the men in woodcraft, and in the ways of the Indians. They will, of course, occupy the tent with the non-commissioned officers, and will mess with them. Being engaged as scouts, only, they will in other respects be free from anything like strictness. I trust that you will do what you can to make them comfortable."

The sergeant saluted, and led the two scouts over to the tent occupied by himself and the other non-commissioned officers, and the roars of laughter that issued from it in the course of the evening, at the anecdotes of the scouts, showed that the newcomers were likely to be highly popular characters in their mess.

Chapter 13: An Abortive Attack.

Three weeks passed. James kept his men steadily at work, and even the scouts allowed that they made great progress. Sometimes they went out in two parties, with an officer and a scout to each, and their pouches filled with blank cartridge. Each would do its best to surprise the other; and, when they met, a mimic fight would take place, the men sheltering behind trees, and firing only when they obtained a glimpse of an adversary.

"I did not think that these pipe-clayed soldiers could have been so spry," Nat said to James. "They have picked up wonderfully, and I wouldn't mind going into an Indian fight with them. They are improving with their muskets. Their shooting yesterday wasn't bad, by no means. In three months' time, they will be as good a lot to handle as any of the companies of scouts."

Besides the daily exercises, the company did scouting work at night, ten men being out, by turns, in the woods bordering the lake. At one o'clock in the morning, on the 19th of March, Nat came into the officers' tent.

"Captain," he said, "get up. There's something afoot."

"What is it, Nat?" James asked, as he threw off his rugs.

"It's the French, at least I don't see who else it can be. It was my turn tonight to go round and look after our sentries. When I came to Jim Bryan, who was stationed just at the edge of the lake, I said to him, 'Anything new, Jim?' and he says, 'Yes; seems to me as I can hear a hammering in the woods.' I listens, and sure enough axes were going. It may be some three miles down. The night is still, and the ice brought the sound.

"'That's one for you, Jim,' says I. 'Them's axes sure enough.' I stands and looks, and then a long way down the lake on the left I sees a faint glare. They had had the sense to light the fires where we couldn't see them; but there were the lights, sure enough. It's the French, captain, the redskins would never have made fires like that, and if it had been a party of our scouts, they would have come on here, and not halted an hour's tramp away.

"You had best get the troops under arms, captain. Who would have thought they would have been such fools as to light their fires within sight of the fort!"

James at once went to Major Eyre's quarters, and aroused him, and in a few minutes the garrison were all under arms. Their strength, including James Walsham's corps, and some scouts of the company of John Stark, numbered three hundred and forty-six men, besides which there were a hundred and twenty-eight invalids in hospital.

Two hours passed, and then a confused sound, as of a great body of men moving on the ice, was heard. The ice was bare of snow, and nothing could be seen, but the cannon on the side facing the lake at once opened fire, with grape and round shot, in the direction of the sound.

After firing for a few minutes, they were silent. The sound on the ice could no longer be heard.

"They have taken to the woods," Nat, who had taken up his station next to James Walsham, said. "It ain't likely they would stop on the ice with the balls pounding it up."

"Do you think they will attack before morning?" James asked.

"It ain't likely," Nat replied. "They won't know the positions, and, such a dark night as this, they wouldn't be able to make out anything about them. If they could have come straight along the ice to the head of the lake here, they would have made a dash, no doubt; but now they find we ain't to be caught asleep, I expect they will wait till morning."

Again the sound of axes was heard in the wood, and the glare of light appeared above the trees.

"There must be a tidy lot of 'em," Nat said.

"Do you think it will be any use to go out and try to surprise them?"

"Not a bit, captain. They are sure to have a lot of redskins with them, and they will be lurking in the woods, in hopes that we may try such a move. No; we have got a strong position here, and can lick them three to one; but in the woods, except Stark's men, and perhaps yours, none of the others wouldn't be no good at all."

Mayor Eyre, shortly afterwards, sent for James, who gave him the opinion of the scout, and the major then ordered the troops to get under shelter again, leaving Stark's men to act as sentries, for the night was bitterly cold.

It was not until ten o'clock next day that the French appeared, and, surrounding the fort on all sides, except on that of the lake, opened heavy musketry fire upon it. They were a formidable body. Vaudreuil, the governor of Canada, had spared no pains to make the blow a successful one. The force had been assembled at Crown Point, and numbered sixteen hundred regulars, Canadians, and Indians. Everything needful for their comfort had been provided–overcoats, blankets, bear skins to sleep on, and tarpaulins to cover them. They had been provided with twelve days' provisions, which were placed on hand sledges and drawn by the troops.

They marched, over the ice of Lake Champlain, down to Ticonderoga, where they rested a week, and constructed three hundred scaling ladders. Three days' further march, up Lake George, brought them to the English fort.

The weak point of the expedition was its leader, for Vaudreuil, who was himself a Canadian, had the greatest jealousy of the French officers, and had intrusted the command of the expedition to his brother, Rigaud.

The fire did no damage, as the garrison lay sheltered behind their entrenchments, replying occasionally whenever the enemy mustered in force, as if with an intention of attacking.

"I don't think they mean business, this time, captain," Nat said in a tone of disgust. "Why, there are enough of them to eat us, if they could but make up their minds to come on. They don't suppose they are going to take William Henry by blazing a way at it half a mile off!"

"Perhaps they are going to make a night attack," James said. "They will have learned all about the position of our works."

"Maybe so," Nat replied; "but I don't think so. When chaps don't attack at once, when there are four or five to one, I reckon that they ain't likely to attack at all. They meant to surprise us, and they haven't, and it seems to me as it has taken all the heart out of them."

As evening approached, the fire ceased. At nightfall, strong guards were placed round the entrenchments, and the troops retired to their quarters, ready to turn out at a minute's notice.

About midnight they were called out. There was again a sound on the lake. The cannon at once opened, and, as before, all was silent again.

"Look, Walsham, look!" Edwards exclaimed. "They have set fire to the sloops."

As he spoke, a tongue of flame started up from one of the two vessels lying in the ice, close to the shore, and, almost simultaneously, flames shot up from among the boats drawn up on the beach.

"That's redskin work," Nat exclaimed.

"Come, lads," James cried, leaping down from the low earthwork into the ditch. "Let us save the boats, if we can."

The scouts followed him and ran down to the shore; but the Indians had done their work well. The two sloops, and many of the boats, were well alight, and it was evident at once that, long before a hole could be broken through the ice, and buckets brought down from the fort, they would be beyond all hopes of saving them.

The French, too, opened fire from the woods bordering the lake, and, as the light of the flames exposed his men to the enemy's marksmen, James at once called them back to the fort, and the sloops and boats burned themselves out.

At noon, next day, the French filed out from the woods on to the ice, at a distance of over a mile.

"What now?" Edwards exclaimed. "They surely don't mean to be fools enough to march across the ice to attack us in broad daylight."

"It looks to me," James replied, "as if they wanted to make a full show of their force. See, there is a white flag, and a party are coming forward."

An officer and several men advanced towards the fort, and Major Eyre sent out one of his officers, with an equal number of men, to meet them. There was a short parley when the parties came together, and then the French officer advanced towards the fort with the English, his followers remaining on the ice.

On nearing the fort, the French officer, Le Mercier, chief of the Canadian artillery, was blindfolded, and led to the room where Major Eyre, with all the British officers, was awaiting him. The handkerchief was then removed from his eyes, and he announced to the commandant that he was the bearer of a message from the officer commanding the French force, who, being desirous of avoiding an effusion of blood, begged the English commander to abstain from resistance, which, against a force so superior to his own, could but be useless. He offered the most favourable terms, if he would surrender the place peaceably, but said that if he were driven to make an assault, his Indian allies would unquestionably massacre the whole garrison.

Major Eyre quietly replied that he intended to defend himself to the utmost.

The envoy was again blindfolded. When he rejoined the French force, the latter at once advanced as if to attack the place, but soon halted, and, leaving the ice, opened a fusillade from the border of the woods, which they kept up for some hours, the garrison contemptuously abstaining from any reply.

At night, the French were heard advancing again, the sound coming from all sides. The garrison stood to their arms, believing that this time the real attack was about to be made.

Nearer and nearer came the sound, and the garrison, who could see nothing in the pitchy darkness, fired wherever they could hear a sound. Presently a bright light burst up. The redskins, provided with faggots of resinous sticks, had crept up towards some buildings, consisting of several store houses, a hospital, and saw mill, and the huts and tents of the rangers, and, having placed their torches against them, set them on fire and instantly retreated. The garrison could do nothing to save the buildings, as their efforts, in the absence of water, must be unavailing, and they would have been shot down by the foe lying beyond the circle of light. They therefore remained lying behind the entrenchment, firing wherever they heard the slightest sound, and momentarily expecting an attack; but morning came without the French advancing, and the garrison were then able to give their whole attention to saving the buildings in the fort.

Some great wood stacks had now ignited, and the burning embers fell thickly on the huts, and for some hours it was only by the greatest exertions that the troops were able to save the buildings from destruction. Every moment they expected to be attacked, for, had the French advanced, the huts must have been left to themselves, in which case the garrison would have found themselves shelterless, and all their provisions and stores would have been consumed; but before noon the danger was over, for not only had the fires begun to burn low, but a heavy snow storm set in. All day it continued.

"Now would be the time for them to attack," James Walsham said to his lieutenant. "We can scarce see twenty yards away."

"Now is their chance," Edwards agreed; "but I don't believe in their attacking. I can't think who they have got in command. He ought to be shot, a man with such a force as he has, hanging about here for four days when he could have carried the place, with a rush, any moment."

"No, I don't think they will attack," James replied. "Men who will stop to light a fire to warm themselves, within sight of an enemy's fort they want to surprise, are not likely to venture out of shelter of their blankets in such a snow as this."

All day and all night the snow came down, till the ground was covered to a depth of over three feet. Early on Tuesday morning, twenty volunteers of the French regulars made a bold attempt to burn a sloop building on the stocks, with several storehouses and other structures near the water, and some hundreds of boats and canoes which were ranged near them. They succeeded in firing the sloop, and some buildings, but James, with his scouts, sallied out and forced them to retreat, with the loss of five of their number; and, by pulling down some of the huts, prevented the fire spreading.

Next morning the sun rose brightly, and the white sheet of the lake was dotted with the French, in full retreat for Canada. Their total loss had been eleven killed and wounded, while, on the English side, seven men had been wounded, all slightly. Never was a worse conducted or more futile expedition.

After this affair, the time passed slowly at Fort William Henry. Until the sun gained strength enough to melt the thick white covering of the earth, James practised his men in the use of snowshoes, and, as soon as spring had fairly commenced, resumed the work of scouting. This was done only as an exercise, for there was no fear that, after such a humiliating failure, the French would, for some time to come, attempt another expedition against the fort.

In the autumn of 1756, General Montcalm had come out from France to take the command of the French troops. Few of the superior officers of the French army cared to take the command, in a country where the work was hard and rough, and little glory was to be obtained. Therefore the minister of war was able, for once, to choose an officer fitted for the post, instead of being obliged, as usual, to fill up the appointment by a court favourite.

The Marquis of Montcalm was born at the chateau of Candiac, near Nimes, on the 29th of February, 1712. At the age of fifteen, up to which time he had studied hard, he entered the army. Two years later he became a captain, and was first under fire at the siege of Philipsbourg. In 1736 he married Mademoiselle Du Boulay, who brought him influential connections and some property. In 1741 Montcalm took part in the campaign in Bohemia. Two years later he was made colonel, and passed unharmed through the severe campaign of 1744.

In the following year he fought in the campaign in Italy, and, in 1746, was wounded at the disastrous action at Piacenza, where he twice rallied his regiment, received five sabre cuts, and was made prisoner. He was soon liberated on parole, and was promoted, in the following year, to the rank of brigadier general, and, being exchanged for an officer of similar rank, rejoined the army, and was again wounded by a musket shot. Shortly afterwards the peace of Aix la Chapelle was signed, and Montcalm remained living quietly with his family, to whom he was tenderly attached, until informed, by the minister of war, that he had selected him to command the troops in North America, with the rank of major general. The Chevalier de Levis was appointed second in command.

No sooner did Montcalm arrive in America, than difficulties arose between him and the Marquis de Vaudreuil, the governor, who had hoped to have himself received the appointment of commander of the French forces, and who, in virtue of his office, commanded the Canadian militia.

From first to last this man opposed and thwarted Montcalm, doing all in his power to injure him, by reports to France in his disfavour. The misfortunes which befell France during the war were, in no slight degree, due to this divided authority, and to the obstacles thrown in the way of Montcalm by the governor.

Montcalm's first blow against the English was struck in August, 1756, six months before the attack on Fort William Henry, which had been arranged by Vaudreuil. Three battalions of regular troops, with 700 Canadians and 250 Indians, with a strong force of artillery, were quietly concentrated at Fort Frontenac, and were intended for an attack upon the important English post of Oswego. Fighting had been going on in this neighbourhood for some time, and it was from Oswego that Shirley had intended to act against Niagara and Frontenac. That enterprise had fallen through, owing to Shirley having been deprived of the command; but a sharp fight had taken place between Colonel Bradstreet and his armed boatmen, and 1100 French, who were beaten off.

Oswego was a place of extreme importance. It was the only English post on Ontario, situated as it was towards the southwest corner of the lake. So long as it remained in their possession, it was a standing menace against the whole line of communications of the French with the south. Owing to gross neglect, the fort had never been placed in a really defensive condition. The garrison was small, and crippled with the fever, which had carried off great numbers of them. The remainder were ill fed and discontented.

On the 12th of August, the Earl of London sent Colonel Webb, with the 44th Regiment and some of Bradstreet's boatmen, to reinforce Oswego. They should have started a month before, and, had they done so, would have been in time; but confusion and misunderstanding had arisen from a change in command. Webb had scarcely made half his march, when tidings of the disaster met him, and he at once fell back with the greatest precipitation.

At midnight on the 10th, Montcalm had landed his force within half a league of the first English fort. Four cannon were at once landed, and a battery thrown up, and so careless of danger were the garrison, that it was not till the morning that the invaders were discovered. Two armed vessels at once sailed down to cannonade them; but their light guns were no match for the heavy artillery of the French, and they were forced to retire.

The attack was commenced without delay. The Indians and Canadians, swarming in the forest round the fort, kept up a hot fire upon it. By nightfall the first parallel was marked out at 180 yards from the rampart.

Fort Ontario, considered the strongest of the three forts at Oswego, stood on a high plateau on the right side of the river, where it entered the lake. It was in the shape of a star, and formed of a palisade of trunks of trees set upright in the ground, hewn flat on both sides, and closely fitted together–an excellent defence against musketry, but worthless against artillery. The garrison of the fort, 370 in number, had eight small cannon and a mortar, with which, all next day, they kept up a brisk fire against the battery which the French were throwing up, and arming with twenty-six pieces of heavy artillery.

Colonel Mercer, the commandant of Oswego, saw at once that the French artillery would, as soon as they opened fire, blow the stockade into pieces, and thinking it better to lose the fort, alone, than the fort and its garrison, he sent boats across the river after nightfall, and the garrison, having spiked their guns, and thrown their ammunition into the well, crossed the river, unperceived by the French.

But Oswego was in no position for defence. Fort Pepperell stood on the mouth of the river, facing Fort Ontario. Towards the west and south the place was protected by an outer line of earthworks, mounted with cannon, but the side facing the river was wholly exposed, in the belief that Fort Ontario would prevent any attack in this direction.

Montcalm lost no time. The next evening, his whole force set to work throwing up a battery, at the edge of the rising ground on which Fort Ontario stood, and, by daybreak, twenty heavy guns were in position, and at once opened fire. The grape and round shot swept the English position, smashing down the mud-built walls, crashing through the stockades, and carrying destruction among the troops. The latter made a shelter of pork barrels, three high and three deep, and planted cannon behind them, and returned the enemy's fire; but the Canadians and Indians had crossed the river, by a ford two miles up, and soon opened fire from all sides.

Colonel Mercer, who had bravely led his men, and inspired them by his example, was cut in two by a cannon shot, and the garrison were seized with despair. A council of officers was held, and the garrison surrendered as prisoners of war, to the number of sixteen hundred, which included sick, the sailors belonging to the shipping, labourers, and upwards of a hundred women.

Montcalm had the greatest difficulty in preventing the Indians, by means of threats, promises, and presents, from massacring the prisoners. Oswego was burned to the ground, the forts and vessels on the stocks destroyed, and, the place having been made a desert, the army returned with their prisoners and spoil to Montreal.

The loss of Oswego had inflicted a very severe blow to the influence and prestige of England, among the Indians of the lake districts, but this was partly restored by the failure of the French expedition against William Henry, early in the following spring.

The expedition against Louisbourg, to strengthen which the western frontier had been denuded of troops, proved a failure. A great delay had taken place at home, in consequence of ministerial changes, and it was not until the 5th of May that fifteen ships of the line and three frigates, under Admiral Holbourne, with 5000 troops on board, sailed from England for Halifax, where Loudon was to meet him with the forces from the colony. But, while the English fleet had been delaying, the French government had obtained information of its destination, and had sent three French squadrons across the Atlantic to Louisbourg.

It was the 10th of July before the united English force assembled at Halifax, and there fresh delays arose. The troops, nearly twelve thousand in number, were landed, and weeks were spent in idle drill.

At the beginning of August the forces were again embarked, when a sloop came in from Newfoundland, bringing letters which had been captured on board a French ship. From these, it appeared that there were twenty-two ships of the line, besides several frigates, in the harbour of Louisbourg, and that 7000 troops were in garrison, in what was by far the strongest fortress on the continent.

Success was now impossible, and the enterprise was abandoned. Loudon, with his troops, sailed back to New York; and Admiral Holbourne, who had been joined by four additional ships, sailed for Louisbourg, in hopes that the French fleet would come out and fight him. He cruised for some time off the port, but Lamotte, the French admiral, would not come out.

In September, a tremendous gale burst upon the British fleet: one ship was dashed on the rocks, a short distance from Louisbourg, and only a sudden shift of the wind saved the rest from a total destruction. Nine were dismasted, and others threw their cannon into the sea. Had Lamotte sailed out on the following day, the English fleet was at his mercy. Fortunately he did not do so, and Holbourne returned to England.

The French in Canada were aware that Loudon had gathered all his troops at New York, and was preparing for an expedition, which was to be aided by a fleet from England; but, thinking it probable that it was directed against Quebec, the most vital point in Canada, since its occupation by the English would entirely cut the colony off from France, Montcalm was obliged to keep his forces in hand near that town, and was unable to take advantage of the unprotected state in which Loudon had left the frontier of the colonies.

As soon, however, as, by despatch received from France, and by the statements of prisoners captured by the Indians on the frontier, Montcalm learned that the expedition, which had just left New York, was destined for Louisbourg, he was at liberty to utilize his army for the invasion of the defenceless colonies, and he determined to commence the campaign by the capture of Fort William Henry.

James Walsham, with his company of Royal Scouts, had spent the spring at Fort William Henry. Loudon had, at first, sent an order for the corps to be broken up, and the men to rejoin their respective regiments, and to accompany them on the expedition; but the earnest representations of Colonel Monro of the 35th Regiment, who was now in command, of the total inadequacy of the garrison to defend itself, should a serious attack be made from Ticonderoga; and of the great value to him of the corps under Captain Walsham, which was now thoroughly trained in forest fighting, induced him to countermand the order.

James was glad that he was not obliged to rejoin his regiment. The independent command was a pleasant one, and although life at Fort William Henry had, since the French repulse, been an uneventful one, there was plenty of fishing in the lake, and shooting in the woods, to vary the monotony of drill.

He and Edwards were now both expert canoemen, and often ventured far down the lake, taking with them one or other of the scouts, and keeping a sharp lookout among the woods on either side for signs of the enemy. Once or twice they were chased by Indian canoes, but always succeeded in distancing them.

"The news has just come in that the expedition has sailed," James said as he one day, towards the end of July, entered the hut which he now occupied with Edwards; for the corps had long since been put under huts, these being better suited for the hot season than tents.

"It is rather a nuisance," Edwards grumbled, "being kept here, instead of going and taking share in a big siege."

"Don't be impatient, Edwards," James replied. "If I am not greatly mistaken, you will have quite as much fighting as you want here before long. Montcalm's sudden attack on Oswego last autumn showed that he is an enterprising general, and I have no doubt that, as soon as he learns that Loudon's expedition is not intended for Quebec, he will be beating us up on the frontier with a vengeance."

Montcalm, indeed, had already prepared to strike a blow. A thousand Indians, lured by the prospect of gifts, scalps, and plunder, had come in from the west and north, and were encamped near Montreal; and, besides these, there were the Mission Indians, and those of the Five Nations who adhered to France.

Early in July, the movement began. Day after day, fleets of boats and canoes rowed up Lake Champlain, and, towards the end of the month, the whole force was gathered at Ticonderoga. Here were now collected eight thousand men, of whom two thousand were Indians, representing forty-one tribes and sub-tribes: among them were Iroquois, Hurons, Nipissings, Abenakis, Algonkins, Micmacs, and Malecites. These were all nominal Christians, and counted eight hundred warriors. With them were the western Indians: Ojibwas, Mississagas, Pottawattamies, Menomonies, Sacs, Foxes, Winnebagoes, Miamis, and Iowas. These were still unconverted.

The French held these savage allies in abhorrence. Their drunkenness, their turbulence, their contempt of all orders, their cruelty to their captives, and their cannibalism, disgusted and shocked Montcalm and his officers; but they were powerless to restrain them, for without them as scouts, guides, and eyes in the forests, the French could have done nothing, and, at the slightest remonstrance, the Indians were ready to take offence, and to march away to their distant homes.

The letters of Montcalm and his officers, to their friends, were full of disgust at the doings of their savage allies, and of regret that they could not dispense with their services, or restrain their ferocity. Vaudreuil and the Canadians, on the other hand, accustomed to the traditions of savage warfare, made no attempt whatever to check the ferocity of the Indians, and were, indeed, the instigators of the raids which the savages made upon the unprotected villages and settlements on the frontier; offered rewards for scalps, and wrote and talked gleefully of the horrible atrocities committed upon the colonists.

Chapter 14: Scouting On Lake Champlain.
One morning, Colonel Monro sent for James.

"Captain Walsham," he said, "there are rumours that the French are gathering at Crown Point in considerable force. Captain Rogers is still disabled by his wound, and his band have suffered so heavily, in their last affair with the enemy, that for the time they are out of action. It is important that I should learn the truth of these rumours, for, if they be true, I must communicate at once to the general, in order that he may get together a sufficient force to relieve us, if Montcalm comes down and lays siege to the fort. Will you undertake the business?"

"I will do my best, sir," James replied. "Do you propose that I should take all my company, or only a picked party?"

"That I will leave to you, Captain Walsham. I want trustworthy news, and how you obtain it for me matters little."

"Then I will take only a small party," James said. "Fifty men would be useless, for purposes of fighting, if the enemy are numerous, while with such a number it would be hopeless to attempt to escape detection by the Indians. The fewer the better for such an enterprise."

On leaving the commandant, James at once summoned the two hunters to his hut, and told them the mission he had received.

"I am ready, captain, that is if you, and I, and Jonathan makes up the party. As to going trapezing about round Crown Point with fifty soldiers, the thing ain't to be thought of. We should be there no more than half an hour before the Indians would know of it, and we should have no show either for fighting or running away. No, captain, the lads are good enough for scouting about round camp here; but, as for an expedition of that sort, we might as well start with a drove of swine."

"That is just what I thought, Nat. One canoe may escape even the eyes of the Indians, but a dozen would have no chance of doing so."

"We might get up the lakes," the scout said; "but the mischief would be in the woods. No, it never would do, captain. If we goes, it must be the three of us and no more. When do you think of starting?"

"The sooner the better, Nat."

"Very well, captain, I will go and get some grub ready, and, as soon as it gets dusk, we will get the canoe into the water."

"I suppose you can't take me with you?" Lieutenant Edwards said, when James told him of the duty he had been requested to perform. "It is dismal here."

"Not exactly," James laughed. "What would become of the company, if it were to lose its two officers and its two scouts at a blow! No, Edwards, you will command during my absence, and I think you will soon have more lively times here, for, if it be true that Montcalm will himself command the troops coming against us, it will be a different business altogether from the last. And now, leave me alone for an hour. I have some letters to write before I start. They will be for you to send off, in case we don't come back again.

"Don't look serious, I have no intention of falling into the hands of Montcalm's savages. Still, there is no doubt the expedition is a risky one, and it is just as well to be prepared."

Just as the sun was setting, Nat came into the officer's hut.

"Everything is ready, captain," he said. "I hope you have made a good dinner, for it's the last hot meal you will eat, till you get back. I have cooked enough meat for the next four days, and that's about as long as it will keep good; after that, dried deer's flesh will have to do for us.

"I expect, I tell you, we shall have to be pretty spry this time. If they are coming down in force, they are sure to send a lot of their Indians through the woods on each side of the lake, and the water will be swarming with their canoes. Jonathan and I have been talking it over, and trying to settle which would be the safest, to foot it all the way, or to go by water. We concluded, as there ain't much difference, and the canoe will be the quickest and easiest, so we had best keep to that plan."

"I would certainly rather go that way, Nat, if you think that the danger is no greater."

"No, I don't think there's much difference, captain. At any rate, we may as well go that way. Like enough, we shall have to tramp back by the woods."

Half an hour later, the canoe put out. Although they had little fear that any of the Indian canoes would be so far up Lake George, there was scarce a word spoken in the boat for some hours after starting. Jonathan was always silent, and Nat, although talkative enough when in camp, was a man of few words when once embarked upon a serious expedition. As for James, he had little inclination for conversation.

The enterprise was, he knew, one of extreme danger. Had it been only a French force he was about to reconnoitre, or even one composed of French and Canadians together, he would have thought little of it; but he knew that the redskins would be roaming thickly in the forest, ahead of the army, and, much as he relied upon the skill and experience of the two scouts, he knew it would be difficult, indeed, to elude their watchful eyes. He thought of the letters he had been writing, and wondered whether he should return to tear them up, or whether they would be read at home.

All the time he was thinking, he worked his paddle vigorously, and at a high rate of speed. The light canoe bounded noiselessly over the water, impelled by three vigorous pairs of arms.

When they approached the narrows connecting Lake George with Lake Champlain, the boat's head was directed towards the shore, for they could not get past Ticonderoga before daylight broke; and it was likely that a good watch would be kept, in the narrows, by the enemy; and it would be dangerous to try to effect a landing there. The canoe was carried ashore, and hidden in some bushes, and all lay down to sleep.

When day broke, Nat rose and went down to the water to see that, in landing, they had left no mark upon the shore, which might betray them to the eye of a passing redskin. Going down on his hands and knees, he obliterated every sign of their footprints, raised the herbage upon which they had trodden, cut short to the ground such stalks as they had bruised or broken in their passage, and then, when confident that all was safe, he returned to his camp. When it again became dark, the canoe was carried down and replaced in the water, and they continued their passage. James had, at Nat's request, laid by his paddle.

"You paddle wonderfully well, captain. I don't say you don't; but for a delicate piece of work like this, one can't be too careful. It ain't often I can hear your paddle dip in the water, not once in a hundred times, but then, you see, that once might cost us our scalps. We have got to go along as silent as a duck swimming. Speed ain't no object, for we shall be miles down Lake Champlain before daylight; but, if the French know their business, they will have half a dozen canoes in these narrows, to prevent us scouting on Lake Champlain; and, you see, they have got all the advantage of us, 'cause they've got just to lie quiet and listen, and we have got to row on. As far as seeing goes, I can make them out as soon as they can make us out; but they can hear us, while they won't give our ears a chance.

"I tell you, captain, I don't expect to get through this narrows without a chase for it. If it come to running, of course you will take your paddle again, and we three can show our heels to any canoe on the lakes, perviding of course as it's only a starn chase. If there are three or four of them, then I don't say as it won't be a close thing."

James accordingly lay quietly back in the boat, while his companions took the paddles. It was not necessary for him either to look out, or to listen, for he knew that his companions' eyes and ears were quicker than his own. It had been agreed, before starting, that they should go along close to the trees, on the left-hand side of the passage, because the keenest lookout would be kept on the right-hand side, as that would naturally be chosen by any boat going up, as being farthest from the French fort.

"There is no fear, whatever, of our being seen from the land," Nat had said. "The redskins would know that so well that they wouldn't trouble to look out. It's only canoes we have got to be afraid of, and, as to them, it's just a chance. They might see us out in the light waters, in the middle; but, under the trees, they can't make us out thirty yards off. They will be lying there, quiet, if they are there at all, and we shall either get past them safe, or we shall pretty nigh run into them. It's just chance, and there's nothing to do for it but to paddle as noiselessly as fish, and trust to our luck."

Having crossed the lake to the left shore, they entered the narrows. The paddles were dipped so quietly into the water, that even James could scarcely hear their sound. Every few strokes the scouts stopped paddling altogether, and sat listening intently. They were keeping close to the trees, so close that, at times, it seemed to James that, by stretching out his hands, he could touch the bushes.

After an hour's paddling they stopped longer than usual.

"What is it?" James whispered in Jonathan's ear, for Nat had taken the bow paddle.

"There are men ahead," the scout whispered back. "We heard them speak just now."

Presently the boat began to move again, but so quietly, that it was only by looking at the dark masses of the boughs, that stretched out overhead, that James knew the boat was in motion. Jonathan now crouched in the bottom of the boat, and placed his hand on Nat's shoulder as a sign for him to do the same. The time seemed endless to James, as he lay there. It was too dark, under the trees, for him even to see the outline of Nat's figure. The boat was, he was sure, moving; for occasionally, as he lay on his back, it grew lighter overhead, as they passed under openings in the trees.

Suddenly his heart gave a bound, and he nearly started, for a guttural voice spoke, seemingly within a few feet of the canoe. He placed his hand on his rifle, in readiness to sit up and fire, but all was still again. It was a passing remark, made by one redskin to another; in a canoe, for the sound was to his right. Another long period passed, and then Jonathan sat up and took to his paddle again, and James judged that the danger was over.

Raising his head, he could see nothing except the vague light of the sheet of water on his right. The boat was still keeping close under the trees, on the left shore of the lake, and he lay back again, and dozed off to sleep. He was awoke by Jonathan touching his foot.

"You can take your paddle now, captain."

He sat up at once, and looked round. They were far out now, on a broad sheet of water. There were some faint lights, as of fires burning low, high up to the left behind them; and he knew that they had already passed Ticonderoga, and were making their way along Lake Champlain. They paddled for some hours, and then landed on the right-hand side of the lake.

"We are not likely to be disturbed here," Nat said, as they lifted the canoe from the water. "The Indians, coming down from Crown Point, would keep on the other side of the lake. They will all make for Ticonderoga, and will not think of keeping a lookout for anyone, as far down the lakes as this."

"That was a close shave with that canoe, Nat. It startled me, when I heard the voice close to us. They must have been within ten yards of us."

"About that," Nat said. "It was lucky they spoke when we were coming along. I expect they had been watching for some nights, and hadn't much idea anyone would come, or else they wouldn't have spoken. As it was, it was easy enough to pass them, on such a dark night. Of course, they were looking outside, and I just kept along as close as I could to the bushes, only just giving a light stroke, now and then, to take her along. Being inside them, I got a sight of 'em some distance away, but I knew they couldn't see us, sharp as their eyes are. The only chance was their hearing, and, as there was no noise for them to hear, I felt safe enough after I had once caught sight of 'em, and saw they were lying out at the edge of the shadow.

"If they had been close under the bushes, as they ought to have been, we should have been in for a fight; for we mightn't have seen each other till the boats touched. Let that be a lesson to you, captain. When you are on the lookout for a canoe, at night, lie in among the bushes. It must pass between you and the light, then, and as they can't see you, you can either grapple or shoot, just as you like.

"If they had a seen us, we should have had a hot time, for I could hear by their calls, right along the other side, that they were looking out for us in earnest, and, if a rifle had been fired, we should have had half a dozen canoes down upon us in no time; and, like enough, should have had to leave the boat, and take to the woods."

"How far is Crown Point away?"

"Not more than ten miles," Nat said. "It is thirty miles from Ticonderoga. It lies out on a point, just where Champlain widens out. I reckon our safest way, tonight, will be to scout along this side, till we are well past the point; then to paddle out well across the lake, and come up again, and land to the left of Crown Point. We shall then be in the track of boats coming up from the lower end of the lake, and can paddle boldly on. No one would be keeping any lookout that way. Our danger won't begin until we get ashore; in course, then we must act according to sarcumstances."

This manoeuvre was carried out. They started as soon as it became dark, and, after paddling along the eastern shore for nearly three hours, struck out into the wide lake till they approached the opposite shore, and then, heading south again, paddled boldly down towards the spot where, at the end of a sweep of land, which seemed to close in the lake, stood the French fort of Crown Point.

Before starting, the two scouts had stripped to the waist, had laid aside their caps, and, fastening a strip of leather round their heads, had stuck some feathers into it. They then painted their faces and bodies.

"You needn't be particular about the flourishes, Jonathan. It's only the redskin outline as one wants to get. If we run against any other canoes coming up the lake, or they get sight of us as we near the shore; so as we look something like redskins, that's near enough. Of course, we can both speak Mohawk well enough to pass muster, and the captain will lay himself down in the bottom.

"Captain, you will do well enough for a Canadian when we have once landed. There ain't much difference between a hunter one side of the frontier and the other, but it's as well that you shouldn't be seen till we land. The less questions asked, the better. Our Mohawk's good enough with any of the other tribes, but it wouldn't pass with a Mohawk, if we got into a long talk with him."

Fortunately, however, these precautions proved unnecessary. No other canoes were seen on the lake, and they landed, unnoticed, at a spot a mile and a half to the west of Crown Point. Before starting from Fort William Henry, James had laid aside his uniform, and had dressed himself in hunting shirt and leggings, similar to those worn by the scouts. He had adopted various little details, in which the Canadian hunters differed from those on the English side of the frontier. The latter wore their hunting shirts loose in Indian fashion, while the Canadians generally wore a leathern belt outside theirs, at the waist.

His cap was made of squirrels' skins, which would pass equally well on both sides of the frontier. The fire bag, in which tobacco, tinder, and other small matters were carried, was of Indian workmanship, as was the cord of his powder horn and bullet pouch. Altogether, his get-up was somewhat brighter and more picturesque than that of English scouts, who, as a rule, despised anything approaching to ornament.

He knew that by disguising himself he would be liable, if captured, to be shot at once as a spy; but this could not be considered, under the circumstances, to add to the risk he ran, for, in any case, he was certain to be killed if detected, and it would have been out of the question to attempt to approach the French camp in the uniform of a British officer. Could he have spoken Canadian French, the mission would have been comparatively easy, but he knew only a few words of the language, and would be detected the instant he opened his lips.

The canoe was hauled up and carefully concealed on land, and then they lay down until daylight; for no information, as to the strength of the enemy, could be gained in the dark. In the morning, the two scouts very carefully made their toilet. They had brought all necessaries with them; and soon, in their Indian hunting shirts and fringed leggings, and with carefully-painted faces, they were in a position to defy the keenest scrutiny.

When, after a careful survey of each other, they felt that their disguise was complete, they moved boldly forward, accompanied by James. After half an hour's walking they emerged from the forest, and the strong fort of Crown Point lay before them.

It was constructed of stone, and was capable of withstanding a long siege, by any force which could be brought against it. Round it was the camp of the French troops, and James judged, from the number of tents, that there must be some 1500 French soldiers there. A short distance away were a large number of roughly-constructed huts, roofed with boughs of trees.

"Them's the Canadians," Jonathan said. "The redskins never build shelters while on the war path. There are a heap of redskins about."

These, indeed, even at the distance of several hundred yards, could be easily distinguished from their white allies, by their plumed headdresses, and by the blankets or long robes of skins which hung from their shoulders.

"I should put them down at three thousand."

"It is a big army," Nat said. "I should think there must be quite as many Canadians as French. How many redskins there are, there ain't no knowing, but we may be sure that they will have got together as many as they could. Put 'em down at 4000, and that makes 7000 altogether, enough to eat up Fort William Henry, and to march to Albany–or to New York, if they are well led and take fancy to it–that is, if the colonists don't bestir themselves smartly.

"Well, so far you have found out what you came to seek, captain. What's the next thing?"

"We must discover, if we can, whether they mean to go up the lakes in boats, or to march through the woods," James replied. "They will have a tremendous job getting any guns through the woods, but, if they are going by water, of course they can bring them."

"Very well," Nat replied. "In that case, captain, my advice is, you stop in the woods, and Jonathan and I will go down past the fort to the shore, and see what provision they are making in that way. You see, the place swarms with Canadians, and you would be sure to be spoken to. Redskins don't talk much to each other, unless there is some need for words, and we can go right through the French camp without fear. The only danger is of some loping Mohawk coming up to us, and I don't reckon there are many of 'em in the camp, perhaps nary a one."

Although James did not like his followers to go into danger, without his sharing it, he saw that his presence would enormously add to their risks, and therefore agreed to their plan. Withdrawing some distance into the wood, and choosing a thick growth of underwood, he entered, and lay down in the bushes, while the two scouts walked quietly away towards the camp.

Two hours passed. Several times he heard footsteps in the wood near him, and, peering through the leaves, caught sight of parties of Indians going towards the camp, either late arrivals from Montreal, or bands that had been out scouting or hunting. At the end of the two hours, to his great relief, he saw two figures coming from the other way through the woods, and at once recognized the scouts. He crawled out and joined them, as they came up.

"Thank God you are back again! I have been in a fever, all the time you have been away."

"I wish I had known the precise place where you were hiding. I should have made a sign to you to keep quiet; but it ain't of no use, now."

"What's the matter then, Nat?"

"I ain't quite sure as anything is the matter," the scout replied; "but I am feared of it. As bad luck would have it, just as we were coming back through the camp, we came upon a Mohawk chief. He looked hard at us, and then came up and said:

"'The Owl thought that he knew all his brothers; but here are two whose faces are strange to him.'

"Of course, I told him that we had been living and hunting, for years, in the English colony, but that, hearing that the Mohawks had joined the French, we had come to fight beside our brothers. He asked a few questions, and then passed on. But I could see the varmin was not satisfied, though, in course, he pretended to be glad to welcome us back to the tribe. So we hung about the camp for another half hour, and then made a sweep before we came out here. I didn't look round, but Jonathan stooped, as if the lace of his moccasin had come undone, and managed to look back, but, in course, he didn't see anything."

"Then you have no reason to believe you are followed, Nat?"

"Don't I tell you I have every reason?" Nat said. "If that redskin, the Owl, has got any suspicion–and suspicion you may be sure he's got–he won't rest till he's cleared the matter up. He is after us, sure enough."

"Then had we not better make for the canoe at full speed?"

"No," Nat said. "If they are behind us, they will be watching our trail; and if they see we change our pace, they will be after us like a pack of wolves; while, as long as we walk slowly and carelessly, they will let us go. If it were dark, we might make a run for it, but there ain't no chance at present. If we took to the lake, we should have a hundred canoes after us, while the woods are full of Indians, and a whoop of the Owl would bring a hundred of them down onto our track."

"Why shouldn't the Owl have denounced you at once, if he suspected you?" James asked.

"Because it ain't redskin nature to do anything, till you are sure," the scout replied. "There is nothing a redskin hates so much as to be wrong, and he would rather wait, for weeks, to make sure of a thing, than run the risk of making a mistake. I don't suppose he takes us for whites. He expects we belong to some other tribe, come in as spies."

"Then what are you thinking of doing?" James asked.

"We will go on a bit further," Nat said, "in hopes of coming across some stream, where we may hide our trail. If we can't find that, we will sit down, before long, and eat as if we was careless and in no hurry."

For a time, they walked on in silence.

"Do you think they are close to us?" James asked, presently.

"Not far away," the scout said carelessly. "So long as they see we ain't hurrying, they will go easy. They will know, by this time, that we have a white man with us, and, like enough, the Owl will have sent back for one or two more of his warriors. Likely enough, he only took one with him, at first, seeing we were but two, and that he reckoned on taking us by surprise; but, when he saw you joined us, he would send back for perhaps a couple more."

"Then what I would suggest," James said, "is, that we should at once stroll down to our canoe, put it in the water, and paddle out a few hundred yards, and there let down the lines we have got on board, and begin to fish. As long as we are quiet there, the redskins may not interfere with us, and, when it gets dark, we can make off. At the worst, we have a chance for it, and it seems to me anything would be better than this sort of wandering about, when we know that, at any time, we may have them down upon us."

"Perhaps that is the best plan," Nat said. "What do you think, Jonathan?"

Jonathan gave an assenting grunt, and they turned their faces towards the lake, still walking at the same leisurely pace. Not once did any of the three look back. As they neared the water, James found the temptation very strong to do so, but he restrained it, and sauntered along as carelessly as ever.

The canoe was lifted from its hiding place and put in the water. As they were about to step in, the bushes parted, and the Owl stood beside them.

"Where are my brothers going?" he asked quietly.

"We are going fishing," Nat answered. "The noise in the woods will have frightened game away."

"There is food in the camp," the Owl said. "The French give food to their brothers, the redskins."

"My white brother wants fish," Nat said quietly, "and we have told him we will catch him some. Will the Owl go with us?"

The Indian shook his head, and in a moment the canoe put off from the shore, the Indian standing, watching them, at the edge of the water.

"That's a badly puzzled redskin," Nat said, with a low laugh. "His braves have not come up yet, or he would not have let us start.

"There, that is far enough. We are out of the range of Indian guns. Now, lay in your paddles, and begin to fish. There are several canoes fishing further out, and the redskin will feel safe. He can cut us off, providing we don't go beyond them."

The Indian was, as Nat had said, puzzled. That something was wrong he was sure; but, as he was alone, he was unable to oppose their departure. He watched them closely, as they paddled out, in readiness to give a war whoop, which would have brought down the fishing canoes outside, and given warning to every Indian within sound of his voice; but, when he saw them stop and begin to fish, he hesitated. If he gave the alarm, he might prove to be mistaken, and he shrank from facing the ridicule which a false alarm would bring upon him. Should they really prove, as he believed, to be spies, he would, if he gave the alarm, lose the honour and glory of their capture, and their scalps would fall to other hands–a risk not to be thought of.

He therefore waited, until six of his braves came up. He had already retired among the trees, before he joined them; but the canoe was still visible through the branches.

"The men we tracked have taken to the water. They are fishing. The Owl is sure that they are not of our tribe; but he must wait, till he sees what they will do. Let three of my brothers go and get a canoe, and paddle out beyond them, and there fish. I will remain with the others here. If they come back again, we will seize them. If they go out further, my brothers will call to the redskins in the other canoes, and will cut them off. The Owl and his friends will soon be with them."

"There is another canoe coming out, Nat," James said. "Hadn't we better make a run for it, at once?"

"Not a bit of it, captain. Dear me, how difficult it is to teach men to have patience! I have looked upon you as a promising pupil; but there you are, just as hasty and impatient as if you had never spent a day in the woods. Where should we run to? We must go up the lake, for we could not pass the point, for fifty canoes would be put out before we got there. We couldn't land this side, because the woods are full of redskins; and if we led them for ten miles down the lake, and landed t'other side, scores of them would land between here and there, and would cut us off.

"No, lad; we have got to wait here till it's getting late. I don't say till it's dark, but till within an hour or so of nightfall. As long as we show no signs of going, the chances is as they won't interfere with us. It's a part of redskin natur to be patient, and, as long as they see as we don't try to make off, they will leave us alone. That's how I reads it.

"You agrees with me, Jonathan?

"In course, you do," he went on, as his companion grunted an assent. "I don't say as they mayn't ask a question or so; but I don't believe as they will interfere with us.

"There is a fish on your line, captain. You don't seem, to me, to be attending to your business."

James, indeed, found it difficult to fix his attention on his line, when he knew that they were watched by hostile eyes, and that, at any moment, a conflict might begin. The canoe that had come out last had shaped its course so as to pass close to those fishing outside them, and a few words had been exchanged with the occupants of each–a warning, no doubt, as to the suspicious character of the fishing party near them. Beyond this, nothing had happened. The Indians in the canoe had let down their lines, and seemed as intent as the others upon their fishing.

The hours passed slowly. Under other circumstances, James would have enjoyed the sport, for the fish bit freely, and a considerable number were soon lying in the canoe. Nat and Jonathan appeared as interested in their work as if no other boat, but their own, were afloat on the lake. Never once did James see them glance towards the canoes. They did not talk much, but when they spoke, it was always in the Indian tongue.

The time seemed endless, before the sun began to sink beyond the low hills on their left. It was an intense relief, to James, when Nat said at last:

"The time is just at hand now, cap. The redskins are tired of waiting. At least, they think that they had better not put it off any longer. They know, as well as we do, that it won't do to wait till it gets dark.

"Do you see that canoe, that came out last, is paddling down towards us? It looks as if it were drifting, but I have seen them dip a paddle in, several times. The others are pulling up their lines, so as to be in readiness to join in. Get your piece ready to pick up, and aim the moment I give the word. They think they are going to surprise us, but we must be first with them. Go on with your fishing, and just drop your line overboard, when you pick up your gun."

The canoe approached slowly, until it was within thirty yards. James and his companions went on with their fishing, as if they did not notice the approach of the other canoe, until one of the Indians spoke.

"Have my Indian brothers caught many fish?"

"A goodish few," Nat replied. "One or two of them are large ones.

"See here," and he stooped as if to select a large fish.

"Now," he said suddenly.

In an instant, the three rifles were levelled to the shoulder, and pointed at the Indians. The latter, taken completely by surprise, and finding themselves with three barrels levelled at them, as by one accord dived overboard.

"Now your paddles," Nat exclaimed.

Three strokes sent the canoe dancing up to that which the Indians had just left. It struck it on the broadside, and rolled it instantly over.

"Those redskin guns are out of the way, anyhow," Nat said. "Now we have got to row for it."

He gave a sharp turn to the canoe as he spoke, and it bounded away towards the right, thereby throwing those outside it on their quarter. Simultaneously with the upset of the canoe, half a dozen rifles rang out from the shore, an Indian war whoop rose at the edge of the woods, and, a minute later, half a dozen canoes shot out from shore.

Chapter 15: Through Many Perils.

The course Nat was taking was not parallel to that of the boats outside him. He was sheering gradually out into the lake, and, although the boat was travelling somewhat faster than its pursuers, James saw that its course would carry it across their bows at a dangerously close distance. The Indians were not long in seeing that the canoe was outstripping them, and in each of the boats one of the redskins laid aside his paddle, and began to fire. The balls struck the water near the canoe, but no one was hit.

"Let them fire," Jonathan said. "It ain't every man as can shoot straight from a canoe going at racing pace. The more they fires the better. They will only fall further behind."

After firing two or three shots each, the Indians appeared to be of the same opinion, and resumed their paddles; but they had lost so much ground that the canoe they were in chase of shot out into the lake fifty yards ahead of the nearest. Some more shots were fired, and then the Indians began hastily to throw the fish, with which their canoes were laden, into the water. After paddling two or three hundred yards farther, Nat laid in his paddle.

"Out with them fish," he said. "You can leave one or two for supper, but the rest must go overboard. Be quick about it, for those canoes from the shore are coming up fast."

The work was concluded just as the canoes with the Owl and his warriors came up with the others, which, having now got rid of their fish, again set out, and, in a close body, the ten canoes started in pursuit.

"Paddle steady," Nat said; "and whatever you do, be keerful of your blades. If one was to break now it would mean the loss of our scalps. Don't gain on 'em; as long as the redskins on shore think as their friends are going to catch us, they won't care to put out and join in the chase; but if they thought we was getting away, they might launch canoes ahead of us and cut us off. The nearer we are to them the better, as long as we are keeping ahead."

For an hour the chase continued. The Indians, although straining every nerve, did not gain a foot upon the fugitives, who, although paddling hard, had still some reserve of strength. The sun, by this time, was touching the tops of the hills.

"Now, cap," Nat said, "it's time to teach 'em as we can bite a bit. They won't be quite so hot over it, if we give them a lesson now. Do you turn round and pepper them a bit."

"Now, old hoss! You and I must row all we know for a bit."

Turning himself in the canoe, resting his elbow on his knee to steady his rifle, James took as careful an aim as the dancing motion of the boat permitted, and fired. A dull sound came back, like an echo, to the crack of the piece, and a paddle in the leading boat fell into the water. A yell arose from the Indians, but no answering shout came back.

The Indians were now paddling even harder than before, in hope of overtaking the canoe, now that it was impelled by but two rowers. But the scouts were rowing their hardest, and proved the justice of their fame, as the best paddlers on the lakes, by maintaining their distance from their pursuers.

Again and again James fired, several of his bullets taking effect. It was now rapidly becoming dusk.

"That will do, captain. We had best be showing them our heels now, and get as far ahead as we can, by the time it is quite dark."

James laid by his rifle and again took his paddle, and, as all were rowing at the top of their speed, they gradually increased the distance between themselves and their pursuers. Rapidly the gap of water widened, and when darkness fell on the lake, the fugitives were more than half a mile ahead of their pursuers. The night was dark, and a light mist rising from the water further aided them. When night had set in, the pursuing canoes could no longer be seen.

For another half hour they paddled on, without intermitting their efforts, then, to James's surprise, Nat turned the head of the canoe to the western shore. He asked no question, however, having perfect faith in Nat's sagacity. They were nearly in the middle of the lake when they altered their course, and it took them half an hour's hard paddling, before the dark mass of trees loomed up in the darkness ahead of him. Ten minutes before, Nat had passed the word that they should paddle quietly and noiselessly. It was certain that the chase would be eagerly watched from the shore, and that any Indians there might be in the wood would be closely watching near the water's edge.

Accordingly, as noiselessly as possible they approached the shore, and, gliding in between the overhanging trees, laid the canoe alongside a clump of bushes. Then, without a word being spoken, they laid in their paddles and stretched themselves full length in the canoe.

James was glad of the rest, for, trained and hard as were his muscles, he was exhausted by the long strain of the row for life. He guessed that Nat would calculate that the Indian canoes would scatter, when they lost sight of them, and that they would seek for them more closely on the eastern shore. At the same time he was surprised that, after once getting out of sight of their pursuers, Nat had not immediately landed on the opposite shore, and started on foot through the woods.

After recovering his breath, James sat up and listened attentively. Once or twice he thought he heard the sound of a dip of a paddle, out on the lake, but he could not be sure of it; while from time to time he heard the croak of a frog, sometimes near, sometimes at a distance along the shore. He would have thought little of this, had not a slight pressure of Jonathan's hand, against his foot, told him that these were Indian signals.

Some hours passed before Nat made a move, then he touched Jonathan, and sat up in the canoe. The signal was passed on to James, the paddles were noiselessly taken up, and, without a sound that could be detected by the most closely-listening ear, the canoe stole out again on to the lake. Until some distance from shore they paddled very quietly, then gradually the strokes grew more vigorous, until the canoe was flying along at full speed up the lake, her course being laid so as to cross very gradually towards the eastern side.

It was not until, as James judged, they must have been several miles from the point at which they had started, that they approached the eastern shore. They did so with the same precautions which had been adopted on the other side, and sat, listening intently, before they gave the last few strokes which took them to the shore. Quietly they stepped out, and the two scouts, lifting the canoe on their shoulders, carried it some fifty yards into the forest, and laid it down among some bushes. Then they proceeded on their way, Nat walking first, James following him so close that he was able to touch him, for, in the thick darkness under the trees, he could not perceive even the outlines of his figure. Jonathan followed close behind. Their progress was slow, for even the trained woodsmen could, with difficulty, make their way through the trees, and Nat's only index, as to the direction to be taken, lay in the feel of the bark of the trunks.

After an hour's progress, he whispered:

"We will stop here till daylight. We can't do any good at the work. We haven't made half a mile since we started."

It was a positive relief, to James, to hear the scout's voice, for not a single word had been spoken since they lost sight of their pursuers in the darkness. The fact that he had ventured now to speak showed that he believed that they were comparatively safe.

"May I speak, Nat?" he asked, after they had seated themselves on the ground.

"Ay, you may speak, captain, but don't you raise your voice above a whisper. There is no saying what redskin ears may be near us. I guess these forests are pretty well alive with them. You may bet there isn't a redskin, or one of the irregular Canadian bands, but is out arter us tonight. The war whoop and the rifles will have put them all on the lookout.

"They will have seen that we were pretty well holding our own, and will guess that, when night came on, we should give the canoes the slip. I guess they will have placed a lot of canoes and flatboats across the lake, opposite Crown Point, for they will know that we should either head back, or take to the woods. I guess most of the redskins near Crown Point will have crossed over at this point, as, in course, we were more likely to land on this side. I had a mighty good mind to land whar we was over there, but there are sure to be such a heap of Indians, making their way up that side from Montreal, that I judge this will be the best; but we shall have all we can do to get free of them."

"Why didn't you land at once, Nat, after we lost sight of them, instead of crossing over?"

"Because that's where they will reckon we shall land, captain. That's where they will look for our tracks the first thing in the morning, and they will know that we can't travel far such a dark night as this, and they will search every inch of the shore for three or four miles below where they lost sight of us, to find where we landed. They would know well enough we couldn't get ashore, without leaving tracks as they would make out, and they would reckon to pick up our trail fast enough, in the wood, and to overtake us before we had gone many miles.

"Now, you see, we have doubled on them. The varmint in the woods will search the edge of the lake in the morning, but it's a good long stretch to go over, and, if we have luck, they mayn't strike on our landing place for some hours after daylight. In course, they may hit on it earlier; still, it gives us a chance, anyhow. Another thing is, we have twenty miles less to travel through the woods than if we had to start up there, and that makes all the difference when you've got redskins at your heels. If we don't have the bad luck to come across some of the varmint in the woods, I expect we shall carry our scalps back to Fort William Henry.

"Now you had best sleep till daybreak. We sha'n't get another chance till we get into the fort again."

With the first dawn of morning, they were on their way. Striking straight back into the woods, they walked fast, but with the greatest care and caution, occasionally making bends and detours, to prevent the redskins following their traces at a run, which they would have been able to do, had they walked in a straight line. Whenever the ground was soft, they walked without trying to conceal their tracks, for Nat knew that, however carefully they progressed, the Indians would be able to make out their trail here. When, however, they came to rocky and broken ground, they walked with the greatest caution, avoiding bruising any of the plants growing between the rocks. After walking ten miles in this direction, they turned to the south.

"We ought to be pretty safe, now," Nat said. "They may be three or four hours before they hit on our landing place, and find the canoe. I don't say as they won't be able to follow our trail–there ain't no saying what redskin eyes can do–but it 'ull take them a long time, anyway. There ain't much risk of running against any of them in the forest, now. I guess that most of them followed the canoe down the lake last night.

"Anyway, we are well out from Lake Champlain now. When we have gone another fifteen mile, we sha'n't be far from the upper arm. There's a canoe been lying hidden there for the last two years, unless some tramping redskin has found it, which ain't likely."

Twenty miles further walking brought them to the shore of the lake. Following this for another hour, they came upon the spot, where a little stream ran into the lake.

"Here we are," Nat said. "Fifty yards up here we shall find the canoe."

They followed the stream up for a little distance, and then Nat, leaving its edge, made for a clump of bushes a few yards away. Pushing the thick foliage aside, he made his way into the centre of the clump.

"Here it is," he said, "just as I left it."

The canoe was lifted out and carried down to the lake, and, taking their seats, they paddled up Lake Champlain, keeping close under the shore.

"We have had good luck, captain," Nat said. "I hardly thought we should har got out without a scrimmage. I expect as the best part of the redskins didn't trouble themselves very much about it. They expect to get such a lot of scalps and plunder, when they take the fort, that the chance of three extra wasn't enough inducement for 'em to take much trouble over it. The redskins in the canoes, who chased us, would be hot enough over it, for you picked out two if not more of them; but those who started from the fort wouldn't have any particular reason to trouble much, especially as they think it likely that those who were chasing us would get the scalps. When a redskin's blood's up there ain't no trouble too great for him, and he will follow for weeks to get his revenge; but, take 'em all in all, they are lazy varmint, and as long as there is plenty of deer's meat on hand, they will eat and sleep away their time for weeks."

By night, they reached the upper end of Lake Champlain, the canoe was carefully hidden away again, and they struck through the woods in the direction of Fort William Henry. They were now safe from pursuit, and, after walking two or three miles, halted for the night, made a fire, and cooked some of the dried meat. When they had finished their meal, Nat said:

"Now we will move away a bit, and then stretch ourselves out."

"Why shouldn't we lie down here, Nat?"

"Because it would be a foolish thing to do, captain. There ain't no saying what redskins may be wandering in the woods in time of war. A thousand nights might pass without one of 'em happening to come upon that fire, but if they did, and we were lying beside it, all the trouble we have taken to slip through their hands would be chucked clean away. No, you cannot be too careful in the woods."

They started early the next morning, and, before noon, arrived at Fort William Henry, where James at once reported, to Colonel Monro, what he had learned of the strength of the French force gathering at Crown Point.

"Thank you, Captain Walsham," the commandant said. "I am greatly indebted to you, for having brought us certain news of what is coming. I will write off at once, and ask for reinforcements. This is a serious expedition, and the colonies will have to make a great effort, and a speedy one, if they are going to save the fort, for, from what we hear of Montcalm, he is not likely to let the grass grow under his feet. I shall report the services you have rendered."

As soon as Colonel Monro received the report James had brought him, he sent to General Webb, who, with two thousand six hundred men, chiefly provincials, was at Fort Edward, fourteen miles away. On the 25th of July that general visited Fort William Henry, and, after remaining there four days, returned to Fort Edward, whence he wrote to the governor of New York, telling him the French were coming, and urging him to send forward the militia at once, saying that he was determined to march himself, with all his troops, to the fort. Instead of doing so, three days later he sent up a detachment of two hundred regulars under Lieutenant Colonel Young, and eight hundred Massachusetts men under Colonel Frye. This raised the force at Fort William Henry to two thousand two hundred men, and reduced that of Webb to sixteen hundred.

Had Webb been a brave and determined man, he would have left a few hundred men, only, to hold Fort Edward, and marched with the rest to assist Monro, when, on the morning of the 3d of August, he received a letter from him, saying that the French were in sight on the lake. But, as he was neither brave nor determined, he remained at Fort Edward, sending off message after message to New York, for help which could not possibly arrive in time.

Already, the garrison of Fort William Henry had suffered one reverse. Three hundred provincials, chiefly New Jersey men, under Colonel Parker, had been sent out to reconnoitre the French outposts. The scouts, under James Walsham, were of the party. They were to proceed in boats down the lake.

"I don't like this business, no way, captain," Nat said, as the company took their place in the boats. "This ain't neither one thing nor the other. If Monro wants to find out about the enemy, Jonathan and I kin do it. If he wants to fight the enemy, this lot ain't enough; besides, these New Jersey men know no more about the forest than so many children. You mark my words, this is going to be a bad business. Why, they can see all these boats halfway down the lake, and, with all these redskins about, they will ambush us as soon as we try to land.

"Look here, captain; you know that I ain't no coward. I don't think no one can say that of me. I am ready to fight when there is a chance of fighting, but I don't see no good in getting myself killed off, when there ain't no good in it. So what I says is this: don't you be in a hurry, captain, with these boats of ours."

"But I must obey orders, Nat," James said, smiling.

"Yes, you must obey orders, captain, no doubt. But there's two ways of obeying orders. The one is to rush in front, and to do a little more than you are told. The other is to take things quiet, and just do what you are told, and no more. Now, my advice is, on this here expedition you go on the last plan. If you are ordered to land first, why land first it must be. If you don't get orders to land first, just let them as is in a hurry land afore you. I ain't been teaching all these lads to know something about the woods, for the last six months, jest to see them killed off like flies, because a blundering wrong-headed colonel sends them out with two hundred and fifty ploughmen, for the redskins to see and attack jest when they fancies."

"Very well, Nat, I will take your advice, and, for once, we won't put ourselves in the front, unless we are ordered."

Satisfied with this, Nat passed quietly round among the men, as they were taking their places in the boats, and told them that there was no occasion for them to row as if they were racing.

"I shall be in the captain's boat," he said. "You keep close to us, and don't you try to push on ahead. When we are once fairly in the woods, then we will do the scouting for the rest, but there ain't no hurry for us to begin that, till we are on shore."

"Look at us," Nat grumbled in James's ear, as the boats started down the lake. "There we are, rowing along the middle, instead of sneaking along close to the shore. Does Parker think that the redskins are as blind as he is, and that, 'cause it's night, a lot of big boats like these can't be seen out in the middle of the lake? I tell you, captain, if we ain't ambushed as soon as we land, I will grant I know nothing of redskin ways."

James had, in fact, before starting, suggested to Colonel Parker that it would be well to keep under the shelter of the bushes; but the officer had replied stiffly:

"When I want your advice, Captain Walsham, I will ask for it."

After which rebuff, James was more willing than he had hitherto been to act in accordance with the advice of the scout. Accordingly, as they rowed down the lake, the boats with the Royal Scouts, although keeping up with the others, maintained their position in the rear of the column.

Towards daybreak, the boats' heads were turned to shore, and, when they neared it, Colonel Parker gave the order for the men to lay in their oars, while the three boats, which happened to be in advance, were told to advance at once and land. The boats passed through the thick curtain of trees, which hung down over the water's edge. A minute passed, and then three others were ordered to follow them.

"Did you hear nothing?" Nat whispered to James.

"No, I didn't hear anything, Nat. Did you?"

"Well, I think I did hear something, captain. It seems to me as I heard a sort of scuffle."

"But they never could surprise some thirty or forty men, without the alarm being given?"

"It depended what sort of men they were," Nat said scornfully. "They wouldn't surprise men that knew their business; but those chaps would just jump out of their boats, as if they was landed on a quay at New York, and would scatter about among the bushes. Why, Lord bless you, the Indians might ambush and tomahawk the lot, before they had time to think of opening their lips to give a shout."

The second three boats had now disappeared among the trees, and Colonel Parker gave the word for the rest to advance in a body.

"Look to your firelocks, lads," James said. "Whatever happens, keep perfectly cool. You at the oars, especially, sit still and be ready to obey orders."

The boats were within fifty yards of the trees when, from beneath the drooping boughs, a volley of musketry was poured out, and, a moment later, a swarm of canoes darted out from beneath the branches, and the terrible Indian war whoop rang in the air.

Appalled by the suddenness of the attack, by the deadly fire, and the terrible yells, the greater portion of the men in the boats were seized with the wildest panic. Many of them jumped into the water. Others threw themselves down in the bottom of the boats. Some tried to row, but were impeded by their comrades.

"Steady, men, steady!" James shouted, at the top of his voice. "Get the boats' heads round, and keep together. We can beat off these canoes, easy enough, if you do but keep your heads."

His orders were obeyed promptly and coolly by the men of his company. The boats were turned with their heads to the lake, as the canoes came dashing up, and the men who were not employed in rowing fired so steadily and truly that the redskins in several of the leading canoes fell, upsetting their boats.

"Don't hurry," James shouted. "There is no occasion for haste. They can go faster than we can. All we have got to do is to beat them off. Lay in all the oars, except the two bow oars, in each boat. All the rest of the men stand to their arms, and let the boats follow each other in file, the bow of one close to the stern of that ahead."

The check, which the volley had given to the canoes, gave time to the men in several of the boats, close to those of the scouts, to turn. They were rowing past James's slowly-moving boats, when he shouted to them:

"Steady, men, your only chance of escape is to show a front to them, as we are doing. They can overtake you easily, and will row you down one after the other. Fall in ahead of our line, and do as we are doing. You need not be afraid. We could beat them off, if they were ten times as many."

Reassured by the calmness with which James issued his orders, the boats took up the positions assigned to them. James, who was in the last boat in the line, shuddered at the din going on behind him. The yells of the Indians, the screams and cries of the provincials, mingled with the sharp crack of rifles or the duller sound of the musket. The work of destruction was soon over. Save his own company and some fifty of the provincials in the boats ahead, the whole of Colonel Parker's force had been killed, or were prisoners in the hands of the Indians, who, having finished their work, set off in pursuit of the boats which had escaped them.

James at once changed the order. The front boat was halted, and the others formed in a line beside it, presenting the broad side to the approaching fleet of canoes. When the latter came within a hundred yards, a stream of fire opened from the boats, the men aiming with the greatest coolness.

The canoes were checked at once. A score of the paddlers had sunk, killed or wounded, into the bottom, and several of the frail barks were upset. As fast as the men could load, they continued their fire, and, in two minutes from the first shot, the canoes were turned, and paddled at full speed towards the shore, pursued by a hearty cheer from the English. The oars were then manned again, and the remains of Parker's flotilla rowed up the lake to Fort William Henry.

Several of the prisoners taken by the Indians were cooked and eaten by them. A few days afterwards a party of Indians, following the route from the head of Lake Champlain, made a sudden attack on the houses round Fort Edward, and killed thirty-two men.

It was an imposing spectacle, as the French expedition made its way down Lake George. General Levis had marched by the side of the lake with twenty-five hundred men, Canadians, regulars, and redskins; while the main body proceeded, the troops in two hundred and fifty large boats, the redskins in many hundreds of their canoes.

The boats moved in military order. There were six regiments of French line: La Reine and Languedoc, La Sarre and Guienne, Bearn and Roussillon. The cannons were carried on platforms formed across two boats. Slowly and regularly the procession of boats made its way down the lake, till they saw the signal fires of Levis, who, with his command, was encamped near the water at a distance of two miles from the fort. Even then, the English were not aware that near eight thousand enemies were gathered close to them. Monro was a brave soldier, but wholly unfitted for the position he held, knowing nothing of irregular warfare, and despising all but trained soldiers.

At daybreak, all was bustle at Fort Henry. Parties of men went out to drive in the cattle, others to destroy buildings which would interfere with the fire from the fort. The English position was now more defensible than it had been when it was attacked in the spring. The forest had been cleared for a considerable distance round, and the buildings which had served as a screen to the enemy had, for the most part, been removed. The fort itself lay close down by the edge of the water. One side and the rear were protected by the marsh, so that it could only be attacked from one side. Beyond the marsh lay the rough ground where Johnson had encamped two years before; while, on a flat hill behind this was an entrenched camp, beyond which, again, was another marsh.

As soon as the sun rose, the column of Levis moved through the forest towards the fort, followed by Montcalm with the main body, while the artillery boats put out from behind the point which had hid them from the sight of the English, and, surrounded by hundreds of Indian canoes, moved slowly forward, opening fire as they went. Soon the sound of firing broke out near the edge of the forest, all round the fort, as the Indians, with Levis, opened fire upon the soldiers who were endeavouring to drive in the cattle.

Hitherto James Walsham, with Edwards and his two scouts, was standing quietly, watching the approaching fleet of boats and canoes; Nat expressing, in no measured terms, his utter disgust at the confusion which reigned in and around the fort.

"It looks more like a frontier settlement suddenly surprised," he said, "than a place filled with soldiers who have been, for weeks, expecting an attack. Nothing done, nothing ready. The cattle all over the place. The tents on that open ground there still standing. Stores all about in the open. Of all the pig-headed, obstinate, ignorant old gentlemen I ever see, the colonel beats them all. One might as well have an old woman in command. Indeed, I know scores of old women, on the frontier, who would have been a deal better here than him."

But if Monro was obstinate and prejudiced, he was brave, cool, and determined, and, now that the danger had come, he felt secure of his ground, and took the proper measures for defence, moving calmly about, and abating the disposition to panic by the calm manner in which he gave his orders. Nat had scarcely finished his grumbling, when the colonel approached.

"Captain Walsham," he said, "you will take your company at once, and cover the parties driving in the cattle. You will fall back with them, and, when you see all in safety, retire into the intrenched camp."

The company were already under arms, waiting for orders and, at the double, James led them up the sloping ground towards the forest, whence the war whoops of the Indians, and the sharp cracks of the rifles, were now ringing out on all sides. James made for the spot where a score of soldiers were driving a number of cattle before them, some hurrying the beasts on across the rough ground, others firing at the Indians, who, as their numbers increased, were boldly showing themselves behind the trees, and advancing in pursuit.

As soon as they neared the spot, James scattered his men in skirmishing order. Each placed himself behind one of the blackened stumps of the roughly-cleared forest, and opened fire upon the Indians. Several of these fell, and the rest bounded back to the forest, whence they opened a heavy fire.

Now the company showed the advantage of the training they had gone through, fighting with the greatest steadiness and coolness, and keeping well in shelter, until, when the soldiers and cattle had got well on their way towards the fort, James gave the order to fall back, and the band, crawling among the stumps, and pausing to fire at every opportunity, made their way back without having lost a man, although several had received slight wounds.

Chapter 16: The Massacre At Fort William Henry.

When the skirmishing round Fort Henry was over, La Corne, with a body of Indians, occupied the road that led to Fort Edward; and Levis encamped close by, to support him, and check any sortie the English might make from their intrenched camp. Montcalm reconnoitred the position. He had, at first, intended to attack and carry the intrenched camp, but he found that it was too strong to be taken by a rush. He therefore determined to attack the fort, itself, by regular approaches from the western side, while the force of Levis would intercept any succour which might come from Fort Edward, and cut off the retreat of the garrison in that direction. He gave orders that the cannon were to be disembarked at a small cove, about half a mile from the fort, and near this he placed his main camp. He now sent one of his aides-de-camp with a letter to Monro.

"I owe it to humanity," he said, "to summon you to surrender. At present I can restrain the savages, and make them observe the terms of a capitulation, but I might not have the power to do so under other circumstances, and an obstinate defence on your part could only retard the capture of the place a few days, and endanger the unfortunate garrison, which cannot be relieved, in consequence of the dispositions I have made. I demand a decisive answer within an hour."

Monro replied simply that he and his soldiers would defend themselves till the last.

The trenches were opened on the night of the 4th. The work was extremely difficult, the ground being covered with hard stumps of trees and fallen trunks. All night long 800 men toiled at the work, while the guns of the fort kept up a constant fire of round shot and grape; but by daybreak the first parallel was made. The battery on the left was nearly finished, and one on the right begun. The men were now working under shelter, and the guns of the fort could do them little harm.

While the French soldiers worked, the Indians crept up through the fallen trees, close to the fort, and fired at any of the garrison who might, for a moment, expose themselves. Sharpshooters in the fort replied to their fire, and all day the fort was fringed with light puffs of smoke, whilst the cannon thundered unceasingly. The next morning, the French battery on the left opened with eight heavy cannon and a mortar, and on the following morning the battery on the right joined in with eleven other pieces.

The fort only mounted, in all, seventeen cannon, for the most part small, and, as some of them were upon the other faces, the English fire, although kept up with spirit, could reply but weakly to that of the French. The fort was composed of embankments of gravel, surmounted by a rampart of heavy logs, laid in tiers, crossing each other, the interstices filled with earth; and this could ill support the heavy cannonade to which it was exposed. The roar of the distant artillery continuing day after day was plainly audible at Fort Edward; but although Monro had, at the commencement of the attack, sent off several messengers asking for reinforcements, Webb did not move.

On the third day of the siege he had received 2000 men from New York, and, by stripping all the forts below, he could have advanced with 4500 men, but some deserters from the French told him that Montcalm had 12,000 men, and Webb considered the task of advancing, through the intervening forests and defiles between him and Fort Henry, far too dangerous an operation to be attempted. Undoubtedly it would have been a dangerous one, for the Indians pervaded the woods as far as Fort Edward. No messenger could have got through to inform Monro of his coming, and Montcalm could therefore have attacked him, on the march, with the greater part of his force. Still, a brave and determined general would have made the attempt. Webb did not do so, but left Monro to his fate.

He even added to its certainty by sending off a letter to him, telling him that he could do nothing to assist him, and advising him to surrender at once. The messenger was killed by the Indians in the forest, and the note taken to Montcalm, who, learning that Webb did not intend to advance, was able to devote his whole attention to the fort. Montcalm kept the letter for several days, till the English rampart was half battered down, and then sent it in by an officer to Monro, hoping that it would induce the latter to surrender. The old soldier, however, remained firm in his determination to hold out, even though his position was now absolutely hopeless. The trenches had been pushed forward until within 250 yards of the fort, and the Indians crept up almost to the wall on this side.

Two sorties were made--one from the fort, the other from the intrenched camp; but both were repulsed with loss. More than 300 of the defenders had been killed and wounded. Smallpox was raging, and the casemates were crowded with sick. All their large cannon had been burst or disabled, and only seven small pieces were fit for service. The French battery in the foremost trench was almost completed, and, when this was done, the whole of Montcalm's thirty-one cannon and fifteen mortars would open fire, and, as a breach had already been effected in the wall, further resistance would have been madness.

On the night of the 8th, it was known in the fort that a council of war would be held in the morning, and that, undoubtedly, the fort would surrender.

James, with his company, had, after escorting the cattle to the fort, crossed the marsh to the intrenched camp, as the fort was already crowded with troops. The company therefore avoided the horrors of the siege. When the report circulated that a surrender would probably be made the next morning, Nat went to James.

"What are you going to do, captain?"

"Do, Nat? Why, I have nothing to do. If Monro and his council decide to surrender, there is an end of it. You don't propose that our company is to fight Montcalm's army alone, do you?"

"No, I don't," Nat said, testily; "there has been a deal too much fighting already. I understand holding out till the last, when there's a hope of somebody coming to relieve you; but what's the use of fighting, and getting a lot of your men killed, and raising the blood of those redskin devils to boiling point? If the colonel had given up the place at once, we should have saved a loss of 300 men, and Montcalm would have been glad enough to let us march off to Fort Edward."

"But probably he will agree to let us do that now," James said.

"He may agree," Nat said, contemptuously; "but how about the redskins? Do you think that, after losing a lot of their braves, they are going to see us march quietly away, and go home without a scalp? I tell you, captain, I know redskin nature, and, as sure as the sun rises tomorrow, there will be a massacre; and I, for one, ain't going to lay down my rifle, and let the first redskin, as takes a fancy to my scalp, tomahawk me."

"Well, but what do you propose, Nat?"

"Well, captain, I have heard you say yours is an independent command, and that you can act with the company wherever you like. While you are here, I know you are under the orders of the colonel; but if you had chosen to march away on any expedition of your own, you could have done it."

"That is so, Nat; but now the siege is once begun, I don't know that I should be justified in marching away, even if I could."

"But they are going to surrender, I tell you," Nat insisted. "I don't see as how it can be your duty to hand over your company to the French, if you can get them clear away, so as to fight for the king again."

"What do you say, Edwards?" James asked his lieutenant.

"I don't see why we shouldn't march away, if we could," Edwards said. "Now that the game is quite lost here, I don't think anyone could blame you for saving the company, if possible, and I agree with Nat that Montcalm will find it difficult, if not impossible, to keep his Indians in hand. The French have never troubled much on that score."

"Well, Nat, what is your plan?" James asked, after a pause.

"The plan is simple enough," Nat said. "There ain't no plan at all. All we have got to do is to march quietly down to the lake, to take some of the canoes that are hauled up at the mouth of the swamp, and to paddle quietly off, keeping under the trees on the right-hand side. There ain't many redskins in the woods that way, and the night is as dark as pitch. We can land eight or ten miles down the lake, and then march away to the right, so as to get clean round the redskins altogether."

"Very well, Nat, I will do it," James said. "It's a chance, but I think it's a better chance than staying here, and if I should get into a row about it, I can't help it. I am doing it for the best."

The corps were quietly mustered, and marched out through the gate of the intrenchments, on the side of the lake. No questions were asked, for the corps had several times gone out on its own account, and driven back the Indians and French pickets. The men had, from their first arrival at the fort, laid aside their heavy boots, and taken to moccasins as being better fitted for silent movement in the forest. Therefore not a sound was heard as, under Nat's guidance, they made their way down the slope into the swamp.

Here they were halted, for the moment, and told to move with the greatest care and silence, and to avoid snapping a bough or twig. This, however, was the less important, as the cannon on both sides were still firing, and a constant rattle of musketry was going on round the fort.

Presently, they reached the point where the canoes were hauled up, and were told off, three to a canoe.

"Follow my canoe in single file," James said. "Not a word is to be spoken, and remember that a single splash of a paddle will bring the redskins down upon us. Likely enough there may be canoes out upon the lake–there are sure to be Indians in the wood."

"I don't think there's much fear, captain," Nat whispered. "There's no tiring a redskin when he's out on the scout on his own account, but when he's acting with the whites he's just as lazy as a hog, and, as they must be sure the fort can't hold out many hours longer, they will be too busy feasting, and counting the scalps they mean to take, to think much about scouting tonight."

"We shall go very slowly. Let every man stop paddling the instant the canoe ahead of him stops," were James's last instructions, as he stepped into the stern of a canoe, while Nat and Jonathan took the paddles. Edwards was to take his place in the last canoe in the line.

Without the slightest sound, the canoes paddled out into the lake, and then made for the east shore. They were soon close to the trees, and, slowly and noiselessly, they kept their way just outside the screen afforded by the boughs drooping down, almost into the water. Only now and then the slightest splash was to be heard along the line, and this might well have been taken for the spring of a tiny fish feeding.

Several times, when he thought he heard a slight sound in the forest on his right, Nat ceased paddling, and lay for some minutes motionless, the canoes behind doing the same. So dark was it, that they could scarce see the trees close beside them, while the bright flashes from the guns from fort and batteries only seemed to make the darkness more intense. It was upwards of an hour before James felt, from the greater speed with which the canoe was travelling, that Nat believed that he had got beyond the spot where any Indians were likely to be watching in the forest.

Faster and faster the boat glided along, but the scouts were still far from rowing their hardest. For, although the whole of the men were accustomed to the use of the paddle, the other boats would be unable to keep up with that driven by the practised arms of the leaders of the file. After paddling for another hour and a half, the scout stopped.

"We are far enough away now," Nat said. "There ain't no chance in the world of any redskins being in the woods, so far out as this. The hope of scalps will have taken them all down close to the fort. We can land safely, now."

The word was passed down the line of canoes, the boats glided through the screen of foliage, and the men landed.

"Better pull the canoes ashore, captain. If we left them in the water, one might break adrift and float out beyond the trees. Some redskin or other would make it out, and we should have a troop of them on our trail, before an hour had passed."

"There's no marching through the forest now, Nat," James said. "I can't see my own hand close to my face."

"That's so, captain, and we'd best halt till daylight. I could make my way along, easy enough, but some of these fellows would be pitching over stumps, or catching their feet in a creeper, and, like enough, letting off their pieces as they went down. We may just as well stay where we are. They ain't likely to miss us, even in the camp, and sartin the redskins can't have known we have gone. So there's no chance whatever of pursuit, and there ain't nothing to be gained by making haste."

James gave the order. The men felt about, till each found a space of ground, sufficiently large to lie down upon, and soon all were asleep except the two scouts, who said, at once, that they would watch by turns till daylight.

As soon as it was sufficiently light to see in the forest, the band were again in motion. They made due east, until they crossed the trail leading from the head of Lake Champlain to Fort Edward; kept on for another hour, and then, turning to the south, made in the direction of Albany, for it would have been dangerous to approach Fort Edward, round which the Indians were sure to be scattered thickly.

For the first two hours after starting, the distant roar of the guns had gone on unceasingly, then it suddenly stopped.

"They have hoisted the white flag," Edwards said. "It is all over. Thank God, we are well out of it! I don't mind fighting, Walsham, but to be massacred by those Indians is a hideous idea."

"I am glad we are out of it too," James agreed; "but I cannot think that Montcalm, with so large a force of French regulars at his command, will allow those fiendish Indians to massacre the prisoners."

"I hope not," Edwards said. "It will be a disgrace indeed to him and his officers if he does; but you know what the Indians are, better than I do, and you have heard Nat's opinion. You see, if Montcalm were to use force against the Indians, the whole of them would go off, and then there would be an end to any hope of the French beating the colonists in the long run. Montcalm daren't break with them. It's a horrible position for an officer and a gentleman to be placed in. Montcalm did manage to prevent the redskins from massacring the garrison of Oswego, but it was as much as he could do, and it will be ten times as difficult, now that their blood is up with this week of hard fighting, and the loss of many of their warriors. Anyhow, I am glad I am out of it, even if the bigwigs consider we had no right to leave the fort, and break us for it. I would rather lose my commission than run the risk of being massacred in cold blood."

James agreed with him.

For two days, they continued their march through the forest, using every precaution against surprise. They saw, however, nothing of the enemy, and emerged from the forest, on the evening of the second day's march, at a distance of a few miles from Albany.

They had not reached that town many hours, when they learned that Nat's sombre predictions had been fulfilled. The council of war in the fort agreed that further resistance was impossible, and Lieutenant Colonel Young went out, with a white flag, to arrange the terms of surrender with Montcalm. It was agreed that the English troops should march out, with the honours of war, and be escorted to Fort Edward by a detachment of French troops; that they should not serve for eighteen months; and that all French prisoners captured in America, since the war began, should be given up within three months. The stores, ammunition, and artillery were to be handed over to the French, except one field piece, which the garrison were to be allowed to retain, in recognition of their brave defence.

Before signing the capitulation, Montcalm summoned the Indian chiefs before him, and asked them to consent to the conditions, and to restrain their young braves from any disorder. They gave their approval, and promised to maintain order.

The garrison then evacuated the fort, and marched to join their comrades in the intrenched camp. No sooner had they moved out, than a crowd of Indians rushed into the fort through the breach and embrasures, and butchered all the wounded who had been left behind to be cared for by the French. Having committed this atrocity the Indians, and many of the Canadians, rushed up to the intrenched camp, where the English were now collected. The French guards, who had been stationed there, did nothing to keep them out; and they wandered about, threatening and insulting the terrified women, telling the men that everyone should be massacred, and plundering the baggage.

Montcalm did his best, by entreaty, to restrain the Indians, but he took no steps whatever to give effectual protection to the prisoners, and that he did not do so will remain an ineffaceable blot upon his fame. Seeing the disposition of the redskins, he should have ordered up all the regular French troops, and marched the English garrison under their protection to Fort Edward, in accordance with the terms of surrender; and he should have allowed the English troops to again fill their pouches with cartridge, by which means they would have been able to fight in their own defence.

The next morning, the English marched at daybreak. Seventeen wounded men were left behind in the huts, having been, in accordance with the agreement, handed over to the charge of a French surgeon; but as he was not there in the morning, the regimental surgeon, Miles Whitworth, remained with them attending to their wants. The French surgeon had caused special sentinels to be placed for their protection, but these were now removed, when they were needed most.

At five in the morning the Indians entered the huts, dragged out the inmates, tomahawked and scalped them before the eyes of Whitworth, and in the presence of La Corne and other Canadian officers, as well as of a French guard stationed within forty feet of the spot–none of whom, as Whitworth declared on oath, did anything to protect the wounded men.

The Indians, in the meantime, had begun to plunder the baggage of the column. Monro complained, to the officers of the French escort, that the terms of the capitulation were broken; but the only answer was that he had better give up all the baggage to the Indians, to appease them. But it had no effect in restraining the passion of the Indians. They rushed upon the column, snatching caps, coats, and weapons from men and officers, tomahawking all who resisted, and, seizing upon shrieking women and children, carried them away or murdered them on the spot. A rush was made upon the New Hampshire men, at the rear of the column, and eighty of them were killed or carried away.

The Canadian officers did nothing at all to try to assuage the fury of the Indians, and the officers of the Canadian detachment, which formed the advance guard of the French escort, refused any protection to the men, telling them they had better take to the woods and shift for themselves. Montcalm, and the principal French officers, did everything short of the only effectual step, namely, the ordering up of the French regular troops to save the English. They ran about among the yelling Indians, imploring them to desist, but in vain.

Some seven or eight hundred of the English were seized and carried off by the savages, while some seventy or eighty were massacred on the spot. The column attempted no resistance. None had ammunition, and, of the colonial troops, very few were armed with bayonets. Had any resistance been offered, there can be no doubt all would have been massacred by the Indians.

Many of the fugitives ran back to the fort, and took refuge there, and Montcalm recovered from the Indians more than four hundred of those they had carried off. These were all sent under a strong guard to Fort Edward. The greater part of the survivors of the column dispersed into the woods, and made their way in scattered parties to Fort Edward. Here cannon had been fired at intervals, to serve as a guide to the fugitives, but many, no doubt, perished in the woods. On the morning after the massacre the Indians left in a body for Montreal, taking with them two hundred prisoners, to be tortured and murdered on their return to their villages.

Few events cast a deeper disgrace on the arms of France than this massacre, committed in defiance of their pledged honour for the safety of their prisoners, and in sight of four thousand French troops, not a man of whom was set in motion to prevent it. These facts are not taken only from English sources, but from the letters of French officers, and from the journal of the Jesuit Roubaud, who was in charge of the Christianized Indians, who, according to his own account, were no less ferocious and cruel than the unconverted tribes. The number of those who perished in the massacre is uncertain. Captain Jonathan Carver, a colonial officer, puts the killed and captured at 1500. A French writer, whose work was published at Montreal, says that they were all killed, except seven hundred who were captured; but this is, of course, a gross exaggeration. General Levis and Roubaud, who were certain to have made the best of the matter, acknowledged that they saw some fifty corpses scattered on the ground, but this does not include those murdered in the fort and camp.

Probably the total number killed was about two hundred, and besides these must be counted the two hundred prisoners carried off to be tortured by the Indians. The greater portion of these were purchased from the Indians, in exchange for rum, by Vaudreuil, the governor at Montreal; but to the eternal disgrace of this man, he suffered many of them to be carried off, and did not even interfere when, publicly, in the sight of the whole town, the Indians murdered some of the prisoners, and, not content with eating them themselves, forced their comrades to partake of the flesh. Bougainville, one of the aides-de-camp of Montcalm, was present, and testified to the fact, and the story is confirmed by the intendant Bigot, a friend of the governor.

The ferocity of the Indians cost them dear. They had dug up and scalped the corpses in the graveyard of Fort William Henry. Many of these had died of smallpox, and the savages took the infection home to their villages, where great numbers perished of the disease.

As soon as their Indian allies had left, the French soldiers were set to work demolishing the English fort, and the operation was completed by the destruction, by fire, of the remains. The army then returned to Crown Point.

In view of the gross breach of the articles of capitulation by the French, the English government refused also to be bound by it, and the French prisoners in their hands were accordingly retained.

Colonel Monro himself was one of those who survived. He had made his way through the savages back to the fort, to demand that the protection of the French troops should be given to the soldiers, and so escaped the massacre.

Upon his arrival at Albany, James reported, to the officer in command there, the reason which had induced him to quit the fort with his company. These reasons were approved of, but the officer advised James to send in a written report to General Webb, and to march at once to Fort Edward, and place himself under that officer's directions.

When he reached the fort, the fugitives were coming in from the woods. James at once reported himself to the general, and handed in his written statement. At the same time he gave his reasons, in a few words, for the course he had taken. Webb was far too much excited by the news of the terrible events which had taken place, and for which, as he could not but be aware, he would be to some extent held responsible, by public opinion, for having refused to move to Monro's assistance, to pay much attention to the young officer's statement.

"You were quite right, sir, quite right to carry off your command," he said hastily. "Thank God there are so many the fewer of his majesty's troops sacrificed! You will please take your company out at once into the woods. They are accustomed to the work, which is more than any of my troops here are. Divide them into four parties, and let them scour the forest, and bring in such of the fugitives as they can find. Let them take as much provisions and rum as they can carry, for many of the fugitives will be starving."

James executed his orders, and, during the next five days, sent in a considerable number of exhausted men, who, hopelessly lost in the woods, must have perished unless they had been discovered by his party.

Had Montcalm marched direct upon Fort Edward, he could doubtless have captured it, for the fall of Fort William Henry had so scared Webb, that he would probably have retreated the moment he heard the news of Montcalm's advance, although, within a day or two of the fall of the fort, many thousands of colonial militia had arrived. As soon, however, as it was known that Montcalm had retired, the militia, who were altogether unsupplied with the means of keeping the field, returned to their homes.

Loudon, on his way back from the unsuccessful expedition against Louisbourg, received the news of the calamity at Fort William Henry. He returned too late to do anything to retrieve that disaster, and determined, in the spring, to take the offensive by attacking Ticonderoga. This had been left, on the retirement of Montcalm, with a small garrison commanded by Captain Hepecourt, who, during the winter, was continually harassed by the corps of Captain Rogers, and James Walsham's scouts.

Toward the spring, receiving reinforcements, Hepecourt caught Rogers and a hundred and eighty men in an ambush, and killed almost all of them; Rogers himself, and some twenty or thirty men, alone escaping.

In the spring there was a fresh change of plans. The expedition against Ticonderoga was given up, as another attempt at Louisbourg was about to be made. The English government were determined that the disastrous delays, which had caused the failure of the last expedition, should not be repeated. Loudon was recalled, and to General Abercromby, the second in command, was intrusted the charge of the forces in the colonies. Colonel Amherst was raised to the rank of major general, and appointed to command the expedition from England against Louisbourg, having under him Brigadier Generals Whitmore, Lawrence, and Wolfe. Before the winter was ended two fleets put to sea: the one, under Admiral Boscawen, was destined for Louisbourg; while the other, under Admiral Osborne, sailed for the Straits of Gibraltar, to intercept the French fleet of Admiral La Clue, which was about to sail from Toulon for America.

At the same time Sir Edward Hawke, with seven ships of the line and three frigates, sailed for Rochefort, where a French squadron with a fleet of transports, with troops for America, were lying.

The two latter expeditions were perfectly successful. Osborne prevented La Clue from leaving the Mediterranean. Hawke drove the enemy's vessels ashore at Rochefort, and completely broke up the expedition. Thus Canada, at the critical period, when the English were preparing to strike a great blow at her, was cut off from all assistance from the mother country, and left to her own resources.

As before, Halifax was the spot where the troops from the colonies were to meet the fleet from England, and the troops who came out under their convoy, and here, on the 28th of May, the whole expedition was collected. The colonies had again been partially stripped of their defenders, and five hundred provincial rangers accompanied the regulars. James Walsham's corps was left for service on the frontier, while the regiments, to which they belonged, sailed with the force destined for the siege of Louisbourg.

This fortress stood, at the mouth of a land-locked bay, on the stormy coast of Cape Breton. Since the peace of Aix la Chapelle, vast sums had been spent in repairing and strengthening it, and it was, by far, the strongest fortress in English or French America. The circuit of its fortifications was more than a mile and a half, and the town contained about four thousand inhabitants. The garrison consisted of the battalions of Artois, Bourgogne, Cambis, and Volontaires Etrangers, with two companies of artillery, and twenty-four of colonial troops; in all, three thousand and eighty men, besides officers. In the harbour lay five ships of the line and seven frigates, carrying five hundred and forty-four guns, and about three thousand men, and there were two hundred and nineteen cannons and seventeen mortars mounted on the ramparts and outworks, and forty-four in reserve.

Of the outworks, the strongest were the grand battery at Lighthouse Point, at the mouth of the harbour; and that on Goat Island, a rocky islet at its entrance. The strongest front of the works was on the land side, across the base of the triangular peninsula on which the town stood. This front, twelve hundred yards in extent, reached from the sea, on the left, to the harbour on the right, and consisted of four strong bastions with connecting works.

The best defence of Louisbourg, however, was the craggy shore, which, for leagues on either side, was accessible only at a few points, and, even there, a landing could only be effected with the greatest difficulty. All these points were watched, for an English squadron, of nine ships of war, had been cruising off the place, endeavouring to prevent supplies from arriving; but they had been so often blown off, by gales, that the French ships had been able to enter, and, on the 2nd of June, when the English expedition came in sight, more than a year's supply of provisions was stored up in the town.

Chapter 17: Louisbourg And Ticonderoga.

All eyes in the fleet were directed towards the rocky shore of Gabarus Bay, a flat indentation some three miles across, its eastern extremity, White Point, being a mile to the west of Louisbourg. The sea was rough, and the white masses of surf were thrown high up upon the face of the rock, along the coast, as far as the eye could reach.

A more difficult coast on which to effect a landing could not have been selected. There were but three points where boats could, even in fine weather, get to shore--namely, White Point, Flat Point, and Fresh Water Cove. To cover these, the French had erected several batteries, and, as soon as the English fleet was in sight, they made vigorous preparations to repel a landing.

Boats were at once lowered, in order to make a reconnaissance of the shore. Generals Amherst, Lawrence, and Wolfe all took part in it, and a number of naval officers, in their boats, daringly approached the shore to almost within musket shot. When they returned, in the afternoon, they made their reports to the admiral, and these reports all agreed with his own opinion–namely, that there was but little chance of success. One naval captain alone, an old officer named Fergusson, advised the admiral to hold no council of war, but to take the responsibility on himself, and to make the attempt at all risks.

"Why, admiral," he said, "the very children at home would laugh at us, if, for a second time, we sailed here with an army, and then sailed away again without landing a man."

"So they would, Fergusson, so they would," the admiral said. "If I have to stop here till winter, I won't go till I have carried out my orders, and put the troops ashore."

In addition to the three possible landing places already named, was one to the east of the town named Lorambec, and it was determined to send a regiment to threaten a landing at this place, while the army, formed into three divisions, were to threaten the other points, and effect a landing at one or all of them, if it should be found possible.

On the next day, however, the 3rd of June, the surf was so high that nothing could be attempted. On the 4th there was a thick fog and a gale, and the frigate Trent struck on a rock, and some of the transports were nearly blown on shore. The sea was very heavy, and the vessels rolled tremendously at their anchors. Most of the troops suffered terribly from seasickness.

The next day, the weather continued thick and stormy. On the 6th there was fog, but towards noon the wind went down, whereupon the signal was made, the boats were lowered, and the troops took their places in them. Scarcely had they done so, when the wind rose again, and the sea got up so rapidly that the landing was postponed.

The next day the fog and heavy surf continued, but in the evening the sea grew calmer, and orders were issued for the troops to take to the boats, at two o'clock next morning. This was done, and the frigates got under sail, and steered for the four points at which the real or pretended attacks were to be made, and, anchoring within easy range, opened fire soon after daylight; while the boats, in three divisions, rowed towards the shore.

The division under Wolfe consisted of twelve companies of Grenadiers, with the Light infantry, Fraser's Highlanders, and the New England Rangers. Fresh Water Cove was a crescent-shaped beach a quarter of a mile long, with rocks at each end. On the shore above lay 1000 Frenchmen under Lieutenant Colonel de Saint Julien, with eight cannons, on swivels, planted to sweep every part of the beach. The intrenchments, behind which the troops were lying, were covered in front by spruce and fir trees, felled and laid on the ground with the tops outward.

Not a shot was fired until the English boats approached the beach, then, from behind the leafy screen, a deadly storm of grape and musketry was poured upon them. It was clear at once that to advance would be destruction, and Wolfe waved his hand as a signal to the boats to sheer off.

On the right of the line, and but little exposed to the fire, were three boats of the Light Infantry under Lieutenants Hopkins and Brown, and Ensign Grant, who, mistaking the signal, or wilfully misinterpreting it, dashed for the shore directly before them. It was a hundred yards or so east of the beach–a craggy coast, lashed by the breakers, but sheltered from the cannon by a small projecting point.

The three young officers leapt ashore, followed by their men. Major Scott, who commanded the Light Infantry and Rangers, was in the next boat, and at once followed the others, putting his boat's head straight to the shore. The boat was crushed to pieces against the rocks. Some of the men were drowned, but the rest scrambled up the rocks, and joined those who had first landed. They were instantly attacked by the French, and half of the little party were killed or wounded before the rest of the division could come to their assistance.

Some of the boats were upset, and others stove in, but most of the men scrambled ashore, and, as soon as he landed, Wolfe led them up the rocks, where they formed in compact order and carried, with the bayonet, the nearest French battery.

The other divisions, seeing that Wolfe had effected a landing, came rapidly up, and, as the French attention was now distracted by Wolfe's attack on the left, Amherst and Lawrence were able to land at the other end of the beach, and, with their divisions, attacked the French on the right.

These, assaulted on both sides, and fearing to be cut off from the town, abandoned their cannon and fled into the woods. Some seventy of them were taken prisoners, and fifty killed. The rest made their way through the woods and marshes to Louisbourg, and the French in the other batteries commanding the landing places, seeing that the English were now firmly established on the shore, also abandoned the positions, and retreated to the town.

General Amherst established the English camp just beyond the range of the cannon on the ramparts, and the fleet set to work to land guns and stores at Flat Point Cove. For some days this work went on; but so violent was the surf, that more than a hundred boats were stove in in accomplishing it, and none of the siege guns could be landed till the 18th. While the sailors were so engaged, the troops were busy making roads and throwing up redoubts to protect their position.

Wolfe, with 1200 men, made his way right round the harbour, and took possession of the battery at Lighthouse Point which the French had abandoned; planted guns and mortars there, and opened fire on the battery on the islet which guarded the entrance to the harbour; while other batteries were raised, at different points along the shore, and opened fire upon the French ships. These replied, and the artillery duel went on night and day, until, on the 25th, the battery on the islet was silenced. Leaving a portion of his force in the batteries he had erected, Wolfe returned to the main army in front of the town.

In the meantime, Amherst had not been idle. Day and night a thousand men had been employed, making a covered road across a swamp to a hillock less than half a mile from the ramparts. The labour was immense, and the troops worked knee deep in mud and water.

When Wolfe had silenced the battery on the islet, the way was open for the English fleet to enter and engage the ships and town from the harbour, but the French took advantage of a dark and foggy night, and sank six ships across the entrance.

On the 25th, the troops had made the road to the hillock, and began to fortify themselves there, under a heavy fire from the French; while on the left, towards the sea, about a third of a mile from the Princess's Bastion, Wolfe, with a strong detachment, began to throw up a redoubt.

On the night of the 9th of July, 600 French troops sallied out and attacked this work. The English, though fighting desperately, were for a time driven back; but, being reinforced, they drove the French back into the town.

Each day the English lines drew closer to the town. The French frigate Echo, under cover of a fog, had been sent to Quebec for aid, but she was chased and captured. The frigate Arethuse, on the night of the 14th of July, was towed through the obstructions at the mouth of the harbour, and, passing through the English ships in a fog, succeeded in getting away. Only five vessels of the French fleet now remained in the harbour, and these were but feebly manned, as 2000 of the officers and seamen had landed, and were encamped in the town.

On the afternoon of the 16th a party of English, led by Wolfe, suddenly dashed forward, and, driving back a company of French, seized some rising ground within three hundred yards of the ramparts, and began to intrench themselves there. All night, the French kept up a furious fire at the spot, but, by morning, the English had completed their intrenchment, and from this point pushed on, until they had reached the foot of the glacis.

On the 21st, the French man of war Celebre was set on fire by the explosion of a shell. The wind blew the flames into the rigging of two of her consorts, and these also caught fire, and the three ships burned to the water's edge. Several fires were occasioned in the town, and the English guns, of which a great number were now in position, kept up a storm of fire night and day.

On the night of the 23rd, six hundred English sailors silently rowed into the harbour, cut the cables of the two remaining French men of war, and tried to tow them out. One, however, was aground, for the tide was low. The sailors therefore set her on fire, and then towed her consort out of the harbour, amidst a storm of shot and shell from the French batteries.

The French position was now desperate. Only four cannon, on the side facing the English batteries, were fit for service. The masonry of the ramparts was shaken, and the breaches were almost complete. A fourth of the garrison were in hospital, and the rest were worn out by toil. Every house in the place was shattered by the English artillery, and there was no shelter either for the troops or the inhabitants.

On the 26th, the last French cannon was silenced, and a breach effected in the wall; and the French, unable longer to resist, hung out the white flag. They attempted to obtain favourable conditions, but Boscawen and Amherst insisted upon absolute surrender, and the French, wholly unable to resist further, accepted the terms.

Thus fell the great French stronghold on Cape Breton. The defence had been a most gallant one; and Drucour, the governor, although he could not save the fortress, had yet delayed the English so long before the walls, that it was too late in the season, now, to attempt an attack on Canada itself.

Wolfe, indeed, urged that an expedition should at once be sent against Quebec, but Boscawen was opposed to this, owing to the lateness of the season, and Amherst was too slow and deliberate, by nature, to determine suddenly on the enterprise. He, however, sailed with six regiments for Boston, to reinforce Abercromby at Lake George.

Wolfe carried out the orders of the general, to destroy the French settlements on the Gulf of Saint Lawrence–a task most repugnant to his humane nature. After this had been accomplished, he sailed for England.

When Amherst had sailed with his expedition to the attack of Louisbourg, he had not left the colonists in so unprotected a state as they had been in the preceding year. They, on their part, responded nobly to the call, from England, that a large force should be put in the field. The home government had promised to supply arms, ammunition, tents, and provisions, and to make a grant towards the pay and clothing of the soldiers.

Massachusetts, as usual, responded most freely and loyally to the demand. She had already incurred a very heavy debt by her efforts in the war, and had supplied 2500 men–a portion of whom had gone with Amherst–but she now raised 7000 more, whom she paid, maintained, and clothed out of her own resources, thus placing in the field one-fourth of her able-bodied men. Connecticut made equal sacrifices, although less exposed to danger of invasion; while New Hampshire sent out one-third of her able-bodied men.

In June the combined British and provincial force, under Abercromby, gathered on the site of Fort William Henry. The force consisted of 6367 officers and soldiers of the regular army, and 9054 colonial troops.

Abercromby himself was an infirm and incapable man, who owed his position to political influence. The real command was in the hands of Brigadier General Lord Howe–a most energetic and able officer, who had, during the past year, thoroughly studied forest warfare, and had made several expeditions with the scouting parties of Rogers and other frontier leaders. He was a strict disciplinarian, but threw aside all the trammels of the traditions of the service. He made both officers and men dress in accordance with the work they had before them. All had to cut their hair close, to wear leggings to protect them from the briars, and to carry in their knapsacks thirty pounds of meal, which each man had to cook for himself. The coats, of both the Regulars and Provincials, were cut short at the waist, and no officer or private was allowed to carry more than one blanket and a bear skin.

Howe himself lived as simply and roughly as his men. The soldiers were devoted to their young commander, and were ready to follow him to the death.

"That's something like a man for a general," Nat said enthusiastically, as he marched, with the Royal Scouts, past the spot where Lord Howe was sitting on the ground, eating his dinner with a pocket knife.

"I have never had much hope of doing anything, before, with the regulars in the forest, but I do think, this time, we have got a chance of licking the French. What do you say, captain?"

"It looks more hopeful, Nat, certainly. Under Loudon and Webb things did not look very bright, but this is a different sort of general altogether."

On the evening of the 4th of July baggage, stores, and ammunition were all on board the boats, and the whole army embarked at daybreak on the 5th. It was indeed a magnificent sight, as the flotilla started. It consisted of 900 troop boats, 135 whale boats, and a large number of heavy flatboats carrying the artillery. They were in three divisions, the regulars in the centre, the provincial troops on either flank.

Each corps had its flags and its music, the day was fair and bright, and, as the flotilla swept on past the verdure-clad hills, with the sun shining brilliantly down on the bright uniforms and gay flags, on the flash of oars and the glitter of weapons, a fairer sight was seldom witnessed.

At five in the afternoon, they reached Sabbath Day Point, twenty-five miles down the lake, where they halted some time for the baggage and artillery. At eleven o'clock they started again, and by daybreak were nearing the outlet of the lake.

An advanced party of the French were watching their movements, and a detachment was seen, near the shore, at the spot where the French had embarked on the previous year. The companies of Rogers and James Walsham landed, and drove them off, and by noon the whole army was on shore.

The troops started in four columns, but so dense was the forest, so obstructed with undergrowth, that they could scarcely make their way, and, after a time, even the guides became confused in the labyrinth of trunks and boughs, and the four columns insensibly drew near to each other.

Curiously, the French advanced party, 350 strong, who had tried to retreat, also became lost in the wood, and, not knowing where the English were, in their wanderings again approached them. As they did so Lord Howe, who, with Major Putnam, and 200 rangers and scouts, was at the head of the principal column, suddenly came upon them. A skirmish followed. Scarcely had it begun when Lord Howe dropped dead, shot through the breast. For a moment, something like a panic seized the army, who believed that they had fallen into an ambush, and that Montcalm's whole force was upon them. The rangers, however, fought steadily, until Rogers' Rangers and the Royal Scouts, who were out in front, came back and took the French in the rear. Only about 50 of these escaped, 148 were captured, and the rest killed or drowned in endeavouring to cross the rapids.

The loss of the English was small in numbers, but the death of Howe inflicted an irreparable blow upon the army. As Major Mante, who was present, wrote:

"In Lord Howe, the soul of General Abercromby's army seemed to expire. From the unhappy moment that the general was deprived of his advice, neither order nor discipline was observed, and a strange kind of infatuation usurped the place of resolution."

The loss of its gallant young general was, indeed, the destruction of an army of 15,000 men. Abercromby seemed paralysed by the stroke, and could do nothing, and the soldiers were needlessly kept under arms all night in the forest, and, in the morning, were ordered back to the landing place.

At noon, however, Bradstreet was sent out to take possession of the sawmill, at the falls which Montcalm had abandoned the evening before. Bradstreet rebuilt the two bridges, which had been destroyed by the enemy, and the army then advanced, and in the evening occupied the deserted encampment of the French.

Montcalm had, for some days, been indecisive as to his course. His force was little more than a fourth of that of the advancing foe. He had, for some time, been aware of the storm which was preparing against him. Vaudreuil, the governor, had at first intended to send a body of Canadians and Indians, under General Levis, down the valley of the Mohawk to create a diversion, but this scheme had been abandoned, and, instead of sending Levis, with his command, to the assistance of Montcalm, he had kept them doing nothing at Montreal.

Just about the hour Lord Howe was killed, Montcalm fell back with his force from his position by the falls, and resolved to make a stand at the base of the peninsula on which Ticonderoga stands. The outline of the works had already been traced, and the soldiers of the battalion of Berry had made some progress in constructing them. At daybreak, just as Abercromby was drawing his troops back to the landing place, Montcalm's whole army set to work. Thousands of trees were hewn down, and the trunks piled one upon another, so as to form a massive breastwork. The line followed the top of the ridge, with many zigzags, so that the whole front could be swept by a fire of musketry and grape. The log wall was eight or nine feet high, and the upper tier was formed of single logs, in which notches were cut to serve as loopholes. The whole space in front was cleared of trees, for the distance of a musket shot, the trees being felled so that their tops turned outwards, forming an almost impenetrable obstacle, while, immediately in front of the log wall, the ground was covered with heavy boughs, overlapping and interlaced, their points being sharpened. This position was, in fact, absolutely impregnable against an attack, in front, by infantry.

It was true that Abercromby might have brought up his artillery, and battered down the breastwork, or he might have planted a battery on the heights which commanded the position, or he might have marched a portion of his army through the woods, and placed them on the road between Ticonderoga and Crown Point, and so have cut off the whole French army, and forced them to surrender, for they had but eight days' provisions. But Howe was dead, there was no longer leading or generalship, and Abercromby, leaving his cannon behind him, marched his army to make a direct attack on the French intrenchment.

In the course of the night Levis, with 400 of his men, arrived, and the French were in readiness for the attack. The battalions of La Sarre and Languedoc were posted on the left under Bourlamaque, Berry and Royal Roussillon in the centre under Montcalm, La Reine, Beam, and Guienne on the right under Levis. A detachment of volunteers occupied the low ground between the breastwork and the outlet of Lake George, while 450 Canadian troops held an abattis on the side towards Lake Champlain, where they were covered by the guns of the fort.

Until noon, the French worked unceasingly to strengthen their position, then a heavy fire broke out in front, as the rangers and light infantry drove in their pickets. As soon as the English issued from the wood, they opened fire, and then the regulars, formed in columns of attack, pushed forward across the rough ground with its maze of fallen trees. They could see the top of the breastwork, but not the men behind it, and as soon as they were fairly entangled in the trees, a terrific fire opened upon them. The English pushed up close to the breastwork, but they could not pass the bristling mass of sharpened branches, which were swept by a terrific crossfire from the intrenchment. After striving for an hour, they fell back. Abercromby, who had remained at the mill a mile and a half in the rear, sent orders for them to attack again.

Never did the English fight with greater bravery. Six times did they advance to the attack, but the task set them was impossible. At five in the afternoon, two English columns made an assault on the extreme right of the French, and, although Montcalm hastened to the spot with his reserves, they nearly succeeded in breaking through, hewing their way right to the very foot of the breastwork, and renewing the attack over and over again, the Highland regiment, which led the column, fighting with desperate valour, and not retiring until its major and twenty-five of the officers were killed or wounded, and half the men had fallen under the deadly fire.

At six o'clock another desperate attempt was made, but in vain; then the regulars fell back in disorder, but, for an hour and a half, the provincials and rangers kept up a fire, while their comrades removed the wounded. Abercromby had lost in killed, wounded, and missing 1944 officers and men, while the loss of the French was 377.

Even now, Abercromby might have retrieved his repulse, for, with 13,000 men still remaining, against 3300 unwounded Frenchmen, he could still have easily forced them to surrender, by planting cannons on the heights, or by cutting off their communication and food.

He did neither, but, at daybreak, re-embarked his army, and retired with all speed down the lake. Montcalm soon received large reinforcements, and sent out scouting parties. One of these caught a party commanded by Captain Rogers in an ambush, but were finally driven back, with such heavy loss that, from that time, few scouting parties were sent out from Ticonderoga.

In October, Montcalm, with the main portion of his army, retired for the winter to Montreal; while the English fell back to Albany.

While Abercromby was lying inactive at the head of Lake George, Brigadier General Forbes had advanced from Virginia against Fort Duquesne, and, after immense labour and hardships, succeeded in arriving at the fort, which the French evacuated at his approach, having burnt the barracks and storehouses, and blown up the fortifications. A stockade was formed, and a fort afterwards built there. This was called Fort Pitt, and the place itself, Pittsburg. A small garrison was left there, and the army, after having collected and buried the bones of Braddock's men, retired to Virginia. The general, who, though suffering terribly from disease, had steadfastly carried out the enterprise in the face of enormous difficulties, died shortly after the force returned to the settlements.

Another successful enterprise, during the autumn, had been the capture of Fort Frontenac, and the gaining of a foothold by the English on Lake Ontario.

Thus, the campaign of 1758 was, on the whole, disastrous to the French. They had held their own triumphantly at Ticonderoga, but they had lost their great fortress of Louisbourg, their right had been forced back by the capture of Fort Duquesne, and their line of communication cut by the destruction of Fort Frontenac.

Chapter 18: Quebec.
In the following spring, the French prepared to resist the serious attack which they expected would be made by way of Lake Champlain and Ontario. But a greater danger was threatening them, for, in the midst of their preparations, the news arrived from France that a great fleet was on its way, from England, to attack Quebec. The town was filled with consternation and surprise, for the Canadians had believed that the

navigation of the Saint Lawrence was too difficult and dangerous for any hostile fleet to attempt. Their spirits rose however when, a few days later, a fleet of twenty-three ships, ladened with supplies from France, sailed up the river.

A day or two later, the British fleet was at the mouth of the Saint Lawrence, and the whole forces of the colony, except three battalions posted at Ticonderoga, and a strong detachment placed so as to resist any hostile movement from Lake Ontario, were mustered at Quebec. Here were gathered five French battalions, the whole of the Canadian troops and militia, and upwards of a thousand Indians, in all amounting to more than sixteen thousand.

The position was an extremely strong one. The main force was encamped on the high ground below Quebec, with their right resting on the Saint Charles River, and the left on the Montmorenci, a distance of between seven and eight miles. The front was covered by steep ground, which rose nearly from the edge of the Saint Lawrence, and the right was covered by the guns of the citadel of Quebec. A boom of logs, chained together, was laid across the mouth of the Saint Charles, which was further guarded by two hulks mounted with cannon. A bridge of boats, crossing the river a mile higher up, connected the city with the camp.

All the gates of Quebec, except that of Saint Charles, which faced the bridge, were closed and barricaded. A hundred and six cannon were mounted on the walls, while a floating battery of twelve heavy pieces, a number of gunboats, and eight fire ships formed the river defences.

The frigates, which had convoyed the merchant fleet, were taken higher up the river, and a thousand of their seamen came down, from Quebec, to man the batteries and gunboats.

Against this force of sixteen thousand men, posted behind defensive works, on a position almost impregnable by nature, General Wolfe was bringing less than nine thousand troops. The steep and lofty heights, that lined the river, rendered the cannon of the ships useless to him, and the exigencies of the fleet, in such narrow and difficult navigation, prevented the sailors being landed to assist the troops.

A large portion of Montcalm's army, indeed, consisted of Canadians, who were of little use in the open field, but could be trusted to fight well behind intrenchments.

Wolfe was, unfortunately, in extremely bad health when he was selected, by Pitt, to command the expedition against Quebec; but under him were Brigadier Generals Monckton, Townshend, and Murray, all good officers.

The fleet consisted of twenty-two ships of war, with frigates and sloops, and a great number of transports. It was, at first, divided into three squadrons. That under Admiral Durell sailed direct for the Saint Lawrence, to intercept the ships from France, but arrived at its destination a few days too late. That of Admiral Holmes sailed for New York, to take on board a portion of the army of Amherst and Abercromby. That of Admiral Saunders sailed to Louisbourg, but, finding the entrance blocked with ice, went on to Halifax, where it was joined by the squadron with the troops from New York. They then sailed again to Louisbourg, where they remained until the 6th of June, 1759, and then joined Durell at the mouth of the Saint Lawrence.

Wolfe's force had been intended to be larger, and should have amounted to fourteen thousand men; but some regiments which were to have joined him from the West

Indies were, at the last moment, countermanded, and Amherst, who no doubt felt some jealousy, at the command of this important expedition being given to an officer who had served under his orders at the taking of Louisbourg, sent a smaller contingent of troops than had been expected.

Among the regiments which sailed was that of James Walsham. After the fight at Ticonderoga, in which upwards of half of his force had fallen, the little corps had been broken up, and the men had returned to duty with their regiments. Owing to the number of officers who had fallen, James now stood high on the list of lieutenants. He had had enough of scouting, and was glad to return to the regiment, his principal regret being that he had to part from his two trusty scouts.

There was great joy, in the regiment, when the news was received that they were to go with the expedition against Quebec. They had formed part of Wolf"s division at Louisbourg, and, like all who had served with him, regarded with enthusiasm and confidence the leader whose frail body seemed wholly incapable of sustaining fatigue or hardship, but whose indomitable spirit and courage placed him ever in the front, and set an example which the bravest of his followers were proud to imitate.

From time to time, James had received letters from home. Communication was irregular; but his mother and Mr. Wilks wrote frequently, and sometimes he received half a dozen letters at once. He had now been absent from home for four years, and his mother told him that he would scarcely recognize Aggie, who was now as tall as herself. Mrs. Walsham said that the girl was almost as interested as she was in his letters, and in the despatches from the war, in which his name had several times been mentioned, in connection with the services rendered by his scouts.

Richard Horton had twice, during James's absence, returned home. The squire, Mrs. Walsham said, had received him very coolly, in consequence of the letter he had written when James was pressed as a seaman, and she said that Aggie seemed to have taken a great objection to him. She wondered, indeed, that he could stay an hour in the house after his reception there; but he seemed as if he didn't notice it, and took especial pains to try and overcome Aggie's feeling against him.

While waiting at the mouth of the Saint Lawrence, Admiral Durell had succeeded in obtaining pilots to take the fleet up the river. He had sailed up the river to the point where the difficult navigation began, and where vessels generally took on board river pilots. Here he hoisted the French flag at the masthead, and the pilots, believing the ships to be a French squadron, which had eluded the watch of the English, came off in their boats, and were all taken prisoners, and forced, under pain of death, to take the English vessels safely up.

The first difficulty of the passage was at Cape Tourmente, where the channel describes a complete zigzag. Had the French planted some guns on a plateau, high up on the side of the mountains, they could have done great damage by a plunging fire; but Vaudreuil had neglected to take this measure, and the fleet passed up in safety, the manner in which they were handled and navigated astonishing the Canadians, who had believed it to be impossible that large ships could be taken up.

On the 26th, the whole fleet were anchored off the Island of Orleans, a few miles below Quebec. The same night, a small party landed on the island. They were opposed by the armed inhabitants, but beat them off, and, during the night, the Canadians crossed to the north shore. The whole army then landed.

From the end of the island, Wolfe could see the full strength of the position which he had come to attack. Three or four miles in front of him, the town of Quebec stood upon its elevated rock. Beyond rose the loftier height of Cape Diamond, with its redoubts and parapets. Three great batteries looked threateningly from the upper rock of Quebec, while three others were placed, near the edge of the water, in the lower town. On the right was the great camp of Montcalm, stretching from the Saint Charles, at the foot of the city walls, to the gorge of the Montmorenci. From the latter point to the village of Beauport, in the centre of the camp, the front was covered with earthworks, along the brink of a lofty height; and from Beauport to the Saint Charles were broad flats of mud, swept by the fire of redoubts and intrenchments, by the guns of a floating battery, and by those of the city itself.

Wolfe could not see beyond Quebec, but, above the city, the position was even stronger than below. The river was walled by a range of steeps, often inaccessible, and always so difficult that a few men could hold an army in check.

Montcalm was perfectly confident of his ability to resist any attack which the British might make. Bougainville had long before examined the position, in view of the possibility of an English expedition against it, and reported that, with a few intrenchments, the city would be safe if defended by three or four thousand men. Sixteen thousand were now gathered there, and Montcalm might well believe the position to be impregnable.

He was determined to run no risk, by advancing to give battle, but to remain upon the defensive till the resources of the English were exhausted, or till the approach of winter forced them to retire. His only source of uneasiness lay in the south, for he feared that Amherst, with his army, might capture Ticonderoga and advance into the colony, in which case he must weaken his army, by sending a force to oppose him.

On the day after the army landed on the island, a sudden and very violent squall drove several of the ships ashore, and destroyed many of the flatboats. On the following night, the sentries at the end of the island saw some vessels coming down the river. Suddenly these burst into flames. They were the fire ships, which Vaudreuil had sent down to destroy the fleet. They were filled with pitch, tar, and all sorts of combustibles, with shell and grenades mixed up with them, while on their decks were a number of cannon, crammed to the mouth with grapeshot and musketballs.

Fortunately for the English, the French naval officer in command lost his nerve, and set fire to his ship half an hour too soon; the other captains following his example. This gave the English time to recover from the first feeling of consternation at seeing the fire ships, each a pillar of flame, advancing with tremendous explosion and noise against them. The troops at once got under arms, lest the French should attack them, while the vessels lowered their boats, and the sailors rowed up to meet the fire ships. When they neared them, they threw grapnels on board, and towed them towards land until they were stranded, and then left them to burn out undisturbed.

Finding that it would be impossible to effect a landing, under the fire of the French guns, Wolfe determined, as a first step, to seize the height of Point Levi opposite

Quebec. From this point he could fire on the town across the Saint Lawrence, which is, here, less than a mile wide.

On the afternoon of the 29th, Monckton's brigade crossed, in the boats, to Beaumont on the south shore. His advanced guard had a skirmish with a party of Canadians, but these soon fell back, and no further opposition was offered to the landing.

In the morning a proclamation, issued by Wolfe, was posted on the doors of the parish churches. It called upon the Canadians to stand neutral in the contest, promising them, if they did so, full protection to their property and religion; but threatening that, if they resisted, their houses, goods, and harvest should be destroyed, and their churches sacked.

The brigade marched along the river to Point Levi, and drove off a body of French and Indians posted there, and, the next morning, began to throw up intrenchments and to form batteries. Wolfe did not expect that his guns here could do any serious damage to the fortifications of Quebec. His object was partly to discourage the inhabitants of the city exposed to his fire, partly to keep up the spirits of his own troops by setting them to work.

The guns of Quebec kept up a continual fire against the working parties, but the batteries continued to rise, and the citizens, alarmed at the destruction which threatened their houses, asked the governor to allow them to cross the river, and dislodge the English. Although he had no belief that they would succeed, he thought it better to allow them to try. Accordingly, some fifteen hundred armed citizens, and Canadians from the camp, with a few Indians, and a hundred volunteers from the regulars, marched up the river, and crossed on the night of the 12th of July.

The courage of the citizens evaporated very quickly, now they were on the same side of the river as the English, although still three miles from them. In a short time a wild panic seized them. They rushed back in extreme disorder to their boats, crossed the river, and returned to Quebec.

The English guns soon opened, and carried destruction into the city. In one day eighteen houses, and the cathedral, were burned by exploding shells; and the citizens soon abandoned their homes, and fled into the country.

The destruction of the city, however, even if complete, would have advanced Wolfe's plans but little. It was a moral blow at the enemy, but nothing more.

On the 8th of July, several frigates took their station before the camp of General Levis, who, with his division of Canadian militia, occupied the heights along the Saint Lawrence next to the gorge of Montmorenci. Here they opened fire with shell, and continued it till nightfall. Owing to the height of the plateau on which the camp was situated, they did but little damage, but the intention of Wolfe was simply to keep the enemy occupied and under arms.

Towards evening, the troops on the island broke up their camp, and, leaving a detachment of marines to hold the post, the brigades of Townshend and Murray, three thousand strong, embarked after nightfall in the boats of the fleet, and landed a little below the Montmorenci, At daybreak, they climbed the heights, and, routing a body of Canadians and Indians who opposed them, gained the plateau and began to intrench themselves there.

A company of rangers, supported by the regulars, was sent into the neighbouring forests; to prevent the parties from cutting bushes for the fascines, to explore the bank of the Montmorenci, and, if possible, to discover a ford across the river.

Levis, with his aide-de-camp, a Jacobite Scotchman named Johnston, was watching the movements of Wolfe from the heights above the gorge. Levis believed that no ford existed, but Johnston found a man who had, only that morning, crossed. A detachment was at once sent to the place, with orders to intrench themselves, and Levis posted eleven hundred Canadians, under Repentigny, close by in support.

Four hundred Indians passed the ford, and discovered the English detachment in the forest, and Langlade, their commander, recrossed the river, and told Repentigny that there was a body of English, in the forest, who might be destroyed if he would cross at once with his Canadians. Repentigny sent to Levis, and Levis to Vaudreuil, then three or four miles distant.

Before Vaudreuil arrived on the spot, the Indians became impatient and attacked the rangers; and drove them back, with loss, upon the regulars, who stood their ground, and repulsed the assailants. The Indians, however, carried thirty-six scalps across the ford.

If Repentigny had advanced when first called upon, and had been followed by Levis with his whole command, the English might have suffered a very severe check, for the Canadians were as much superior to the regulars, in the forest, as the regulars to the Canadians in the open.

Vaudreuil called a council of war, but he and Montcalm agreed not to attack the English, who were, on their part, powerless to injure them. Wolfe's position on the heights was indeed a dangerous one. A third of his force was six miles away, on the other side of the Saint Lawrence, and the detachment on the island was separated from each by a wide arm of the river. Any of the three were liable to be attacked and overpowered, before the others could come to its assistance.

Wolfe, indeed, was soon well intrenched, but, although safe against attack, he was powerless to take the offensive. The fact, however, that he had taken up his position so near their camp, had discomfited the Canadians, and his battery played, with considerable effect, on the left of their camp.

The time passed slowly. The deep and impassable gulf of the Montmorenci separated the two enemies, but the crests of the opposite cliffs were within easy gunshot of each other, and men who showed themselves near the edge ran a strong chance of being hit. Along the river, from the Montmorenci to Point Levi, continued fighting went on between the guns of the frigates, and the gunboats and batteries on shore. The Indians swarmed in the forest, near the English camp, and constant skirmishing went on between them and the rangers.

The steady work of destruction going on in the city of Quebec, by the fire from Point Levi, and the ceaseless cannonade kept up by the ships and Wolfe's batteries; added to the inactivity to which they were condemned, began to dispirit the Canadian militia, and many desertions took place, the men being anxious to return to their villages and look after the crops; and many more would have deserted, had it not been for the persuasion of the priests, and the fear of being maltreated by the Indians, whom the governor threatened to let loose upon any who should waver in their resistance.

On the 18th of July a fresh move was made by the English. The French had believed it impossible for any hostile ships to pass the batteries of Quebec; but, covered by a furious cannonade from Point Levi, the man of war Sutherland, with a frigate and several small vessels, aided by a favouring wind, ran up the river at night and passed above the town. Montcalm at once despatched six hundred men, under Dumas, to defend the accessible points in the line of precipices above Quebec, and on the following day, when it became known that the English had dragged a fleet of boats over Point Levi, and had launched them above the town, a reinforcement of several hundreds more was sent to Dumas.

On the night of the 20th Colonel Carleton, with six hundred men, rowed eighteen miles up the river, and landed at Pointe aux Trembles on the north shore. Here, many of the fugitives from Quebec had taken refuge, and a hundred women, children and old men were taken prisoners by Carleton, and brought down the next day with the retiring force. Wolfe entertained the prisoners kindly, and sent them, on the following day, with a flag of truce into Quebec.

On the night of the 28th, the French made another attempt to burn the English fleet, sending down a large number of schooners, shallops, and rafts, chained together, and filled, as before, with combustibles.

This time, the fire was not applied too soon, and the English fleet was for some time in great danger, but was again saved by the sailors, who, in spite of the storm of missiles, vomited out by cannon, swivels, grenades, shell, and gun and pistol barrels loaded up to the muzzle, grappled with the burning mass, and towed it on shore.

It was now the end of July, and Wolfe was no nearer taking Quebec than upon the day when he first landed there. In vain he had tempted Montcalm to attack him. The French general, confident in the strength of his position, refused to leave it.

Wolfe therefore determined to attack the camp in front. The plan was a desperate one, for, after leaving troops enough to hold his two camps, he had less than five thousand men to attack a position of commanding strength, where Montcalm could, at an hour's notice, collect twice as many to oppose him.

At a spot about a mile above the gorge of the Montmorenci a flat strip of ground, some two hundred yards wide, lay between the river and the foot of the precipices, and, at low tide, the river left a flat of mud, nearly half a mile wide, beyond the dry ground.

Along the edge of the high-water mark, the French had built several redoubts. From the river, Wolfe could not see that these redoubts were commanded by the musketry of the intrenchments along the edge of the heights above, which also swept with their fire the whole face of the declivity, which was covered with grass, and was extremely steep. Wolfe hoped that, if he attacked one of the redoubts, the French would come down to defend it, and that a battle might be so brought on; or that, if they did not do so, he might find a spot where the heights could be stormed with some chance of success. At low tide, it was possible to ford the mouth of the Montmorenci, and Wolfe intended that the troops from his camp, on the heights above that river, should cross here, and advance along the strand to cooperate with Monckton's brigade, who were to cross from Point Levi.

On the morning of the 31st of July, the Centurion, of 64 guns; and two armed transports, each with 14 guns, stood close in to one of the redoubts, and opened fire upon it; while the English batteries, from the heights of the Montmorenci, opened fire across the chasm upon the French lines.

At eleven o'clock, the troops from Point Levi put off in their boats, and moved across the river, as if they intended to make a landing between Beauport and the city. For some hours, Montcalm remained ignorant as to the point on which the English attack was to be made, but became presently convinced that it would be delivered near the Montmorenci, and he massed the whole of his army on that flank of his position.

At half-past five o'clock the tide was low, and the English boats dashed forward, and the troops sprang ashore on to the broad tract of mud, left bare by the tide; while, at the same moment, a column 2000 strong moved down from the height towards the ford at the mouth of the Montmorenci. The first to land were thirteen companies of Grenadiers, and a detachment of Royal Americans, who, without waiting for the two regiments of Monckton's brigade, dashed forward against the redoubt at the foot of the hill. The French at once abandoned it, but the Grenadiers had no sooner poured into it, than a storm of bullets rained down upon them, from the troops who lined the heights above.

Without a moment's hesitation, the Grenadiers and Americans dashed forward, and strove to climb the steep ascent, swept as it was by a terrific hail of bullets and buckshot from the French and Canadians. Numbers rolled, dead or wounded, to the bottom of the hill, but the others struggled on.

But at this moment, the cloud, which had been threatening all day, suddenly opened, and the rain poured down in a torrent. The grassy slopes instantly became so slippery that it was absolutely impossible to climb them, and the fire from above died away, as the wet rendered the firelocks unserviceable.

The Grenadiers fell back into the redoubt. Wolfe, who had now arrived upon the spot, saw that it was absolutely impossible to carry the heights under the present conditions, and ordered the troops to retreat. Carrying off many of the wounded with them, they fell back in good order. Those of the Grenadiers and Americans who survived recrossed, in their boats, to the island; the 15th Regiment rowed back to Point Levi; and the 78th Highlanders, who belonged to Monckton's brigade, joined the column from below the Montmorenci, and slowly retired along the flats and across the ford.

The loss fell entirely upon the Grenadiers and Americans, and was, in proportion to their number, enormous–four hundred and forty-three, including one colonel, eight captains, twenty-one lieutenants, and three ensigns, being killed, wounded, or missing. The blow to the English was a severe one, and even Wolfe began to despair, and meditated leaving a portion of his troops on Isle aux Coudres and fortifying them there, and sailing home, with the rest, to prepare another expedition in the following year.

In the middle of August, he issued a third proclamation to the Canadians, declaring, as they had refused his offers of protection, and had practised the most unchristian barbarity against his troops on all occasions, he could no longer refrain, in justice to himself and his army, in chastising them as they deserved. The barbarities consisted in the frequent scalping and mutilating of sentinels, and men on outpost duty, which were perpetrated alike by the Canadians and Indians.

Wolfe's object was twofold: first, to cause the militia to desert, and secondly, to exhaust the colony. Accordingly the rangers, light infantry and Highlanders were sent out, in all directions, to waste the settlements wherever resistance was offered. Farm houses and villages were laid in ashes, although the churches were generally spared. Wolfe's orders were strict that women and children were to be treated with honour.

"If any violence is offered to a woman, the offender shall be punished with death."

These orders were obeyed, and, except in one instance, none but armed men, in the act of resistance, were killed.

Vaudreuil, in his despatches home, loudly denounced these barbarities; but he himself was answerable for atrocities incomparably worse, and on a far larger scale, for he had, for years, sent his savages, red and white, along a frontier of 600 miles, to waste, burn, and murder at will, and these, as he was perfectly aware, spared neither age nor sex.

Montcalm was not to be moved from his position by the sight of the smoke of the burning villages. He would not risk the loss of all Canada, for the sake of a few hundred farm houses.

Seeing the impossibility of a successful attack below the town, Wolfe determined to attempt operations on a large scale above it. Accordingly, with every fair wind and tide, ships and transports ran the gauntlet of the batteries of Quebec, and, covered by a hot fire from Point Levi, generally succeeded, with more or less damage, in getting above the town. A fleet of flatboats was also sent up, and 1200 troops marched overland, under Brigadier Murray, to embark in them.

To meet this danger above the town, Bougainville was sent from the camp at Beaufort with 1500 men. Murray made another descent at Pointe-aux-Trembles, but was repulsed with loss. He tried a second time at another place, but a body of ambushed Canadians poured so heavy a fire into the boats, that he was forced to fall back again with considerable loss. His third attempt was more successful, for he landed at Deschambault, and burned a large building filled with stores, and with all the spare baggage of the officers of the French regular troops.

Vaudreuil now regretted having sent the French frigates up the river, and withdrawing their crews to work in the batteries. Had they been kept just above the town, they could have overpowered the English vessels as they passed up. The sailors were now sent up to man their ships again; but Admiral Holmes, who had taken command of the ships of war above Quebec, was already too strong for them, and the sailors were recalled to Quebec.

Both armies were suffering. Dysentery and fever had broken out in the English camp, and the number of effective men was greatly reduced. Upon the other hand, the French were suffering from shortness of supplies. The English frigates above the town prevented food being brought down from Montreal in boats, and the difficulties of land carriage were very great.

The Canadians deserted in great numbers, and Montcalm's force had been weakened by the despatch of Levis, to assist in checking the advance of Amherst. The latter had captured Ticonderoga and Crown Point. Niagara had also been taken by the English. Amherst, however, fell back again, and Levis was able to rejoin Montcalm.

But the greatest misfortune which befell the English was the dangerous illness of Wolfe, who, always suffering from disease, was for a time utterly prostrate. At the end of August, however, he partially recovered, and dictated a letter to his three brigadier generals, asking them to fix upon one of three plans, which he laid before them, for attacking the enemy. The first was that the army should march eight or ten miles up the Montmorenci, ford the river, and fall upon the rear of the enemy. The second was to cross the ford at the mouth of the Montmorenci, and march along the shore, until a spot was found where the heights could be climbed. The third was to make a general attack from the boats upon Beauport.

Monckton, Townshend, and Murray met in consultation, and considered all the plans to be hopeless; but they proposed that an attempt should be made to land above the town, and so to place the army between Quebec and its base of supplies, thereby forcing Montcalm to fight or to surrender.

The attempt seemed a desperate one, but Wolfe determined to adopt it. He had not much hope of its succeeding, but should it not do so, there was nothing for him but to sail, with his weakened army, back to England. He therefore determined at last to make the attempt, and implored his physician to patch him up, so that he could, in person, take the command.

"I know perfectly well that you cannot cure me," he wrote; "but pray make me up, so that I may be without pain for a few days, and able to do my duty. That is all I want."

On the 3rd of September, Wolfe took the first steps towards the carrying out of his plans, by evacuating the camp at Montmorenci. Montcalm sent a strong force to attack him, as he was moving; but Monckton at Point Levi saw the movement, and, embarking two battalions in boats, made a feint of landing at Beauport. Montcalm recalled his troops to repulse the threatened attack, and the English were able to draw off from Montmorenci without molestation.

On the night of the 4th, a fleet of flatboats passed above the town, with the baggage and stores. On the 5th the infantry marched up by land, and the united force, of some 3600 men, embarked on board the ships of Admiral Holmes.

The French thought that the abandonment of Montmorenci, and the embarkation of the troops, was a sign that the English were about to abandon their enterprise, and sail for England. Nevertheless, Montcalm did not relax his vigilance, being ever on the watch, riding from post to post, to see that all was in readiness to repel an attack. In one of his letters at this time, he mentioned that he had not taken off his clothes since the 23d of June.

He now reinforced the troops under Bougainville, above Quebec, to 3000 men. He had little fear for the heights near the town, believing them to be inaccessible, and that a hundred men could stop a whole army. This he said, especially, in reference to the one spot which presented at least a possibility of being scaled. Here Captain de Vergor, with a hundred Canadian troops, were posted. The battalion of Guienne had been ordered to encamp close at hand, and the post, which was called Anse du Foulon, was but a mile and a half distant from Quebec. Thus, although hoping that the

English would soon depart, the French, knowing the character of Wolfe, made every preparation against a last attack before he started.

From the 7th to the 12th, Holmes' fleet sailed up and down the river, threatening a landing, now at one point and now at another, wearing out the French, who were kept night and day on the qui vive, and were exhausted by following the ships up and down, so as to be ready to oppose a landing wherever it might be made.

James Walsham's regiment formed part of Monckton's brigade, and his colonel had frequently selected him to command parties who went out to the Canadian villages, as, from the knowledge he had acquired of irregular warfare, he could be trusted not to suffer himself to be surprised by the parties of Canadians or Indians, who were always on the watch to cut off detachments sent out from the British camp. There were still ten men in the regiment who had formed part of his band on the lakes. These were drafted into his company, and, whatever force went out, they always accompanied him.

Although James had seen much, and heard more, of the terrible barbarities perpetrated by the Canadians and their Indian allies on the frontier, he lamented much the necessity which compelled Wolfe to order the destruction of Canadian villages; and when engaged on this service, whether in command of the detachment, or as a subaltern if more than one company went out, he himself never superintended the painful work; but, with his ten men, scouted beyond the village, and kept a vigilant lookout against surprise. In this way, he had several skirmishes with the Canadians, but the latter never succeeded in surprising any force to which he was attached. Walsham and his scouts were often sent out with parties from other regiments, and General Monckton was so pleased with his vigilance and activity, that he specially mentioned him to General Wolfe, at the same time telling him of the services he had performed on the lakes, and the very favourable reports which had been made by Johnson, Monro, Lord Howe, and Abercromby, of the work done by the corps which he had organized and commanded.

"I wish we had a few more officers trained to this sort of warfare," General Wolfe said. "Send him on board the Sutherland tomorrow. I have some service which he is well fitted to carry out."

James accordingly repaired on board the Sutherland, and was conducted to the general's cabin.

"General Monckton has spoken to me in high terms of you, Lieutenant Walsham, and he tells me that you have been several times mentioned in despatches, by the generals under whom you served; and you were with Braddock as well as with Johnson, Howe, and Abercromby, and with Monro at the siege of Fort William Henry. How is it that so young an officer should have seen so much service?"

James informed him how, having been pressed on board a man of war, he had been discharged, in accordance with orders from home, and, hearing that his friends were going to obtain a commission for him, in a regiment under orders for America, he had thought it best to utilize his time by accompanying General Braddock as a volunteer, in order to learn something of forest warfare; that, after that disastrous affair, he had served with Johnson in a similar capacity, until, on his regiment arriving, he had been selected to drill a company of scouts, and had served with them on the lakes, until the corps was broken up when the regiment sailed for Canada.

"In fact, you have seen more of this kind of warfare than any officer in the army," General Wolfe said. "Your special services ought to have been recognized before. I shall have you put in orders, tomorrow, as promoted to the rank of captain. And now, I am about to employ you upon a service which, if you are successful, will give you your brevet majority.

"There must be some points at which those precipices can be climbed. I want you to find out where they are. It is a service of great danger. You will go in uniform, otherwise, if caught, you would meet with the fate of a spy; but at the same time, even in uniform you would probably meet with but little mercy, if you fell into the hands of the Canadians or Indians. Would you be willing to undertake such a duty?"

"I will try, sir," James said. "Do you wish me to start tonight?"

"No," the general replied. "You had better think the matter over, and let me know tomorrow how you had best proceed. It is not an enterprise to be undertaken without thinking it over in every light. You will have to decide whether you will go alone, or take anyone with you; when and how you will land; how you will regain the ships. You will, of course, have carte blanche in all respects."

After James had returned on shore, he thought the matter over in every light. He knew that the French had many sentries along the edge of the river, for boats which, at night, went over towards that side of the river, were always challenged and fired upon. The chance of landing undetected, therefore, seemed but slight; nor, even did he land, would he be likely, at night, to discover the paths, which could be little more than tracks up the heights.

Had he been able to speak Canadian French, the matter would have been easy enough, as he could have landed higher up the river and, dressed as a Canadian farmer, have made his way through the French lines without suspicion. But he knew nothing of French, and, even had he spoken the language fluently, there was sufficient difference between the Canadian French and the language of the old country, for the first Canadian who spoke to him to have detected the difference.

Nor could he pass as an Indian; for, although he had picked up enough of the language to converse with the redskin allies of the English on the lakes, the first Indian who spoke to him would detect the difference; and, indeed, it needed a far more intimate acquaintance with the various tribes, than he possessed, for him to be able to paint and adorn himself so as to deceive the vigilant eyes of the French Indians.

Had his two followers, Nat and Jonathan, been with him, they could have painted and dressed him so that he could have passed muster, but, in their absence, he abandoned the idea as out of the question. The prospect certainly did not seem hopeful.

After long thought, it seemed to him that the only way which promised even a chance of success would be for him to be taken prisoner by the French soldiers. Once fairly within their lines, half the difficulty was over. He had learned to crawl as noiselessly as an Indian, and he doubted not that he should be able to succeed in getting away from any place of confinement in which they might place him. Then he could follow the top of the heights, and the position of the sentries or of any body of men encamped there would, in itself, be a guide to him as to the existence of paths to the strand below.

The first step was the most difficult. How should he manage to get himself taken prisoner? And this was the more difficult, as it was absolutely necessary that he should fall into the hands of French regulars, and not of the Canadians, who would finish the matter at once by killing and scalping him.

The next morning, he again went off to the Sutherland. He was in high spirits, for his name had appeared in orders as captain, and as appointed assistant quartermaster general on the headquarter staff. On entering the general's cabin, he thanked him for the promotion.

"You have earned it over and over again," the general said. "There are no thanks due to me. Now, have you thought out a plan?"

James briefly stated the difficulties which he perceived in the way of any other scheme than that of getting himself taken prisoner by the French, and showed that that was the only plan that seemed to offer even a chance of success.

"But you may not be able to escape," Wolfe said.

"I may not," James replied, "and in that case, sir, I must of course remain a prisoner until you take Quebec, or I am exchanged. Even then you would be no worse off than you are at present, for I must, of course, be taken prisoner at some point where the French are in force, and where you do not mean to land. My presence there would give them no clue whatever to your real intentions, whereas, were I taken prisoner anywhere along the shore, they would naturally redouble their vigilance, as they would guess that I was looking for some way of ascending the heights."

"How do you propose being taken?" Wolfe asked.

"My idea was," James replied, "that I should land with a party near Cap Rouge, as if to reconnoitre the French position there. We should, of course, be speedily discovered, and would then retreat to the boats. I should naturally be the last to go, and might well manage to be cut off."

"Yes," Wolfe replied, "but you might also, and that far more easily, manage to get shot. I don't think that would do, Captain Walsham. The risks would be twenty to one against your escaping being shot. Can you think of no other plan?"

"The only other plan that I can think of," James said, "might involve others being taken prisoners. I might row in towards Cap Rouge in broad daylight, as if to examine the landing place, and should, of course, draw their fire upon the boat. Before starting, I should fire two or three shots into the boat close to the water line, and afterwards plug them up with rags. Then, when their fire became heavy, I should take the plugs out and let the boat fill. As she did so, I could shout that I surrendered, and then we could drift till we neared the shore in the water-logged boat, or swim ashore. I can swim well myself, and should, of course, want four men, who could swim well also, picked out as the crew."

"The plan is a dangerous one," Wolfe said, "but less so than the other."

"One cannot win a battle without risking life, sir," James said quietly. "Some of us might, of course, be hit, but as we risk our lives whenever we get within range of the enemy, I do not see that that need be considered; at any rate, sir, I am ready to make the attempt, if the plan has your approval."

"I tell you frankly, Captain Walsham, that I think your chances of success are absolutely nil. At the same time, there is just a faint possibility that you may get ashore alive, escape from the French, discover a pathway, and bring me the news; and, as the only chance of the expedition being successful now depends upon our discovering such a path, I am not justified in refusing even this faint chance."

The general touched a bell which stood on the table before him.

"Will you ask the captain to come here," he said to the officer who answered the summons.

"Captain Peters," he said when the captain appeared, "I want you to pick out for me four men, upon whom you can thoroughly rely. In the first place they must be good swimmers, in the second place they must be able to hold their tongues, and lastly they must be prepared to pass some months in a French prison. A midshipman, with the same qualifications, will be required to go with them."

The captain naturally looked surprised at so unusual a request.

"Captain Walsham is going to be taken prisoner by the French," General Wolfe explained, "and the only way it can be done is for a whole boat's crew to be taken with him," and he then detailed the plan which had been arranged. "Of course, you can offer the men any reward you may think fit, and can promise the midshipman early promotion," he concluded.

"Very well, general. I have no doubt I can find four men and a midshipman willing to volunteer for the affair, especially as, if you succeed, their imprisonment will be a short one. When will the attempt be made?"

"If you can drift up the river as far as Cap Rouge before daylight," James said, in answer to an inquiring look from the general, "we will attempt it tomorrow morning. I should say that the best plan would be for me to appear opposite their camp when day breaks, as if I was trying to obtain a close view of it in the early morning."

"The sooner the better," General Wolfe said. "Every day is of importance. But how do you propose to get back again, that is, supposing that everything goes well?"

"I propose, general, that I should conceal myself somewhere on the face of the heights. I will spread a handkerchief against a rock or tree, so that it will not be seen either from above or below, but will be visible from the ships in the river. I cannot say, of course, whether it will be near Cap Rouge or Quebec; but, if you will have a sharp lookout kept through a glass, as the ships drift up and down, you are sure to see it, and can let me know that you do so by dipping the ensign. At night I will make my way down to the shore, and if, at midnight exactly, you will send a boat for me, I shall be ready to swim off to her, when they show a lantern as they approach the shore. Of course, I cannot say on what day I may be in a position to show the signal, but at, any rate, if a week passes without your seeing it, you will know that I have failed to make my escape, or that I have been killed after getting out."

Chapter 19: A Dangerous Expedition.

The details of the proposed expedition being thus arranged, the captain left the cabin with James, and the latter paced to and fro on the quarterdeck, while the captain sent for the boatswain and directed him to pick out four men who could swim well, and who were ready to volunteer for desperate service.

While the captain was so engaged, James saw a naval officer staring fixedly at him. He recognized him instantly, though more than four years had elapsed since he had last seen him. He at once stepped across the quarterdeck.

"How are you, Lieutenant Horton? It is a long time since we last parted on the Potomac."

Horton would have refused the proffered hand, but he had already injured himself very sorely, in the eyes of the squire, by his outburst of ill feeling against James, so he shook hands and said coldly:

"Yes, your position has changed since then."

"Yes," James said with a laugh, "but that was only a temporary eclipse. That two months before the mast was a sort of interlude for which I am deeply thankful. Had it not been for my getting into that smuggling scrape, I should have been, at the present moment, commencing practice as a doctor, instead of being a captain in his majesty's service."

The words were not calculated to improve Horton's temper. What a mistake he had made! Had he interfered on James Walsham's behalf–and a word from him, saying that James was the son of a medical man, and was assuredly mixed up in this smuggling affair only by accident–he would have been released. He had not spoken that word, and the consequence was, he had himself fallen into bad odour with the squire, and James Walsham, instead of drudging away as a country practitioner, was an officer of rank equal to himself, for he, as second lieutenant in the Sutherland, ranked with a captain in the army.

Not only this, but whenever he went to Sidmouth he had heard how James had been mentioned in the despatches, and how much he was distinguishing himself. Everything seemed to combine against him. He had hated James Walsham from the day when the latter had thrashed him, and had acted as Aggie's champion against him. He had hated him more, when he found Aggie installed as the squire's heiress, and saw how high James stood in her good graces, and that he had been taken up by the squire.

He had hoped that he had gained the advantage over him, when he had come back a naval officer, while James was still a schoolboy, and had kept aloof from the house while he devoted himself to the young heiress. Everything had seemed going on well with his plans, until the very circumstance which, at the time, seemed so opportune, namely, the pressing James as a seaman on board the Thetis, had turned out so disastrous. The letter, in which he had suffered his exultation to appear, had angered the squire, had set Mrs. Walsham and her friend the ex-sergeant against him, and had deeply offended Aggie. It had, too, enabled the squire to take instant measures for procuring James's discharge, and had now placed the latter in a position equal to his own.

James, on his part, did not like Richard Horton, but he felt no active animosity against him. He had got the best of it in that first quarrel of theirs, and, although he had certainly felt very sore and angry, at the time Richard was staying at the Hall, and seemed to have taken his place altogether as Aggie's friend, this feeling had long since died away, for he knew, from the letters of Mr. Wilks, that Aggie had no liking whatever for Richard Horton.

"You were at Sidmouth in the spring, I heard," he said. "You found my mother looking well, I hope?"

"Yes, I was there a fortnight before we sailed," Richard said. "I think she was looking about as usual."

For a few minutes, they talked in a stiff and somewhat constrained tone, for Richard could not bring himself to speak cordially to this man, whom he regarded as a dangerous rival. Presently, the captain came up to them.

"I have picked four volunteers for your work, Captain Walsham. They were somewhat surprised, at first, to find that they were required for a bout in a French prison; but sailors are always ready for any hare-brained adventure, and they made no objection whatever, when I explained what they would have to do. Next to fighting a Frenchman, there's nothing a sailor likes so much as taking him in. Young Middleton goes in command of the boat. He is a regular young pickle, and is as pleased at the prospect as if a French prison were the most amusing place in the world. He knows, of course, that there will be some considerable danger of his being shot before he is taken prisoner; but I need hardly say that the danger adds to the interest of the scheme. It's a risky business you have undertaken, Captain Walsham, terribly risky; but, if you succeed, you will have saved the expedition from turning out a failure, and we shall all be under obligations to you for the rest of our lives.

"Has Captain Walsham told you what he is undertaking, Mr. Horton?"

"No, sir."

"He is going to get taken prisoner, in the gig, in order that he may, if possible, give the French the slip again, find out some way down that line of cliffs, and so enable the general to get into the heart of the French expedition. It is a grand scheme, but a risky one."

"The chances are a hundred to one against you, Captain Walsham."

"That is just what the general said," James replied, with a smile. "I don't think, myself, they are more than five to one against me; but, even if they were a thousand, it would be worth trying, for a thousand lives would be cheaply sacrificed to ensure the success of this expedition."

"There are not many men who would like to try it," the captain said. "I say honestly I shouldn't, myself. Anything in the nature of duty, whether it's laying your ship alongside a Frenchman of twice her weight of metal, or a boat expedition to cut out a frigate from under the guns of the battery, I should be ready to take my share in; but an expedition like yours, to be carried out alone, in cold blood and in the dark, I should have no stomach for. I don't want to discourage you, and I honour your courage in undertaking it; but I am heartily glad that the general did not propose to me, instead of to you, to undertake it."

"You would have done it if he had, sir," James said, smiling, "and so would any officer of this expedition. I consider myself most highly honoured in the general entrusting me with the mission. Besides, you must remember that it is not so strange, to me, as it would be to most men. I have been for four years engaged in forest warfare, scouting at night in the woods, and keeping my ears open to the slightest sound which might tell of a skulking redskin being at hand. My eyes have become so accustomed to darkness, that, although still very far short of those of the Indians,

I can see plainly where one unaccustomed to such work would see nothing. I am accustomed to rely upon my own senses, to step noiselessly, or to crawl along on the ground like an Indian. Therefore, you see, to me this enterprise does not present itself in the same light as it naturally would to you."

"You may make light of it," the captain said, "but it's a dangerous business, look at it as you will. Well, if you go through it safely, Captain Walsham, you will be the hero of this campaign."

Late in the afternoon the tide turned, and the vessels began to drift up the river. The four sailors had, of course, mentioned to their comrades the service upon which they were about to be engaged. The captain had not thought it necessary to enjoin secrecy upon them, for there was no communication with the shore, no fear of the knowledge spreading beyond the ship; besides, the boat had to be damaged, and this alone would tell the sailors, when she was lowered in the water, that she was intended to be captured.

A marine was called up to where the captain's gig was hanging from the davits. James pointed out a spot just below the waterline, and the man, standing a yard or two away, fired at it, the ball making a hole through both sides of the boat. Another shot was fired two or three inches higher, and the four holes were then plugged up with oakum.

All was now in readiness for the attempt. James dined with Captain Peters, the first lieutenant and four officers of the general's staff being also present, General Wolfe himself being too ill to be at table, and Admiral Holmes having, early in the morning, gone down the river to confer with Admiral Saunders.

"I drink good health and a safe return to you, Captain Walsham, for our sake as well as yours. As a general thing, when an officer is chosen for dangerous service, he is an object of envy by all his comrades; but, for once, I do not think anyone on board would care to undertake your mission."

"Why, sir, your little midshipman is delighted at going with me. He and I have been chatting the matter over, and he is in the highest glee."

"Ah! He has only got the first chance of being shot at," Captain Peters said. "That comes in the line of duty, and I hope there isn't an officer on board a ship but would volunteer, at once, for that service. But your real danger only begins when his ends.

"By the way," he asked, as, after dinner was over, he was walking up and down the quarterdeck, talking to James, "have you and Lieutenant Horton met before? I thought you seemed to know each other when I came up, but, since then I have noticed that, while all the other officers of the ship have been chatting with you, he has kept aloof."

"We knew each other at home, sir," James said, "but we were never very good friends. Our acquaintanceship commenced, when we were boys, with a fight. I got the best of it, and Horton has never, I think, quite forgiven me."

"I don't like the young fellow," Captain Peters said shortly. "I know he was not popular in the Thetis, and they say he showed the white feather out in the East. I wouldn't have had him on board, but the first lord asked me, as a personal favour, to take him. I have had no reason to complain of him, since he joined, but I know that he is no more popular, among my other officers, than he was in the Thetis."

"I never heard a word against him, sir," James said earnestly. "His uncle, Mr. Linthorne, has large estates near Sidmouth, and has been the kindest friend to me and mine. At one time, it was thought that Horton would be his heir, but a granddaughter, who had for years been missing, was found; but still Horton will take, I should think, a considerable slice of the property, and it would grieve the squire, terribly, if Horton failed in his career. I think it's only a fault of manners, sir, if I may say so, and certainly I myself know nothing whatever against him."

"I don't know," Captain Peters replied thoughtfully. "Just before I sailed, I happened to meet an old friend, and over our dinner I mentioned the names of my officers. He told me he knew this Mr. Linthorne well, and that Horton had gone to sea with him for the first time as a midshipman, and that there was certainly something queer about him as a boy, for Linthorne had specially asked him to keep his eye upon him, and had begged him, frankly, to let him know how he conducted himself. That rather set me against him, you know."

"I don't think that was anything," James urged. "I do not much like Horton, but I should not like you to have a false impression of him. It was a mere boyish affair, sir–in fact, it was connected with that fight with me. I don't think he gave a very strictly accurate account of it, and his uncle, who in some matters is very strict, although one of the kindest of men, took the thing up, and sent him away to sea. Horton was certainly punished severely enough, for that stupid business, without its counting against him afterwards."

"I like the way you speak up in his defence, Captain Walsham, especially as you frankly say you don't like him, and henceforth I will dismiss the affair from my mind, but I should say that he has never forgiven it, although you may have done so."

"That's natural enough," James laughed, "because I came best out of it."

To Richard Horton, the news that James Walsham was about to undertake a desperate enterprise, which, if he succeeded in it, would bring him great honour and credit, was bitter in the extreme, and the admiration expressed by the other officers, at his courage in undertaking it, added to his anger and disgust. He walked moodily up and down the quarterdeck all the afternoon, to think the matter over, and at each moment his fury increased. Could he in any way have put a stop to the adventure, he would instantly have done so, but there was no possible way of interfering.

The thought that annoyed him most was of the enthusiasm with which the news of the successful termination of the enterprise would be received at Sidmouth. Already, as he knew, Aggie regarded James as a hero, and the squire was almost as proud of his mention in despatches as if he had been his own son; but for this he cared but little. It was Aggie's good opinion Richard Horton desired to gain. James Walsham still thought of her as the girl of twelve he had last seen, but Richard Horton knew her as almost a woman, and, although at first he had resolved to marry her as his uncle's heiress, he now really cared for her for herself.

On the visit before James had left home, Richard had felt certain that his cousin liked him; but, since that time, he had not only made no progress, but he felt that he had lost rather than gained ground. The girl was always friendly with him, but it was the cool friendliness of a cousin, and, somehow, Richard instinctively felt James Walsham was the cause.

In vain he had angrily told himself that it was absurd to suppose that his cousin could care for this fellow, whom she had only seen as an awkward boy, who had been content to stop away from the house, and never go near her for weeks. Still, though he told himself it was absurd, he knew that it was so. When the conversation happened to turn upon James, she seldom took any part in it; but Richard knew that it was not from indifference as to the subject. There was a soft flush on her cheek, a light in her eyes, which he had never been able to call up; and, many a time, he had ground his teeth in silent rage, when the squire and Mr. Wilks were discussing the news received in James's last letter, and expressing their hopes that, ere long, he would be back from foreign service.

Although by no means fond of encountering danger, Richard felt that he would gladly pick an open quarrel with the man he regarded as his rival, and shoot him like a dog–for in those days, duels were matters of everyday occurrence–but there was no possibility of doing this, at the present juncture; and, moreover, he knew that this would be the worst possible way of ridding himself of him; for, were James to fall by his hands, his chances of winning Aggie would be hopelessly extinguished.

"No," he said to himself, "that is out of the question; but I will do something. Come what may, he shall never go back to Sidmouth."

The squadron drifted up beyond Cap Rouge, and anchored, at the top of the flood, an hour before daybreak. The gig was lowered, and James Walsham, amid many good wishes and hearty farewells from the officers, took his place in her, by the side of the midshipman.

"Look out for my signal," he said. "Any time, after today, you may see it."

"We will see it if you make it, my boy," said the captain, who had come on deck to see him off. "Don't you fear about that. If you make your signal, you may rely upon it, our boat will be ashore for you that night."

Another moment, and the boat pulled away from the side of the ship.

"Take it easy, lads," young Middleton said, "only just dip your oars in the water. We have but three miles to row, with the stream, and don't want to be there till the day begins to show."

The oars had been muffled, and, noiselessly, the boat dropped down the stream, until she neared Cap Rouge, then they rowed in towards the French shore. The day was just beginning to break, in the east, as they neared the spot where the French camp was situated. It stood high up on the plateau; but there were a small number of tents on the low ground, by the river, as some batteries had been erected here. They were but two hundred yards from the shore when a French sentry challenged. They gave no answer, and the soldier at once fired.

"Keep about this distance out," James ordered. "Row quietly. I will stand up, as if I were watching the shore."

As soon as the shot was fired, it was answered by shots from other sentries. A minute later, a drum was heard to beat sharply, and then, in the faint light, a number of French soldiers could be seen, running at full speed towards the shore. The shots fell thickly round the boat, and one of the men dropped his oar, as a bullet struck him on the shoulder.

"Pull out the plugs," James said.

The oakum was pulled out and thrown overboard, and the water rushed in.

"Now turn her head from the shore, as if we were trying to escape."

So rapidly did the water rush in through the four holes that, in a minute, the gunwale was nearly level with the water.

"Turn her over now," James said, and in a moment the boat was upset, and the men clinging to the bottom.

A shout of exultation rose from the shore, as the boat was seen to upset, and the firing at once ceased.

"Swim towards the shore, and push the boat before you," the young midshipman said. "They won't fire any more now, and we have finished the first part of our business."

Pushing the boat before them, the men made their way slowly towards the shore, striking the land half a mile below the point where they had overturned. The French soldiers had followed them down the bank, and surrounded them as they landed. The holes in the boat explained for themselves the cause of the disaster.

An officer stepped forward.

"You are our prisoners," he said to James.

The latter bowed.

"It is the fortune of war," he said. "Your men are better shots than I gave them credit for," and he pointed to the holes in the boat.

He spoke in English, but the officer guessed his meaning.

Some of the Indians and Canadians soon came flocking down, and, with angry gestures, demanded that the prisoners should be shot; but the French officer waived them off, and placed a strong guard of his own men around them, to prevent their being touched by the Indians. The young midshipman spoke French fluently, having been specially selected by the captain for that reason; but it had been agreed, between him and James, that he should not betray his knowledge of the language, as he might, thereby, pick up information which might be useful.

They were at once conducted before Bougainville.

"Do you speak French?" he asked.

James shook his head. The midshipman looked as if he had not understood the question.

"It is clear," the French officer said to those standing around him, "that they came in to reconnoitre the landing place, and thought, in the dim light, they could run the gauntlet of our sentries' fire. It was more accurate than they gave them credit for."

"The boat was struck twice, you say?"

"Yes, general," the officer who conducted them into the tent replied. "Two balls right through her, and one of the men was hit on the shoulder."

"The reconnaissance looks as if Wolfe meant to attempt a landing here," Bougainville said. "We must keep a sharp lookout. I will send them on to Quebec, for the general to question them. He will find someone there who speaks their language. I will send, at once, to tell him we have captured them. But I can't very well do so, till we have a convoy going, with regulars to guard it. If they were to go in charge of Canadians, the chances of their arriving alive in Quebec would be slight.

"Let the sailors be placed in a tent in your lines, Chateaudun, and place a sentry over them, to see that the Indians don't get at them. The two officers can have the tent that Le Boeuf gave up yesterday. You can put a sentry there, but they can go in and out as they like. There is no fear of their trying to escape; for, if they once went outside the lines of the regulars, the Indians and Canadians would make short work of them."

The officer led James and the midshipman to a tent in the staff lines, whose owner had ridden to Quebec, on the previous night, with despatches, and motioned to them that it was to be theirs. He also made signs to them that they could move about as they chose; but significantly warned them, by a gesture, that if they ventured beyond the tents, the Indians would make short work of them.

For a time, the prisoners made no attempt to leave the tent, for the Indians stood scowling at a short distance off, and would have entered, had not the sentry on duty prevented them from doing so.

"Do not talk too loudly," James said. "It is probable that, in a camp like this, there is someone who understands English. Very likely they are playing the same game with us that we are with them. They pretend there is no one who can speak to us; but, very likely, there may be someone standing outside now, trying to listen to what we say."

Then, raising his voice he went on:

"What abominable luck I have! Who could have reckoned upon the boat being hit, twice, at that distance? I thought we had fairly succeeded. The general will be in a nice way, when he finds we don't come back."

"Yes," Middleton rejoined, "and to think that we are likely to spend the winter in prison, at Quebec, instead of Old England. I am half inclined to try and escape!"

"Nonsense!" James replied. "It would be madness to think of such a thing. These Indians can see in the dark, and the moment you put your foot outside the lines of these French regulars, you would be carried off and scalped. No, no, my boy; that would be simply throwing away our lives. There is nothing for it, but to wait quietly, till either Wolfe takes Quebec, or you are exchanged."

The prisoners were treated with courtesy by the French officers, and comfortable meals were provided. In the evening, they went outside the tent for a short time, but did not venture to go far, for Indians were still moving about, and the hostile glances, which they threw at the prisoners, were sufficient to indicate what would happen to the latter, if they were caught beyond the protection of the sentry.

"Bougainville was right in supposing that prisoners would not be likely to attempt to escape," James said, in a low voice. "The look of those Indians would be quite sufficient to prevent anyone from attempting it, under ordinary circumstances. It is well that my business will take me down the river towards Quebec, while they will make sure that I shall have made up the river, with a view of making my way off to the ships, the next time they go up above Cap Rouge."

"It will be risky work getting through them," the midshipman remarked; "but all the same, I wish I was going with you, instead of having to stick here in prison."

"It would be running too great a risk of spoiling my chance of success," James said. "I am accustomed to the redskins, and can crawl through them as noiselessly as they could themselves. Besides, one can hide where two could not. I only hope that, when they find I have gone, they won't take it into their heads to revenge my escape upon you."

"There is no fear of that," the midshipman said. "I shall be sound asleep in the tent, and when they wake me up, and find you are gone, I shall make a tremendous fuss, and pretend to be most indignant that you have deserted me."

The two prisoners had eaten but little of the meals served to them that day, putting the greater portion aside, and hiding it in the straw which served for their beds, in order that James might take with him a supply, for it might be three or four days before he could be taken off by the ships' boats.

"I suppose you won't go very far tonight?" the midshipman said, suddenly.

"No," James replied. "I shall hide somewhere along the face of the cliff, a mile or so away. They are not likely to look for me down the river at all; but, if they do, they will think I have gone as far as I can away, and the nearer I am to this place, the safer."

"Look here," the midshipman said. "I am going strictly to obey orders; but, at the same time, it is just possible that something may turn up that you ought to know, or that might make me want to bolt. Suppose, for instance, I heard them say that they meant to shoot us both in the morning–it's not likely, you know; still, it's always as well to be prepared for whatever might happen–if so, I should crawl out of camp, and make my way along after you. And if so, I shall walk along the edge, and sometimes give two little whistles like this; and, if you hear me, you answer me."

"Don't be foolish, Middleton," James said seriously. "You would only risk your life, and mine, by any nonsense of that sort. There can't be any possible reason why you should want to go away. You have undertaken to carry this out, knowing that you would have, perhaps, to remain a prisoner for some time; and having undertaken it, you must keep to the plans laid down."

"But I am going to, Captain Walsham. Still, you know, something might turn up."

"I don't see that anything possibly could turn up," James insisted; "but, if at any future time you do think of any mad-brained attempt of escaping, you must take off your shoes, and you must put your foot down, each time, as gently as if the ground were covered with nails; for, if you were to tread upon a twig, and there were an Indian within half a mile of you, he would hear it crack. But don't you attempt any such folly. No good could possibly come of it, and you would be sure to fall into the hands of the savages or Canadians; and you know how they treat prisoners."

"I know," the boy said; "and I have no wish to have my scalp hanging up in any of their wigwams."

It was midnight, before the camp was perfectly still, and then James Walsham quietly loosened one of the pegs of the canvas, at the back of the tent, and, with a warm grasp of the midshipman's hand, crawled out. The lad listened attentively, but he could not hear the slightest sound. The sentinel was striding up and down in front of the tent, humming the air of a French song as he walked. Half an hour passed without the slightest stir, and the midshipman was sure that James was, by this time, safely beyond the enemy's camp.

He was just about to compose himself to sleep, when he heard a trampling of feet. The sentry challenged, the password was given, and the party passed on towards the general's tent. It was some thirty yards distant, and the sentry posted there challenged.

"I wonder what's up?" the midshipman said to himself; and, lifting the canvas, he put his head out where James had crawled through.

The men had halted before the general's tent, and the boy heard the general's voice, from inside the tent, ask sharply, "What is it?"

"I regret to disturb you, Monsieur le General; but we have here one of the Canadian pilots, who has swam ashore from the enemy's fleet higher up the river, and who has important news for you."

The midshipman at once determined to hear what passed. He had already taken off his shoes; and he now crawled out from the tent, and, moving with extreme caution, made his way round to the back of the general's tent, just as the latter, having thrown on his coat and lighted a candle, unfastened the entrance. The midshipman, determined to see as well as hear what was going on, lifted up the flap a few inches behind, and, as he lay on the ground, peered in. A French officer had just entered, and he was followed by a Canadian, whom the midshipman recognized at once, as being the one who piloted the Sutherland up and down the river.

"Where do you come from?" Bougainville asked.

"I swam ashore two hours ago from the English ship Sutherland," the Canadian said.

"How did you manage to escape?"

"I would have swam ashore long ago, but at night I have always been locked up, ever since I was captured, in a cabin below. Tonight the door opened quietly, and someone came in and said:

"'Hush!–can you swim?'

"'Like a fish,' I said.

"'Are you ready to try and escape, if I give you the chance?'

"'I should think so,' I replied.

"'Then follow me, but don't make the slightest noise.'

"I followed him. We passed along the main deck, where the sailors were all asleep in their hammocks. A lantern was burning here, and I saw, by its light, that my conductor was an officer. He led me along till we entered a cabin–his own, I suppose.

"'Look,' he whispered, 'there is a rope from the porthole down to the water. If you slide quietly down by it, and then let yourself drift till you are well astern of the ship, the sentry on the quarterdeck will not see you. Here is a letter, put it in your cap. If you are fired at, and a boat is lowered to catch you, throw the paper away at once. Will you swear to do that?'

"I said I would swear by the Virgin.

"'Very well,' he went on; 'if you get away safely and swim to shore, make your way without a minute's delay to the French camp at Cap Rouge, and give this letter to the general. It is a matter of the most extreme importance.'

"This is the letter, general."

He handed a small piece of paper, tightly folded up, to Bougainville, who opened it, and read it by the light of the candle.

He gave a sharp exclamation.

"Quick!" he exclaimed. "Come along to the tent of the prisoners. I am warned that the capture was a ruse, and that the military officer is a spy, whose object here is to discover a landing place. He is to escape the first opportunity."

The three men at once ran out from the tent. The instant they did so, the midshipman crawled in under the flap, rushed to the table on which the general had thrown the piece of paper, seized it, and then darted out again, and stole quietly away in the darkness. He had not gone twenty yards, when a volley of angry exclamations told him that the French general had discovered that the tent was empty.

The night was a dark one, and to prevent himself from falling over tent ropes, the midshipman threw himself down and crawled along on his hands and knees, but he paused, before he had gone many yards, and listened intently. The general was returning to his tent.

"It is no use doing anything tonight," he said. "Even an Indian could not follow the track of a waggon. At daybreak, Major Dorsay, let the redskins know that the prisoners have escaped, and offer a reward of fifty crowns for their recapture, dead or alive–I care not which. Let this good fellow turn in at the guard tent. I will talk to him in the morning. Good night!"

The midshipman kept his eyes anxiously on the dim light that could be faintly seen through the tent. If the general missed the paper, he might guess that it had been taken by the fugitives, and might order an instant search of the camp. He gave a sigh of relief, when he saw the light disappear the moment the French officer had entered the tent, and then crawled away through the camp.

Chapter 20: The Path Down The Heights.

As the midshipman crawled away from the tent of the French general, he adopted the precautions which James had suggested, and felt the ground carefully for twigs or sticks each time he moved. The still-glowing embers of the campfires warned him where the Indians and Canadians were sleeping, and, carefully avoiding these, he made his way up beyond the limits of the camp. There were no sentries posted here, for the French were perfectly safe from attack from that quarter, and, once fairly beyond the camp, the midshipman rose to his feet, and made his way to the edge of the slopes above the Saint Lawrence. He walked for about a mile, and then paused, on the very edge of the sharp declivity, and whistled as agreed upon.

A hundred yards further, he repeated the signal. The fourth time he whistled he heard, just below him, the answer, and a minute later James Walsham stood beside him.

"You young scamp, what are you doing here?"

"It was not my fault, Captain Walsham, it wasn't indeed; but I should have been tomahawked if I had stayed there a moment longer."

"What do you mean by 'you would have been tomahawked,'" James asked angrily, for he was convinced that the midshipman had made up his mind, all along, to accompany him.

"The pilot of the Sutherland swam ashore, with the news that you had been taken prisoner on purpose, and were really a spy."

"But how on earth did he know that?" James asked. "I took care the man was not on deck, when we made the holes in the boat, and he does not understand a word of English, so he could not have overheard what the men said."

"I am sorry to say, sir, that it is a case of treachery, and that one of our officers is concerned in it. The man said that an officer released him from his cell, and took him to his cabin, and then lowered him by a rope through the porthole."

"Impossible!" James Walsham said.

"It sounds impossible, sir; but I am afraid it isn't, for the officer gave him a note to bring to the general, telling him all about it, and that note I have got in my pocket now."

The midshipman then related the whole circumstances of his discovery.

"It is an extraordinary affair," James said. "However, you are certainly not to blame for making your escape when you did. You could not have got back into your tent till too late; and, even could you have done so, it might have gone hard with you, for of course they would have known that you were, what they would call an accomplice, in the affair."

"I will go on if you like, sir," the boy said, "and hide somewhere else, so that if they track me they will not find you."

"No, no," James said, "I don't think there's any fear of our being tracked. Indian eyes are sharp; but they can't perform miracles. In the forest it would be hopeless to escape them, but here the grass is short and the ground dry, and, without boots, we cannot have left any tracks that would be followed, especially as bodies of French troops have been marching backwards and forwards along the edge of these heights for the last fortnight. I won't say that it is impossible that they can find us, but it will not be by our tracks.

"Now, come down to this bush where I was lying. We will wait there till daylight breaks. It is as far down as I dare go by this light, but, when we can see, we will find a safer place further down."

Cautiously they made their way down to a clump of bushes, twenty feet below the edge, and there, lying down, dozed until it became light enough to see the ground. The slope was very steep, but bushes grew here and there upon it, and by means of these, and projecting rocks, they worked their way down some thirty feet lower, and then sat down among some bushes, which screened them from the sight of anyone who might be passing along the edge of the river, while the steep slope effectually hid them from anyone moving along above.

"Is there any signature to that letter," James asked presently.

The midshipman took the piece of paper out and looked at it.

"No, there is no signature," he said; "but I know the handwriting. I have seen it in orders, over and over again."

James was silent a few minutes.

"I won't ask you who it is, though I fear I know too well. Look here, Middleton, I should like you to tear that letter up, and say no more about it."

"No, sir," the boy said, putting the paper in his pocket. "I can't do that. Of course I am under your orders, for this expedition; but this is not an affair in which I consider that I am bound to obey you. This concerns the honour of the officers of my ship, and I should not be doing my duty if I did not, upon my return, place this letter in the hands of the captain. A man who would betray the general's plans to the enemy, would betray the ship, and I should be a traitor, myself, if I did not inform the captain. I am sorry, awfully sorry, that this should happen to an officer of the Sutherland, but it will be for the captain to decide whether he will make it public or not.

"There is one thing. If it was to be anyone, I would rather that it was he than anyone else, for there isn't a man on board can abide him. No, sir, I am sorry, but I cannot give up the letter, and, even if you had torn it up when you had it in your hand just now, I should have reported the whole thing to the captain, and say I could swear to the handwriting."

James was silent. The boy was right, and was only doing his duty in determining to denounce the act of gross treachery which had been perpetrated. He was deeply grieved, however, to think of the consequences of the discovery, and especially of the blow that it would be, to the squire, to hear that his nephew was a traitor, and indeed a murderer at heart, for, had not his flight taken place before the discovery was made, he would certainly have been executed as a spy.

The day passed quietly. That the Indians were searching for him, far and wide, James Walsham had no doubt, and indeed, from their hiding place he saw several parties of redskins moving along on the river bank, carefully examining the ground.

"It's lucky we didn't move along there," he said to his companion, "for the ground is so soft that they would assuredly have found our tracks. I expect that they think it possible that we may have been taken off, in a boat, during the night."

"I hope they will keep on thinking so," the midshipman said. "Then they will give up looking for us."

"They won't do that," James replied; "for they will be sure that they must have seen our tracks, had we passed along that muddy bank. Fortunately, they have no clue to where we really are. We might have gone east, west, or north, and the country is so covered with bush that anything like a regular search is absolutely impossible."

"I hope we ain't going to be very long, before we get on board again," the midshipman said, as he munched the small piece of bread James served out to him for his dinner. "The grub won't last more than two days, even at this starvation rate, and that one bottle of water is a mockery. I could finish it all, straight off. Why, we shall be as badly off as if we were adrift at sea, in a boat."

"Not quite so bad," James replied. "We can chew the leaves of some of these bushes; besides, people don't die of hunger or thirst in four days, and I hope, before that, to be safely on board."

Not until it was perfectly dark did they leave their hiding place, and, by the aid of the bushes, worked their way up to the top of the ascent again. James had impressed on his companion that, on no account, was he to speak above a whisper, that he was to stop whenever he did, and, should he turn off and descend the slope, he was at once to follow his example. The midshipman kept close to his companion, and marvelled how assuredly the latter walked along, for he himself could see nothing.

Several times, James stopped and listened. Presently, he turned off to the right, saying "hush!" in the lowest possible tone, and, proceeding a few paces down the slope, noiselessly lay down behind the bush. The midshipman imitated his example, though he wondered why he was so acting, for he could hear nothing. Two or three minutes later he heard a low footfall, and then the sound of men speaking in a low voice, in some strange tongue. He could not see them, but held his breath as they were passing. Not till they had been gone some minutes did James rise, and pursue his course.

"Two Indians," he said, "and on the search for us. One was just saying to the other he expected, when they got back to camp, to find that some of the other parties had overtaken us."

Another mile further, and they saw the light of several fires ahead.

"That is a French battery," James said. "We must make a detour, and get to the other side of it; then I will crawl back, and see if there is any path down to the river."

The detour was made, and then, leaving the midshipman in hiding a few paces from the edge, James crawled back. He soon saw, by the fires, that the battery was manned by sailors from the French fleet, and he had little fear of these discovering him. Keeping well below them, he came presently upon a narrow path. Above him, he could hear a French sentry walking. He followed the path down, with the greatest caution, stepping with the most extreme care, to avoid displacing a stone. He found the path was excessively steep and rugged, little more, indeed, than a sheep track. It took him half an hour to reach the bottom, and he found that, in some places, sappers had been lately at work obliterating the path, and that it could scarcely be considered practicable for men hampered with their arms and ammunition.

Another half hour's work took him to the top again, and a few minutes later he rejoined his companion.

"That won't do," he said. "We must try again. There is a path, but the troops could scarcely climb it if unopposed, and certainly could not do so without making such a noise as would attract the notice of the sentinels above."

"That is the battery they call Sillery," the midshipman said. "They have fired at us over and over again from there, as we went up or down the river. There is another about a mile further on. It is called Samos."

Upon reaching the Samos battery, James again crept up and reconnoitred. The way down, however, was even more difficult than at Sillery. There was, indeed, no regular path, and so steep was the descent that he doubted whether it would be possible for armed men to climb it. Even he, exceptionally strong and active as he was, and unencumbered with arms, had the greatest difficulty in making his way down and up again and, indeed, could only do so by grasping the trunks of trees and strong bushes.

"It can't be done there," he said to the midshipman when he joined him again. "And now we must look for a hiding place. We must have been five or six hours since we started, and the nights are very short. At any rate, we cannot attempt another exploration before morning."

"I wish we could explore the inside of a farm house and light upon something to eat and drink," the midshipman said.

"It's no use wishing," James replied. "We can't risk anything of that sort and, probably, all the farm houses are full of troops. We have got a little bread left. That will hold us over tomorrow comfortably."

"It may hold us," Middleton said; "but it certainly won't hold me comfortably. My idea of comfort, at the present time, would be a round of beef and a gallon of ale."

"Ah! You are an epicure," James laughed. "If you had had three or four years of campaigning in the forest, as I have had, you would learn to content yourself on something a good deal less than that."

"I might," the boy said; "but I have my doubts about it. There's one comfort. We shall be able to sleep all day tomorrow, and so I sha'n't think about it. As the Indians did not find our tracks yesterday, they are not likely to do so today."

They were some time before they found a hiding place, for the descent was so steep that they had to try several times, before they could get down far enough to reach a spot screened by bushes, and hidden from the sight of anyone passing above. At last they did so, and soon lay down to sleep, after partaking of a mouthful of water each, and a tiny piece of bread. They passed the day for the most part in sleep, but the midshipman woke frequently, being now really parched with thirst. Each time, he chewed a few leaves from the bush in which they were lying, but derived but small comfort from it.

"It's awful to think of tomorrow," he said, as evening approached. "Even supposing you find a way down tonight, it must be midnight tomorrow before we are taken off."

"If I find a way down," James said, "I will, if possible, take you down with me, and then we can take a long drink at the river; but, at any rate, I will take the bottle down with me, and bring it up full for you. The next place to try is the spot where we saw some tents, as we went up the river. There is no battery there, and the tents can only have been pitched there because there was some way down to the water. It cannot be more than half a mile away, for it was not more than a mile from Fort Samos."

"Can't I go with you?" the midshipman said. "I will be as quiet as a cat; and, if you find it is a good path, and come up to fetch me down, you see there will be a treble risk of being seen."

"Very well," James agreed. "Only mind, if you set a stone rolling, or break a twig, it will cost us both our lives, to say nothing of the failure of our expedition."

"I will be as quiet as a mouse. You see if I ain't," the midshipman said confidently; "and I will try not to think, even once, of the water below there, so as not to hurry."

Together they crept cautiously along the edge of the ridge, until they came to a clump of some fifteen tents. As they approached they could see, by the light of the fires, that the encampment was one of Canadian troops.

James had not intended to move forward until all were asleep, but the men were all chatting round the fires, and it did not seem to him that a sentry had, as yet, been placed on the edge of the descent. He therefore crept forward at once, followed closely by the midshipman, keeping, as far as possible, down beyond the slope of the descent.

Presently, he came to a path. He saw at once that this was very different from the others--it was regularly cut, sloping gradually down the face of the sharp descent, and was wide enough for a cart to pass. He at once took his way down it, moving with the greatest caution, lest a sentry should be posted some distance below. It was very dark, for, in many places, the trees met overhead.

About halfway down he suddenly came to a stop, for, in front of him, rose a bank breast high. Here, if anywhere, a sentry should have been placed, and, holding his companion's arm, James listened intently for some time.

"Mind what you are doing," he said in a whisper. "This is a breastwork and, probably, the path is cut away on the other side. Fortunately, we are so far down the hill now, that there is not much risk of their hearing any slight noise we might make. You stand here, till I find out what's on the other side."

James climbed over the breastwork, and cautiously let himself go on the other side. He fell some five or six feet.

"Come on," he said in a low voice. "Lower yourself down by your arms. I can reach your legs then."

The gap cut in the path was some ten feet across, and six feet deep. When, with some difficulty, they clambered up on the other side, they found the path obstructed by a number of felled trees, forming a thick abattis. They managed to climb the steep hillside, and kept along it until past the obstruction. Then they got on to the path again, and found it unbroken to the bottom.

"So far, so good," James said. "Now, do you stop here, while I crawl forward to the water. The first thing to discover is whether they have a sentinel stationed anywhere near the bottom of this path."

The time seemed terribly long to Middleton before James returned, though it was really but a few minutes.

"All right!" he said, as he approached him. "There is no one here, though I can hear some sentries farther up the river. Now you can come forward, and have a drink. Fortunately, the river is high."

After having satisfied their thirst, Middleton asked:

"Where are you going now? I don't care how far we have got to march, for, after that drink, I feel ready for anything."

"It won't do to hide anywhere near," James said; "for, if the boat which comes to take us off were to be seen, it would put them on their guard, and there would be plenty of sentries about here in future. No, we will keep along at the foot of the precipice till we are about halfway, as far as we can tell, between Samos and Sillery, and then we will climb up, as high as we can get, and show our signal in the morning. But you must be careful as we walk, for, as I told you, there are some sentries posted by the water's edge, higher up."

"I will be careful, don't you fear," the midshipman said. "There is not much fear of a fellow, walking about in the dark without boots, not being careful. I knocked my toe against a rock, just now, and it was as much as I could do not to halloa. I will be careful in future, I can tell you."

An hour's walking brought them to a spot where the hill was rather less steep than usual. They climbed up, until they gained a spot some fifty feet above the level of the river, and there sat down in a clump of bushes.

"As soon as it's daylight, we will choose a spot where we can show a signal, without the risk of it's being seen from below," James said. "We mustn't go to sleep, for we must move directly the dawn commences, else those sentries below might make us out."

At daybreak they shifted their position, and gained a spot completely hidden from below, but from which an entire view of the river could be obtained.

"Tide will be low in a couple of hours," the midshipman said. "There are the fleet below. They will come up with the first flood, so, in three or four hours, they will be abreast of us. I hope they will make out our signal."

"I have no fear of that," James replied. "They are sure to keep a sharp lookout for it."

Presently the tide grew slacker, and, half an hour later, the ships were seen to hoist their sails, and soon began to drop slowly up the river. When they approached, James fastened his handkerchief against the trunk of a tree, well open to view from the river, and then stood with his eyes fixed on the approaching ships. Just as the Sutherland came abreast of the spot where they were standing, the ensign was dipped. James at once removed his handkerchief.

"Now," he said, "Middleton, you can turn in and take a sleep. At twelve o'clock tonight there will be a boat below for us."

Two or three hours after darkness had fallen, James and his companion made their way down the slope, and crawled out to the water's edge. There was no sentry within hearing, and they sat down, by the edge of the river, until suddenly a light gleamed for an instant, low down on the water, two or three hundred yards from the shore.

They at once stepped into the river, and, wading out for some little distance, struck out towards where they had seen the light. A few minutes' swimming, and they saw something dark ahead. Another few strokes took them alongside, and they were hauled into the boat.

The slight noise attracted the attention of a sentry, some little distance along the shore, and his qui vive came sharply across the water, followed a few seconds later by the flash of his gun.

The crew now bent to their oars, and, a quarter of an hour later, the boat was alongside the Sutherland, which, with her consorts, was slowly drifting up the stream. General Wolfe and the admiral were on deck, and anxiously waiting the arrival of the boat. The former, in his anxiety, hailed the boat as it approached.

"Is Captain James Walsham on board?"

"Yes, sir," James replied.

"Bravo, bravo!" the general cried, delighted.

"Bravo!" he repeated, seizing James Walsham's hand as he stepped on deck. "I did not expect to see you again, Captain Walsham, at least until we took Quebec. Now, come to my cabin at once and tell me all about it. But perhaps you are hungry."

"I am rather hungry, general," James said quietly. "We have had nothing to eat but a crust of bread for three days."

"We? Who are we?" the general asked quickly.

"Mr. Middleton and myself, sir. He escaped after I had left, and joined me."

"The galley fires are out," the admiral said, "but you shall have some cold meat in my cabin, instantly."

James was at once led to the cabin, where, in two or three minutes, food and a bottle of wine were placed before him. The general would not allow him to speak a word, till his hunger was satisfied. Then, when he saw him lay down his knife and fork, he said:

"Now, Captain Walsham, in the first place, have you succeeded–have you found a practicable path down to the river?"

"I have found a path, sir. It is cut in one place, and blocked with felled trees, but the obstacles can be passed. There are some Canadians, in tents, near the top of the path, but they seem to keep a very careless watch, and no sentry is placed at the bottom, or on the edge of the river anywhere near."

"Admirable, admirable!" Wolfe exclaimed. "At last there is a chance of our outreaching Montcalm. And you were not seen examining the path? Nothing occurred to excite their suspicion, and lead them to keep a better lookout in future?"

"No, sir," James replied. "They have had no suspicion of my presence anywhere near. The spot where I was taken off was two miles higher. I moved away in order that, if we were seen swimming off to the boat, no suspicion should occur that we had been reconnoitring the pathway."

"That is right," the general said. "Now, tell me the whole story of what you have been doing, in your own way."

James related his adventures, up to the time when he was joined by the midshipman.

"But what made Mr. Middleton escape?" the admiral asked. "I thought that his instructions were precise, that he was to permit himself to be taken prisoner, and was to remain quietly in Quebec, until we could either exchange him or take the place."

"That was how he understood his instructions, sir," James said; "but I would rather that you should question him, yourself, as to his reasons for escaping. I may say they appear to me to be perfectly valid, as an occurrence took place upon which it was impossible for Captain Peters to calculate, when he gave them."

James then finished the report of his proceedings, and General Wolfe expressed his great satisfaction at the result.

"I will put you in orders, tomorrow, for your brevet-majority," he said; "and never was the rank more honourably earned."

The admiral rang a hand bell.

"Send Mr. Middleton to me. Where is he?"

"He is having supper in Captain Peters' cabin."

"Ask Captain Peters if he will be good enough to come in with him."

A minute later Captain Peters entered, followed by the midshipman.

"I suppose, Peters, you have been asking young Middleton the reason why he did not carry out his instructions?"

"I have, admiral," Captain Peters said gravely, "and I was only waiting until you were disengaged to report the circumstance to you. He had better tell you, sir, his own way."

Captain Peters then took a seat at the table, while the midshipman related his story, in nearly the same words in which he had told it to James. When he told of the account the Canadian pilot had given of his escape, the admiral exclaimed:

"But it seems altogether incredible. That some one has unbolted the man's cabin from the outside seems manifest, and it is clear that either gross treachery, or gross carelessness, enabled him to get free. I own that, although the sergeant of marines declares positively that he fastened the bolts, I think that he could not have done so, for treachery seems almost out of the question. That an officer should have done this seems impossible; and yet, what the man says about the cabin, and being let out by a rope, would seem to show that it must have been an officer."

"I am sorry to say, sir," Middleton said, "that the man gave proofs of the truth of what he was saying. The officer, he said, gave him a paper, which I heard and saw the general reading aloud. It was a warning that Captain Walsham had purposely allowed himself to be captured, and that he was, in fact, a spy. The French officer, in his haste, laid down the paper on the table when he rushed out, and I had just time to creep under the canvas, seize it, and make off with it. Here it is, sir. I have showed it to Captain Peters."

The admiral took the paper and read it, and handed it, without a word, to General Wolfe.

"That is proof conclusive," he said. "Peters, do you know the handwriting?"

"Yes," Captain Peters said gravely. "I recognized it at once, as did Mr. Middleton. It is the handwriting of Lieutenant Horton."

"But what on earth could be the motive of this unhappy young man?" the admiral asked.

"I imagine, sir, from what I saw on the evening before Captain Walsham set out, and, indeed, from what Captain Walsham said when I questioned him, that it was a case of private enmity against Captain Walsham."

"Is this so, Captain Walsham?" General Wolfe asked.

"I have no enmity against him, sir," James said, "though I own that his manner impressed me with the idea that he regarded me as an enemy. The fact is, we lived near each other as boys, and we had a fight. I got the best of it. He gave an account of the affair, which was not exactly correct, to his uncle, Mr. Linthorne, a wealthy landowner and a magistrate. The latter had me up at the justice room; but I brought forward witnesses, who gave their account of the affair. Mr. Linthorne considered that his nephew–whom he had at that time regarded as his heir–had not given a correct account, and was so angry that he sent him to sea.

"I would say, sir," he said earnestly, "that, were it possible, I should have wished this unhappy affair to be passed over."

"Impossible!" the admiral and general said together.

"I fear it is impossible now, sir," James said gravely; "but it might have been stopped before."

"Captain Walsham wanted me to tear up the note," the midshipman put in; "but, though I was awfully sorry such a thing should happen to an officer of the Sutherland, I was obliged to refuse to do so, as I thought it was my duty to hand the note to you."

"Certainly it was, Mr. Middleton," the admiral said. "There can be no question about that."

"I wonder that you even suggested such a thing, Captain Walsham," the general remarked. "This was not a private affair. The whole success of the enterprise was jeopardized."

"It was, sir," James said quietly; "but you must remember that, at the time I asked Mr. Middleton to tear up the note, it had ceased to be jeopardized, for I had got fairly away. I am under great obligations to Mr. Linthorne, and would do much to save him pain. I regarded this act, not as one of treason against the country, but as one of personal enmity to myself, and I am sure that Lieutenant Horton, himself, did not think of the harm that his letter might do to the cause, but was blinded by his passion against me."

"Your conduct does credit to your heart, Captain Walsham, if not to your head," General Wolfe said.

The admiral rang the bell.

"Tell Lieutenant Horton that I wish to speak to him, and order a corporal, with a file of marines, to be at the door."

The messenger found Lieutenant Horton pacing the quarterdeck with hurried steps. On the receipt of the message, instead of going directly to the admiral's cabin, he ran down below, caught something from a shelf by his berth, placed it in the breast of his coat, and then went to the admiral's cabin. The corporal, with the two marines, had already taken his station there. The young officer drew a deep breath, and entered.

A deadly fear had seized him, from the moment he saw the signal of James Walsham, although it seemed impossible to him that his treachery could have been discovered. The sudden summons at this hour of the night confirmed his fears, and it was with a face almost as pale as death that he entered the cabin.

"Lieutenant Horton," the admiral said, "you are accused of having assisted in the escape of the pilot, who was our prisoner on board this ship. You are further accused of releasing him with the special purpose that the plans which General Wolfe had laid, to obtain information, might be thwarted."

"Who accuses me?" Richard Horton asked. "Captain Walsham is my enemy. He has for years intrigued against me, and sought to do me harm. He was the companion of smugglers, and was captured by the Thetis, and had the choice of being sent to prison, and tried for his share in the killing of some of the coast guards, or of going before the mast. I was a lieutenant in the Thetis at the time, and I suppose, because I did not then interfere on his behalf, he has now trumped up this accusation against me, an accusation I defy him to prove."

"You are mistaken, Lieutenant Horton," the admiral said. "Captain Walsham is not your accuser. Nay, more, he has himself committed a grave dereliction of duty in trying to screen you, and by endeavouring to destroy the principal evidence against you. Mr. Middleton overheard a conversation between the Canadian pilot and the French general, and the former described how he had been liberated by an English officer, who assisted him to escape by a rope from the porthole in his cabin."

"I do not see that that is any evidence against me," Richard Horton said. "In the first place, the man may have been lying. In the second place, unless he mentioned my name, why am I suspected more than any other officer? And, even if he did mention my name, my word is surely as good as that of a Canadian prisoner. It is probable that the man was released by one of the crew–some man, perhaps, who owed me a grudge–who told him to say that it was I who freed him, in hopes that some day this outrageous story might get about."

"Your suggestions are plausible, Mr. Horton," the admiral said coldly. "Unfortunately, it is not on the word of this Canadian that we have to depend.

"There, sir," he said, holding out the letter; "there is the chief witness against you. Captain Peters instantly recognized your handwriting, as Mr. Middleton had done before him."

Richard Horton stood gazing speechlessly at the letter. So confounded was he, by the unexpected production of this fatal missive, that he was unable to utter a single word of explanation or excuse.

"Lay your sword on the table, sir," the admiral said, "and retire to your cabin, where you will remain, under close arrest, till a court martial can be assembled."

Richard Horton unbuckled his sword and laid it on the table, and left the cabin without a word.

"It would have been better to send a guard with him," Captain Peters said; "he might jump overboard, or blow his brains out."

"Quite so, Peters," the admiral said. "The very thing that was in my mind, when I told him to retire to his cabin–the very best thing he could do, for himself and for the service. A nice scandal it would be, to have to try and hang a naval officer for treachery.

"I am sure you agree with me, general?"

"Thoroughly," the general said. "Let him blow his brains out, or desert; but you had best keep a sharp lookout that he does not desert at present. After we have once effected our landing, I should say keep as careless a watch over him as possible; but don't let him go before. It is bad enough that the French know that Captain Walsham went ashore for the purpose of discovering a landing place; but it would be worse were they to become aware that he has rejoined the ships, and that he was taken off by a boat within a couple of miles of the spot where we mean to land."

The admiral was right. Richard Horton had, when summoned to the cabin, hastily placed a pistol in his bosom, with the intention of blowing out his brains, should he find that the discovery he dreaded had been made. Had the marines posted outside the cabin been ordered to accompany him, he would at once have carried his purpose into execution; but, finding himself free, he walked to his cabin, still determined to blow out his brains before morning; but, the impulse once past, he could not summon up resolution to carry his resolve into effect. He would do it, he said to himself, before the court martial came on. That would be time enough.

This was the decision he arrived at when the morning dawned upon him, lying despairing in his cot.

Chapter 21: The Capture Of Quebec.

On the day on which he received James' report, Wolfe issued his orders for the attack. Colonel Burton, at Point Levi, was to bring up every man who could be spared, to assist in the enterprise, and that officer accordingly marched to the spot indicated for embarkation, after nightfall, with 1200 men.

As night approached, the main fleet, under Admiral Saunders, below Quebec, ranged itself opposite Beauport, and opened a tremendous cannonade, while the boats were lowered, and filled with sailors and marines. Montcalm, believing that the movements of the English above the town were only a feint, and that their main body was still below it, massed his troops in front of Beauport, to repel the expected landing.

To Colonel Howe, of the Light Infantry, was given the honour of leading the little party, who were to suddenly attack Vergor's camp, at the head of the path. James Walsham, knowing the way, was to accompany him as second in command. Twenty-four picked men volunteered to follow them. Thirty large troop boats, and some boats belonging to the ships, were in readiness, and 1700 men took their places in them.

The tide was still flowing, and, the better to deceive the French, the vessels and boats were allowed to drift upwards for a little distance, as if to attempt to effect a landing above Cap Rouge. Wolfe had, that day, gained some intelligence which would assist him to deceive the enemy, for he learned that a number of boats, laden with provisions from Quebec, were coming down with the tide.

Wolfe was on board the Sutherland. He was somewhat stronger than he had been for some days, but felt a presentiment that he would die in the approaching battle. About two o'clock, the tide began to ebb, and two lanterns–the signal for the troops to put off–were shown in the rigging of the Sutherland.

Fortune favoured the English. Bougainville had watched the vessels, until he saw them begin to drift down again with the stream, and, thinking that they would return again with the flood, as they had done for the last seven days, allowed his weary troops to retire to their camp. The battalion of Guienne, instead of encamping near the heights, had remained on the Saint Charles; and Vergor, an incapable and cowardly officer, had gone quietly to bed, and had allowed a number of the Canadians under him to go away to their village, to assist in getting in the harvest.

For two hours, the English boats drifted down with the stream. As they neared their destination, they suddenly were challenged by a French sentry. An officer, who spoke the language replied, "France."

"A quel regiment?"

"De la reine," the officer replied, knowing that a part of that regiment was with Bougainville. The sentry, believing that they were the expected provision boats, allowed them to pass on.

A few hundred yards further, another sentry challenged them. The same officer replied in French, "Provision boats. Don't make a noise; the English will hear us."

A few minutes later, the boats rowed up to the strand, at the foot of the heights. Vergor had placed no sentry on the shore, and the troops landed unchallenged. Guided by James Walsham, Colonel Howe, with his twenty-four volunteers, led the way. As silently as they could, they moved up the pathway, until they gained the top, and saw before them the outline of the tents. They went at them with a rush. Vergor leaped from his bed, and tried to run off, but was shot in the heel and captured. His men, taken by surprise, made little resistance. One or two were caught, but the rest fled.

The main body of the troops were waiting, for the most part, in the boats by the edge of the bank. Not a word was spoken as the men listened, almost breathlessly, for a sound which would tell them whether the enterprise had succeeded. Suddenly the stillness was broken by the musketry on the top of the heights, followed by a loud British cheer. Then all leapt from the boats, and each man, with his musket slung at his back, scaled the rocks as best he might. The narrow path had been made impassable by trenches and abattis, but the obstructions were soon cleared away, and the stream of soldiers poured steadily up.

As soon as a sufficient number had gained the plateau, strong parties were sent off to seize the batteries at Samos and Sillery, which had just opened fire upon the boats and ships. This was easily done, and the English footing on the plateau was assured. As fast as the boats were emptied of the men, they rowed back to the ships to fetch more, and the whole force was soon on shore. The day began to break a few minutes after the advanced troops had gained the heights, and, before it was fairly daylight, all the first party were drawn up in line, ready to resist attack. But no enemy was in sight. A body of Canadians, who had sallied from the town on hearing the firing, and moved along the strand towards the landing place, had been quickly driven back, and, for the present, no other sign of the enemy was to be seen.

Wolfe reconnoitred the ground, and found a suitable place for a battle, at a spot known as the Plains of Abraham, from a pilot of that name who had owned a piece of land there, in the early days of the colony. It was a tract of grass, with some cornfields here and there, and studded by clumps of bushes. On the south, it was bounded by the steep fall down to the Saint Lawrence; on the north, it sloped gradually down to the Saint Charles.

Wolfe led his troops to this spot and formed them in line, across the plateau and facing the city. The right wing rested on the edge of the height, along the Saint Lawrence, but the left did not extend far enough to reach the slopes down to the Saint Charles. To prevent being outflanked on this wing, Brigadier Townshend was stationed here, with two battalions, drawn up at right angles to the rest, and facing the Saint Charles. Webb's regiment formed the reserve, the 3d battalion of Royal Americans were left to guard the landing, and Howe's light infantry occupied a wood, far in the rear of the force, to check Bougainville should he approach from that direction. Wolfe, with his three brigadiers, commanded the main body, which, when all the troops had arrived, numbered less than three thousand five hundred men.

Quebec was less than a mile distant from the spot where the troops were posted, in order of battle, but an intervening ridge hid it from the sight of the troops. At six o'clock, the white uniforms of the battalion of Guienne, which had marched up in hot haste from their camp on the Saint Charles, made their appearance on the ridge, and halted there, awaiting reinforcements. Shortly afterwards, there was an outbreak of hot firing in the rear, where the light troops, under Colonel Howe, repulsed a detachment of Bougainville's command, which came up and attacked them.

Montcalm had been on the alert all night. The guns of Saunders' fleet thundered unceasingly, opposite Beauport, and its boats hovered near the shore, threatening a landing. All night, the French troops remained in their intrenchments. Accompanied by the Chevalier Johnston, he remained all night in anxious expectation. He felt that the critical moment had come, but could not tell from which direction the blow was to arrive. He had sent an officer to Vaudreuil, whose quarters were near Quebec, begging him to send word instantly, should anything occur above the town.

Just at daybreak, he heard the sound of cannon from that direction. This was the battery at Samos, opening fire upon the English ships. But no word came from Vaudreuil and, about six o'clock, Montcalm mounted and, accompanied by Johnston, rode towards the town. As he approached the bridge across the Saint Charles, the country behind the town opened to his view, and he presently saw the red line of

British troops, drawn up on the heights above the river, two miles away. Instantly, he sent Johnston off, at full gallop, to bring up the troops from the centre and left. Vaudreuil had already ordered up those on the right. Montcalm rode up to Vaudreuil's quarters, and, after a few words with the governor, galloped over the bridge of the Saint Charles towards the seat of danger.

It must have been a bitter moment for him. The fruits of his long care and watching were, in a moment, snatched away, and, just when he hoped that the enemy, foiled and exhausted, were about to return to England, he found that they had surmounted the obstacles he had deemed impregnable, and were calmly awaiting him on a fair field of battle. One who saw him said that he rode towards the field, with a fixed look, uttering not a word.

The army followed in hot haste, crossed the Saint Charles, passed through Quebec, and hurried on to the ridge, where the battalion of Guienne had taken up its position. Nothing could have been stronger than the contrast which the two armies afforded. On the one side was the red English line, quiet and silent, save that the war pipes of the Highlanders blew loud and shrilly; on the other were the white-coated battalions of the regular army of France, the blue-clad Canadians, the bands of Indians in their war paint and feathers, all hurried and excited by their rapid march, and by the danger which had so unexpectedly burst upon them.

Now the evils of a divided command were apparent. Vaudreuil countermanded Montcalm's orders for the advance of the left of the army, as he feared that the English might make a descent upon Beauport. Nor was the garrison of Quebec available, for Ramesay, its commander, was under the orders of Vaudreuil and, when Montcalm sent to him for twenty-five field guns from one of its batteries, he only sent three, saying that he wanted the rest for his own defence.

Montcalm held a council of war with all his officers, and determined to attack at once. For this he has been blamed. That he must have fought was certain, for the English, in the position which they occupied, cut him off from the base of his supplies; but he might have waited for a few hours, and in that time he could have sent messengers, and brought up the force of Bougainville, which could have marched, by a circuitous route, and have joined him without coming in contact with the English.

Upon the other hand, Montcalm had every reason to believe that the thirty-five hundred men he saw before him formed a portion, only, of the English army, that the rest were still on board the fleet opposite Beauport, and that a delay would bring larger reinforcements to Wolfe than he could himself receive. He was, as we know, mistaken, but his reasoning was sound, and he had, all along, believed the English army to be far more numerous than it really was. He was doubtless influenced by the fact that his troops were full of ardour, and that any delay would greatly dispirit the Canadians and Indians.

He therefore determined to attack at once. The three field pieces, sent by Ramesay, opened fire upon the English line with canister, while fifteen hundred Canadians and Indians crept up among the bushes and knolls, and through the cornfield, and opened a heavy fire. Wolfe threw out skirmishers in front of the line, to keep these assailants in check, and ordered the rest of the troops to lie down to avoid the fire.

On the British left, the attack was most galling. Bands of the sharpshooters got among the thickets, just below the edge of the declivity down to the Saint Charles, and from these, and from several houses scattered there, they killed and wounded a considerable number of Townshend's men.

Howe was called up, with his light troops, from the rear; and he, and the two flank battalions of Townshend, dashed at the thickets, and, after some sharp fighting, partially cleared them, and took and burned some of the houses.

Towards ten o'clock, the French advanced to the attack. Their centre was formed of regular troops, only, with regulars and Canadian battalions on either flank. Two field pieces which, with enormous labour, the English had dragged up the path from the landing place, at once opened fire with grape upon the French line.

The advance was badly conducted. The French regulars marched steadily on, but the Canadians, firing as they advanced, threw themselves on the ground to reload, and this broke the regularity of the line. The English advanced some little distance, to meet their foes, and then halted.

Not a shot was fired until the French were within forty paces, and then, at the word of command, a volley of musketry crashed out along the whole length of the line. So regularly was the volley given, that the French officers afterwards said that it sounded like a single cannon shot. Another volley followed, and then the continuous roar of independent firing.

When the smoke cleared off a little, its effects could be seen. The French had halted where they stood, and, among them, the dead and wounded were thickly strewn. All order and regularity had been lost under that terrible fire, and, in three minutes, the line of advancing soldiers was broken up into a disorderly shouting mob. Then Wolfe gave the order to charge, and the British cheer, mingled with the wild yell of the Highlanders, rose loud and fierce. The English regiments advanced with levelled bayonets. The Highlanders drew their broadswords and rushed headlong forward.

The charge was decisive. The French were swept helplessly before it, and the battle was at an end, save that the scattered parties of Canadians and Indians kept up, for some time, a fire from the bushes and cornfields.

Their fire was heaviest on the British right, where Wolfe himself led the charge, at the head of the Louisbourg Grenadiers. A shot shattered his wrist. He wrapped his handkerchief around it and kept on. Another shot struck him, but he still advanced. When a third pierced his breast, he staggered and sat down. Two or three officers and men carried him to the rear, and then laid him down, and asked if they should send for a surgeon.

"There is no need," he said. "It is all over with me."

A moment later, one of those standing by him cried out:

"They run, see how they run!"

"Who run?" Wolfe asked.

"The enemy, sir. They give way everywhere."

"Go, one of you, to Colonel Burton," Wolfe said. "Tell him to march Webb's regiment down to the Charles River, to cut off their retreat from the bridge;" then, turning on his side, he said:

"Now, God be praised, I will die in peace!" and, a few minutes later, he expired.

Montcalm, still on horseback, was borne by the tide of fugitives towards the town. As he neared the gate, a shot passed through his body.

It needed some hard work before the Canadians, who fought bravely, could be cleared out from the thickets. The French troops did not rally from their disorder till they had crossed the Saint Charles. The Canadians retired in better order.

Decisive as the victory was, the English, for the moment, were in no condition to follow it up. While on the French side Montcalm was dying, and his second in command was mortally wounded; on the English, Wolfe was dead and Monckton, second in rank, badly wounded, and the command had fallen upon Townshend, at the moment when the enemy were in full flight. Knowing that the French could cut the bridge of boats across the Saint Charles, and so stop his pursuit, and that Bougainville was close at hand, he halted his troops, and set them to work to intrench themselves on the field of battle.

Their loss had been six hundred and sixty-four, of all ranks, killed and wounded; while the French loss was estimated at about double that number. In point of numbers engaged, and in the total loss on both sides, the fight on the Plains of Abraham does not deserve to rank as a great battle, but its results were of the most extreme importance, for the victory transferred Canada from France to England.

Vaudreuil, after joining his force with that of Bougainville, would have still vastly outnumbered the English, and could, by taking up a fresh position in their rear, have rendered himself impregnable, until the winter forced the English to retire; while the latter had no means of investing or besieging Quebec. But his weakness was now as great as his presumption had been before, and, on the evening of the battle, he abandoned the lines of Beauport, and, leaving all his tents and stores behind him, retreated hastily, or rather it may be said fled, for as the Chevalier Johnston said of it:

"It was not a retreat, but an abominable flight, with such disorder and confusion that, had the English known it, three hundred men sent after us would have been sufficient to have cut all our army to pieces. The soldiers were all mixed, scattered, dispersed, and running as hard as they could, as if the English army were at their heels."

The flight was continued, until they reached the impregnable position of Jacques Cartier on the brink of the Saint Lawrence, thirty miles from the scene of action.

Montcalm died in Quebec the next morning. Levis soon arrived at Jacques Cartier from Montreal, and took the command, and at once attempted to restore order, and persuaded Vaudreuil to march back to join Bougainville, who had remained firmly with his command, at Cap Rouge, while the horde of fugitives swept by him. Vaudreuil, before leaving, had given orders to Ramesay to surrender, if Quebec was threatened by assault, and Levis, on his march to its relief, was met by the news that, on the morning of the 18th, Ramesay had surrendered.

The garrison was utterly dispirited, and unwilling to fight. The officers were even more anxious to surrender than the men, and, on the fleet approaching the walls Ramesay obeyed Vaudreuil's orders, and surrendered. Townshend granted favourable conditions, for he knew that Levis was approaching, and that his position was dangerous in the extreme. He therefore agreed that the troops and sailors of the garrison should march out from the place, with the honours of war, and were to be carried to France, and that the inhabitants should have protection in person and property, and free exercise of religion.

The day after the capture of Quebec, James Walsham returned on board ship. The thought of Richard Horton, awaiting the court martial, which would assuredly award him the sentence of death for his treachery, was constantly in his mind. He remembered the conversation between Captain Peters and the admiral, and General Wolfe's words: "I should say, keep as careless a watch over him as possible," and he determined, if possible, to aid him in making his escape, confident that, in the general exultation at the success of the enterprise, no one would trouble greatly about the matter, and that the admiral would be only too pleased that an inquiry should be avoided, which could but end in the disgrace and execution of a naval officer.

James was relieved when, on his arrival, he found that Richard Horton was still in confinement, for he feared that he might have carried out the other alternative spoken of by the admiral, and might have committed suicide.

"Captain Peters," he said, going up to that officer, "I should be obliged if you would give me an order to see Lieutenant Horton."

"Can't do it, my lad. The admiral's orders are precise. Nobody is to be admitted to see him, without an order signed by himself."

James accordingly sought the admiral's cabin.

"What do you want to see him for, eh?" the admiral asked.

James hesitated. He would not tell an untruth in the matter, and yet he could think of no excuse which could answer, without doing so.

"I want to see him, sir, to have some conversation with him."

"Ah!" the admiral said, looking at him keenly. "Conversation, eh! You are not going to take him a pistol, or poison, or anything of that sort, to help him to put an end to his wretched existence?"

"No, indeed, sir," James said warmly.

"Humph! You are not thinking, I hope," he said, with a twinkle of the eye, "of helping him to escape?"

James was silent.

"Well, well," the admiral said hastily, "that's not a fair question to ask. However, I will tell you in confidence that, if he should escape, which is the most unlikely thing in the world, you know, no one would be particularly sorry, and there would be no great fuss made about it. Everyone in the navy here would feel it cast a slur upon the service if, at a time like this, a naval officer were tried and shot for treachery. However, if it must be it must.

"Here is an order for you to see him. If it was anyone else, I might have my doubts about granting it, but as you are the man against whom he played this scurvy trick, I feel safe in doing so.

"There you are, my lad. Give me your hand. You are a fine fellow, Major Walsham, a very fine fellow."

Immediately upon entering Quebec, James had purchased a large turn-screw, some ten yards of fine but strong rope, and three or four bladders. When he procured the order, he went to his cabin, took off his coat, wound the rope round his body, and then, putting on his coat, placed the flattened bladders under it and buttoned it up, slipping the turn-screw up his sleeve, and then proceeded to the prisoner's cabin. The sentry at once admitted him, on producing the admiral's order.

Richard Horton was lying down on his berth, and started with surprise as his visitor entered.

"I am glad you have come to see me, James Walsham, for I have been wishing to speak to you, and I thought you would come. I have been thinking much for the last two days. I know that it is all up with me. The proofs are too strong, and I will not face a court martial, for I have the means—I know I may tell you safely—of avoiding it. The hour that brings me news that the court is ordered to assemble, I cease to live.

"When a man is at that point, he sees things more clearly, perhaps, than he did before. I know that I have wronged you, and, when the admiral said that you had done all in your power to shield me, I felt more humiliated than I did when that fatal letter was produced. I know what you have come for—to tell me that you bear me no malice. You are a fine fellow, Walsham, and deserve all your good fortune, just as I deserve what has befallen me. I think, if it had not been for the squire taking me up, I should never have come to this, but might have grown up a decent fellow. But my head was turned. I thought I was going to be a great man, and this is what has come of it."

"I have come partly, as you suppose, to tell you that I bear you no malice, Richard Horton. I, too, have thought matters over, and understand your feeling against me. That first unfortunate quarrel, and its unfortunate result, set you against me, and, perhaps, I never did as much as I might to turn your feelings the other way. However, we will not talk more of that. All that is past and over. I come to you, now, as the nephew of the man who has done so much for me. I have brought with me the means of aiding your escape."

"Of aiding my escape, Walsham! You must be mad! I am too securely fastened here; and, even were it not so, I would not accept a kindness which would cost you your commission, were it known."

"As to the second reason, you may make your mind easy. From words which dropped, from the admiral, I am sure that everyone will be so glad, at your escape, that no very strict inquiry will be made. In the next place, your fastenings are not so very secure. The porthole is screwed down as usual."

"Yes," Horton said; "but, in addition, there are a dozen strong screws placed round it."

"Here is a long turn-screw which will take them out as quickly as the carpenter put them in," James said, producing the tool; "and here," and he opened his coat, "is a rope for lowering yourself down into the water."

"You are very good, James," Horton said quietly; "but it is no use. I can't swim."

"I know you could not, as a boy," James replied, "and I thought it likely enough that you have not learned since; but I think, with these, you may make a shift to get ashore," and he produced four bladders and some strong lashing. "If you blow these out, fasten the necks tightly, and then lash them round you, you can't sink. The drift of the tide will take you not very far from the point below, and, if you do your best to strike out towards the shore, I have no doubt you will be able to make it. You must lower yourself into the water very quietly, and allow yourself to float down, till you are well astern of the vessel."

Richard Horton stood for a minute or two, with his hand over his eyes; then he said in a broken voice:

"God bless you, Walsham. I will try it. If I am shot, 'tis better than dying by my own hand. If I escape, I will do my best to retrieve my life. I shall never return to England again, but, under a new name, may start afresh in the colonies. God bless you, and make you happy."

The young men wrung each other hands, with a silent clasp, and James returned to his own cabin.

The next morning, the officer of marines reported to Captain Peters that the prisoner was missing. The porthole was found open, and a rope hanging to the water's edge. The captain at once took the report to the admiral.

"A bad job," the admiral said, with a twinkle of the eye. "A very bad job! How could it have happened?"

"The sentries report, sir, that they heard no noise during the night, and that the only person who visited the cabin, with the exception of the sergeant with the prisoner's food, was Major Walsham, with your own order."

"Yes, now I think of it, I did give him an order; but, of course, he can have had nothing to do with it. Horton must have managed to unscrew the porthole, somehow, perhaps with a pocketknife, and he might have had a coil of rope somewhere in his cabin. Great carelessness, you know. However, at a time like this, we need not bother our heads about it. He's gone, and there's an end of it."

"He could not swim, sir," the captain said. "I heard him say so, once."

"Then most likely he's drowned," the admiral remarked briskly. "That's the best thing that could happen. Enter it so in the log book: 'Lieutenant Horton fell out of his cabin window, while under arrest for misconduct; supposed to have been drowned.' That settles the whole matter."

Captain Peters smiled to himself, as he made the entry. He was convinced, by the calm manner in which the admiral took it, that he more than suspected that the prisoner had escaped, and that James Walsham had had a hand in getting him off.

Shortly after Quebec surrendered, Townshend returned to England with the fleet, leaving Murray in command of the army at Quebec. In the spring, Levis advanced with eight or nine thousand men against Quebec; and Murray, with three thousand, advanced to meet him, and gave battle nearly on the same ground on which the previous battle had been fought. The fight was a desperate one; but the English, being outflanked by the superior numbers of the French, were driven back into Quebec, with the loss of a third of their number.

Quebec was now besieged by the French until, in May, an English fleet arrived, and destroyed the vessels which had brought down the stores and ammunition of Levis from Montreal. The French at once broke up their camp, and retreated hastily; but all hope was now gone, the loss of Quebec had cut them off from France.

Amherst invaded the country from the English colonies, and the French were driven back to Montreal, before which the united English forces, 17,000 strong, took up their position; and, on the 8th of September, 1760, Vaudreuil signed the capitulation, by which Canada and all its dependencies passed to the English crown. All the French officers, civil and military, and the French troops and sailors, were to be sent back to France, in English ships.

James Walsham was not present at the later operations round Quebec. He had been struck, in the side, by a shot by a lurking Indian, when a column had marched out from Quebec, a few days after its capture; and, for three or four weeks, he lay between life and death, on board ship. When convalescence set in, he found that he was already on blue water, all the serious cases being taken back by the fleet when, soon after the capture of Quebec, it sailed for England.

The voyage was a long one, and, by the time the fleet sailed with their convoy into Portsmouth harbour, James had recovered much of his strength. An hour after landing, he was in a post chaise on his way home. It seemed strange, indeed, to him, as he drove through the little town, on his way up to the Hall. He had left it, in the beginning of 1755, a raw young fellow of eighteen. He returned, in the last month of 1759, a man of twenty-three, with the rank of major, and no inconsiderable share of credit and honour.

He stopped the vehicle at the lodge gate, had his baggage taken out there, and proceeded on foot towards the Hall, for he was afraid that, if he drove straight up to the door, the sudden delight of seeing him would be too much for his mother.

John Petersham opened the door, and, recognizing him at once, was about to exclaim loudly, when James made a motion for him to be silent.

"Show me quietly into the squire's study, John," he said, grasping the butler's hand with a hearty squeeze, "and don't say anything about my being here, until he has seen my mother. They are all well, I hope?"

"All well, sir, and right glad they will be to see you; for Mrs. Walsham, and all of them, have been fretting sorely since the news came that you were badly wounded."

"I have had a narrow shave of it," James said; "but, thank God, I am as well now as ever!"

As he spoke, he opened the door of the study, and entered. The squire, who was reading the paper, looked up, and leapt to his feet with a cry of satisfaction.

"My dear boy, I am glad–thank God you are back again! What a relief your coming will be to us all!"

And he shook James warmly by both hands.

"I should hardly have known you, and yet you are not so much changed, either. Dear, dear, how delighted your mother will be! You have not seen her yet?"

"No, sir," James said. "I dismissed the post chaise at the gate, and walked up quietly. I was afraid, if I drove suddenly up, the shock might be too much for her."

"Quite right!" the squire said. "We must break it to her quietly. Wilks must do it–or no, he shall tell Aggie, and she shall tell your mother."

He rang the bell, and John, who had been expecting a summons, instantly appeared.

"Tell Mr. Wilks I want to speak to him, John."

The old soldier speedily appeared, and his delight was as great as if James had been his son. He went off to break the news, and, in a short time, Mrs. Walsham was in the arms of her son.

Major Walsham went no more to the wars, nor did he follow his original intention of entering the medical profession. Indeed, there was no occasion for him to do either.

For Aggie insisted on his leaving the army; and she had a very strong voice in the matter. James had not long been home before he and the young lady came to an understanding. Before speaking to her, James had consulted his old friend.

"You know how I feel," he said; "but I don't know whether it would be right. You see, although I am major in the service, I have nothing but my pay. I owe everything to the squire, and he would naturally look very much higher for a husband for his granddaughter."

"Don't you be a fool, James Walsham," Mr. Wilks said. "I made up my mind that you should marry Aggie, ever since the day when you got her out of the sea. The squire has known, for years, what I thought on the subject. You will meet with no opposition from him, for he is almost as proud of you as I am. Besides, he thinks only of Aggie's happiness, and, unless I am greatly mistaken, that young lady has fully made up her mind on the subject."

This was indeed the case, for Aggie, when James had settled the point with her, made no hesitation in telling him that she had regarded him as her special property since she had been a child.

"I considered it all settled, years and years ago," she said demurely, "and I was quite aggrieved, I can tell you, when, on your arrival, you just held out your hand to me, instead of–well, instead of doing the same to me as to your mother."

"You shall have no reason for complaint, that way, in the future, Aggie, I promise you. But how could I tell? The last time I saw you, you were flirting, as hard as you could, with someone else."

"Well, sir, whose fault was that? You chose to make yourself disagreeable, and stay away, and what was I to do? I should do the same in the future, I can tell you, if you neglected me in the same way."

"I sha'n't give you the chance, Aggie. You can rely upon that."

The squire was fully prepared for the communication which James had to make to him, and, as there were no reasons for waiting, the ceremony took place very shortly afterwards.

The squire never asked any questions about his nephew. The official report had come home that Lieutenant Horton had died of drowning, while under arrest, but the squire forbore all inquiry, and, to the end of his life, remained in ignorance of the disgraceful circumstances.

Perhaps, in his heart, the news was a relief to him. He had never been fond of Richard as a lad, and his confidence, once shaken, had never been restored. He had intended to carry out his promise to leave him twenty thousand pounds; but he was well pleased that all that belonged to him should descend to his granddaughter. Mr. Wilks was the only resident at the Hall who ever learned, from James, the facts of Richard Horton's disgrace.

Years afterwards a few lines, without signature or address, came to James from America. The writer said that he was sure that he would be glad to hear that, under a changed name, he was doing very well.

"I shall never return to England," he ended, "nor ever forget your kindness and generosity."

The marriage of the young people made but few changes at the Hall. The squire proposed to give Aggie, at once, a sum which would have purchased an estate in the neighbourhood; but he was delighted to find that she, and James, had made up their minds that the party at the Hall should not be broken up.

"What do you want to send us away for, grandpapa?" she asked. "You three will be happier for having us with you, and James and I will be happier for having you with us. What nonsense to talk about buying another estate! We might get a little house up in London. It would make a change, for James and me to spend two or three months every year there, but of course this will be our home."

And so it was arranged, and so matters continued until, in the lapse of time, the seniors passed away, and James Walsham and his wife, and it may be said their children, became the sole occupants of the Hall, the estate having been largely increased, by the purchase of adjoining property, by the squire before his death. James Walsham might have represented his county in Parliament had he chosen, but he was far too happy in his country life, varied by a few months passed every year in town, to care about taking part in the turmoil of politics. He did much for Sidmouth, and especially for its fishermen, and, to the end of his life, retained a passionate love for the sea.

CPSIA information can be obtained at www.ICGtesting.com
Printed in the USA
268018BV00001B/21/P